# The Debt of the Living

SUNY series in Contemporary Italian Philosophy
Silvia Benso and Brian Schroeder, editors

# The Debt of the Living

## Ascesis and Capitalism

Elettra Stimilli
Translated by Arianna Bove
Foreword by Roberto Esposito

Original Italian edition: *Il debito del vivente. Ascesi e capitalismo* (Quodlibet, 2011)

The translation of this work has been funded

by SEPS

Segretariato Europeo per le Pubblicazioni Scientifiche

Via Val d'Aposa 7 - 40123 Bologna - Italy
seps@seps.it — www.seps.it
by "Scuola Normale Superiore" and "Ministero dell'Istruzione,
dell'Università e della Ricerca Italiano"

Published by State University of New York Press, Albany

© 2017 State University of New York

All rights reserved

Printed in the United States of America

For information, contact State University of New York Press, Albany, NY
www.sunypress.edu

Production, Jenn Bennett
Marketing, Fran Keneston

Library of Congress Cataloging-in-Publication Data

Names: Stimilli, Elettra, author.
Title: The debt of the living : ascesis and capitalism / by Elettra Stimilli ; translated
    by Arianna Bove.
Other titles: Debito del vivente. English
Description: Albany : State University of New York Press, [2017] | Series: SUNY
    series in contemporary Italian philosophy | Includes bibliographical references
    and index.
Identifiers: LCCN 2016031442 (print) | LCCN 2016046321 (ebook) |
    ISBN 9781438464152 (hardcover : alk. paper) | ISBN 9781438464169 (e-book)
Subjects: LCSH: Capitalism—Religious aspects. | Religion and sociology. |
    Asceticism.
Classification: LCC HB501 .S915513 2017 (print) | LCC HB501 (ebook) |
    DDC 330.12/2—-dc23
LC record available at https://lccn.loc.gov/2016031442

10 9 8 7 6 5 4 3 2 1

# Contents

*Foreword to the English Translation*

Roberto Esposito

It might be said that much of contemporary Italian theory situates itself in the gap of what Michel Foucault has not said, a research building site that his great oeuvre opened but left interrupted. This space is filled and redeveloped primarily with reference to some other author who provides an interpretative framework destined to retroact on Foucauldian categories and point them into different directions. The first author in this role of theoretical intersection was Carl Schmitt, used in a manner that articulates the biopolitical regime jointly with that of sovereignty, which Foucault had actually very sharply distinguished it from. In another influential interpretation, Schmitt's place is taken up by Gilles Deleuze, and this results in conferring to biopolitics an affirmative force that was not always discernible as such in Foucault's texts. A further vector of discourse proposed an approach of Foucault and Martin Heidegger on the basis of a symmetrical relation between the concept of *dispositif* and that of "Gestell," which led to a new definition of political theology as a machine that reduces two to one.

*In the Debt of the Living: Ascesis and Capitalism*, Elettra Stimilli embarks on an original and fruitful path of research without the aid of any of these authors. Instead, associated to Foucault is the work of Max Weber, keeping the Walter Benjamin's fragment on "Capitalism as Religion" in sight. Read in conjunction with Weber's essay on the spirit of capitalism, this work provides definitive support to the thesis that was later developed by Foucault on the connection between pastoral power and the dispositif of governmentality. Stimilli puts forward an acute interpretation of the asceticism discussed by Weber that reads it not merely as a premise, but as the content of capitalist productivity. Beyond the sacrificial paradigm that subjects the accumulation of commodities to renunciation and defers their immediate enjoyment, the productive praxis of production we are confronted with today contains, in itself, its own end: a purposiveness without purpose, ultimately coinciding with the flow of life that contemporary modes of production have been able to put to work. What this means is that the figure of being in debt, now the very condition of our existence, cannot be seen as a mere contingent outcome of the current crisis, but needs to be rethought as the form that human life takes on thanks to the close intertwining of the economy and politics that for a long time has turned the former into both a presupposition and an outcome of the latter.

From this perspective, which Stimilli manages to activate effectively by way of a rich series of anthropological and textual references, both of the paradigms that lay at the center of the current debate, political theology, and biopolitics, take an epistemological leap.

Political theology is pushed beyond Schmitt's definition, where it was linked to the category of sovereignty, and made to encounter what might be named "economic theology," as found in Benjamin's Fragment as well as Patristic texts. The economy of neoliberal societies is a realm where the early Christian life form develops according to an increasingly close juxtaposition of guilt and debt, one that had already been observed by Friedrich Nietzsche in "On the Genealogy of Morality" and that would later be turned upside down by the logic of what Jacques Lacan called the "capitalist discourse." Enjoyment, rather than being repressed or deferred, is now the sole purpose of economic praxis; but it is also an effected mode of political control that is one and the same as the government of the living. In this sense, the antinomy at the core of the dialectics Foucault theorized between subjectivation and subjection becomes manifest. Caught in the economic-political dispositif of governmentality, human beings become as separate from what unites them as they are made subservient to what liberates them.

In this framework, even the paradigm of biopolitics leaps forward with respect to the current debate. Biopolitics is intended neither as the sovereign power over a life stripped of its form, nor as an immunizing procedure that tries to preserve life by imbuing it with a fragment of the evil from which it seeks to defend it. Rather, it is an internal dispositif that operates on the actual ability of human beings to valorize their own life according to a purposiveness without purpose. In this sense, biopower does not merely work toward the politicization of private life or even of naked and bare living matter, but rather responds to the need of a subjectivity separated from itself and put to work in a theological-political and theological-economic mechanism that both precedes and determines it.

Stimilli evinces two indications from this reconstruction, enriched by her new book *Debt and Guilt* (Rome, 2015): first, that confronting the crisis simply by opposing policies of growth to policies of austerity does not make sense because both are part of the same dispositif. Debt is not a contingent technical datum, but a political operator of global governance that releases life from its obedience to a transcendent norm and welds it to its productive impulse. Inside this mechanism, as the product of our investment and as that which we reproduce in a sort of paradoxical dialectic with credit, debt cannot be settled. Like the trust that feeds it, debt became infinite the moment capital started becoming one and the same as the existence of each one of us. Naturally, this comes at a high price, its most external symptom being contemporary psychopathologies. How is it possible to exit this mechanism? How does one leave behind an economic theology that is also a political theology, the metaphysical structure of our time? The desire to turn from a financial economy back to a real one is inadequate because still internal to the "general economy" George Bataille spoke of in his time. The suggestion that the law of this regime could be made inactive by means of a sort of destituent power also seems internal to the same language it tries to dismantle.

Instead, the author suggests, one ought to reactivate the purposiveness without purpose that feeds debt and disentangle it from the dispositif it is currently captured by. But is it possible to separate something from its very life force, freeing it from the potentiality it contains? Is it possible to dislocate the power of the act without flattening it onto the apolitical space of a pure testimony? Or is it necessary to place back in the field the category of conflict that, like that of power, lays at the heart of Italian theory, and make them interact? I believe this is the question to be asked today, and that Elettra Stimilli's work places it right at the center of the contemporary debate.

*Preface to the English Translation*

Elettra Stimilli

This work is primarily concerned with a reflection on the unknown relationship between individual lives and the management of the global economy as it has emerged over the past thirty years and seen its most recent manifestation in widespread indebtedness, for example, in the United States with the subprime mortgage crisis between 2006 and 2008, and with the sheer amount of debt accumulated by the American students to enroll in university degrees, which exceeded even the credit card as a major source of debt in the country; or, in Europe, in the sovereign debt crisis erupted in 2012 in some EU member states. This book was published first in Italy, when the crisis had already shown its most disturbing aspects in the United States, but before it also spread to European countries.

In many ways, from the beginning the capitalist economy has established an intimate connection with individual lives, formerly based on the exploitation of specific skills in the form of work. The real change is that today at stake are not only specific services, but the whole of life and the very capacity of human living to assign a value to it. This phenomenon has emerged in all its radicalism with the affirmation of neoliberal policies, basically designed to turn the market into the very principle of political government and to thus turn economic rationality into a normative logic able to comprehend all areas both public and private, from the state to the most intimate aspects of human subjectivity. This aspect was rendered even more acute by the consequent process of financialization of the economy.

On the one hand, economic transactions have become increasingly abstract and dependent on financial transactions that have determined the global trend in a relation seemingly independent of the real economy and individual lives. On the other hand, however, at the heart of the new forms of entrepreneurship that characterized the neoliberal turn of the economy and the predominance of finance there is an investment on individual lives that has not seen any precedents in previous eras. Its basic assumption is the fact that the enterprise—capitalist company—is at the heart of all social relations, individuated in the form of the "self-enterprise." Each person enters the process of exploitation at the foundation of the capitalist economy through an investment in their own lives.

The tremendous influence that the economic theories of "human capital" have had in contemporary modes of production leads, then, to a renewed reflection that takes into account the collapse of the distinction between "work" and "action" built into them, the consequent introduction of economic discourse into the ethical and political one, and the absorption of these under global economic governance.

At stake here is a constant accumulation, not connected with specific work activities, but with the very capacity of the living human being to give shape and value to life. Particularly relevant for an analysis of this process are the findings of the latest studies of Michel Foucault, his research on the links between "governmental techniques" as forms of government adopted by economic power and "technologies of the self," the ways and practices through which subjects are constituted as such. As evidenced by his courses at the Collège de France in the late 1970s, Foucault was among the first to recognize the power and danger of neoliberal policies, as a source of new dynamics of governance and subjugation. Particularly interesting for the path that I have followed in this work is the connection, investigated by Foucault, among the most recent mode of subjection and subjectivation practices.

Foucault on this path has opened a research field on the asceticism of late Antiquity, Pagan, and Christian, which proved very useful to focus the question I wanted to investigate. Retracing this path has led me to reconsider in a new light the thesis on the origin of capitalism in worldly Protestant asceticism, that Max Weber elaborated in his famous essay "The Protestant Ethic and the Spirit of Capitalism of 1905." A cross-reading of the two approaches is, therefore, the inspiration of this book, which intends to further explore the relationship between Christian religion and the economy, both investigated by Weber, with particular reference to Protestant Christianity, and by Foucault, who located in the "Christian pastoral power" the origin of "governmental power."

In the first part of the book I present a genealogical analysis of Christian asceticism as a matrix of economic power: from its origins in the early

Christian community to its development in medieval monastic rules, where the latter, following a recent trend of historical studies, are taken to represent the paradigm of Western economic discourse. As the first explicit example of forms of regulation and institutional organization of desires and pleasures, monastic rules are shown to be intimately connected with the disturbing modes of reproducing desires and pleasures on which the contemporary practice of consumption that sustains the global marketplace is now founded.

In this sense, a paradoxical form of asceticism can be called into play even in the production of enjoyment as an end in itself that is involved in the consumption characterizing contemporary capitalist production. In the second part of the book, instead, the need for a direct confrontation with philosophical discourse has led to an investigation on ascetic practice as an anthropological device, as is analyzed by Friedrich Nietzsche and Sigmund Freud, as well as by Weber himself.

A constitutive excess of human life is here identified as an original debt that should not be filled, but rather reproduced in order to be governed. A process similar to that described by Walter Benjamin in the fragment Capitalism as religion—on which I also dwell in this part of the book—according to which the capitalist economy is nothing more than a permanent cult that spreads itself through a perpetual form of borrowing and blame.

With the worsening of the current economic crisis the prophetic words of Benjamin increasingly become the focus of daily experience. In Europe, a period of waste and consumption has been countered by an era of savings and sacrifices, almost like a state of retaliation or the expiatory phase for a wrong committed. The "guilt" of having spent too much—on the basis of forms of virtual wealth based on ever more complex modes of debt—has become the slogan of the austerity policies that are imposed on major indebted European countries: debt has definitely emerged as the mechanism at the basis of the world economy.

In the same year this book was published in Italy other important writings on the subject came out: for example, that of Richard Dienst, *The Bonds of Debt: Borrowing Against the Common Good* (Verso, London 2011); or, in particular, that of David Graeber, *Debt. The First 5,000 Years* (Melville House, New York 2011) and that of Maurizio Lazzarato, *La fabrique de l'homme endetté. Essai sur la condition neoliberal* (Editions Amsterdam, Paris 2011).

The question of "debt," that in this work on the relationship between "asceticism and capitalism" had already emerged as the central condition of our times, then became the main theme of a second book, which follows this and entirely focuses on the link between debt and guilt—implicit in the very German word Schuld/Schulden—which was published in 2015 (E. Stimilli *Debito e colpa*, Ediesse, Rome 2015).

The intention was, here, to develop a comparison with the most important studies published on the subject in recent years, starting with what happened after the release of this work. Now, thanks to its English translation, this first research becomes accessible to a wider audience I hope to be able to provide, at least in part, useful food for thought in view of an investigation that, from what Foucault calls "ontology of the present" is able to outline possible alternative routes to what appears to be a path with no way out.

*Acknowledgments*

It would have been impossible to write this book without the direct experience of a "government of the living," both in the active and passive sense. But only now that the text has taken on an autonomous form have I realized the extent of the influence of my confrontation with Sebastiano on some of its essential parts; as for our children, Emilio and Simone, they have been able in their way to understand me and remind me of the reasons for facts when necessary. But I owe this work also to the fundamental help of my mother, who has first taught me the meaning of oikonomía.

The existence of this work is also essentially linked to the trust and the esteem granted to me by the old department of philosophy and by the current department of Human, Philosophical, and Formative Sciences at the University of Salerno, and by the Scuola Normale Superiore of Pisa.

In particular, I would like to thank Massimo De Carolis, Enrica Lisciani Petrini, and Davide Tarizzo who have read the manuscript at different stages and in different ways. Thanks to their critical comments and the discussions we had, I was able to find the strength to rework the material until it found a form that I hope will come close to their intentions.

The advice of Paolo Virno has been fundamental: He had the patience to read my book at various points and encourage me to move on.

I also owe much to the reading of Roberto Esposito who crucially convinced me to leave behind what I had written. I thank him particularly for the interest he has shown in my work.

I am very grateful to Gabriele Guerra who read the first draft. I also thank Giuliano Milani who, between one and the other school errand of our children, allowed me to talk about the economy, monasteries, and much more. Thanks to him I approached the middle ages in a new way.

Many of the single parts of this book have been discussed at seminars and conferences, where I took the opportunity to change and further reflect on the arguments presented. For one of these precious occasions

I sincerely thank Giovanni Filoramo who invited me to discuss the text that was the original nucleus of this book at the Peterson Library in Turin, with ideal interlocutors for the themes discussed. I also thank, for similar opportunities, Bazzicalupo; Adalgiso Amendola; Federico Chicchi; Giacomo Marramao; the Doctoral School of the Department of Historical and Political Studies at the University of Padua; the Doctoral School of the Department of Law at the University of Turin; Paolo Napoli, as a friend and director of the Centre d'étude des normes juridiques Yan Thomas at the École des Hautes Etudes en Sciences Sociales; the friends of the seminar on Benjamin studies, and those from seminars organized by the journal Forme di Vita.

Finally, a special thanks to the smile of those who listened to me in moments of crisis: Elisabetta Baiocco, who gave me precious help with final advice; my Italian editors Stefano Verdicchio and Gino Giometti, whose reading motivated renewed discussions; and the translator Arianna Bove and the publishing house SUNY Press for their availability and collaboration.

# Introduction

Modernity and its forms of power have often been interpreted through the paradigm of sacrifice: the renunciation of individual freedom for the preservation of life is regarded as a foundation stone of the creation of the nation state, a form of compensation exchanged at the price of repression is the hallmark of modern civilization. But now this model no longer seems to work: it cannot describe the present condition. Recent studies claim that the most common psychopathologies and contemporary malaises (such as anorexia, bulimia, new forms of addiction, depression, panic attacks) can no longer be referred to the dissonances originating from the removal of desire or the renunciation of instinctual drives that Sigmund Freud had diagnosed in the last century, nor can they be seen as the effects of sacrifices imposed by civilization; instead, they are deemed to result from an intricate process where seeking opportunities of enjoyment becomes a social imperative. Performance increasingly takes the place of the "reality principle" and desires are made completely adequate to the competitive logic of profit forcibly becoming conditions of self-affirmation. Jacques Lacan speaks of "discourse of capitalism" coining an expression that is particularly effective to confront one of the characteristic phenomena of the essence of our times: that is, that power has taken on the form of an economy in the era of globalization.

The main intention of this book is to carry out an analysis of the mechanisms that have engendered and continue to perpetrate this form of power. One of the most renowned views on this topic is Max Weber's thesis on the way capitalism originates from inner-worldly asceticism. The investigation carried out in my work starts from the premise that accumulation and profit are no longer retraceable to renunciation, that is, to the ability to delay the gratification of needs and desires for the sake of the accumulation of wealth, contrary to Weber's analysis, which is in line with the sacrificial paradigm. Instead, I claim that they are traceable to the

compulsive drive to enjoy and consume and that there is no ascetic practice lurking in the background.

Not only will I try to demonstrate the present relevance of the aspects
of Weber's thesis that do not make recourse to the sacrificial model, I will
also try to investigate the anthropological foundations of ascetic practice,
with a particular focus on Christian asceticism, because I am convinced
that it contributes to a reading of the present. My work follows the path
traced by Michel Foucault's studies on "governmental power" and the
asceticism of Late Antiquity.

Underlining my investigation of the anthropological foundations of
ascetic practice is a philosophical problem concerning human action and
the fact that, as Aristotle claimed, while the goal (*télos*) of production (*poíesis*) is different from production, the goal of practice (*prâxis*) is not. In the
*Ethics* Aristotle claims that "good action (*eupraxía*) itself is its end (*télos*)"
(Aristotle, *Ethics* 6.1140b). Each end or finality outlined by human action
presupposes the ability to have a goal that cannot be deduced from the
external environment and as such is not necessarily resolved in its extrinsic
realization. A finality of this kind is not limited to its teleological value; by
its nature, it is "purposiveness without end," to use an expression coined by
Kant that conveys both the obscurity and the intimate complexity of this
question. In this framework, identifying the ascetic nature of action only
makes sense in so far as the asceticism of praxis does not resolve itself in
sacrifice but confronts instead the "purposiveness without end" that appears
to be a determining feature of human action. This feature nurtures both the
ability of action to be innovative and the possibility of it being subjugated
by a mechanism that is its own end.

My thesis then is that in contemporary forms of production, something other than the ability to produce as such or goal-directed action is at
stake, and it characterizes human action more intrinsically. This is the fact
that human beings are not only given the ability to act in the pursuit of
determined goals, but also the possibility to engage in a practice that contains its own end in itself. The question of power in its current economic
form refers to the modes of government Foucault has already outlined: the
path he traced entails a reflection on the economy where the question of
work, production, and profit concerns planning, costs, and sacrifices, but
is also traceable to "ascetic" techniques of the self-production of human
life, the aimless productivity that intimately characterizes it and the ability of human action to possess its own end that is equally characteristic

of asceticism. This is the "force" that contemporary modes of production were capable of putting to work the most.

Unlike animal behavior, human praxis can be an action without end, or not predetermined by its actualization, and this potentiality of action has been central to Western political and ethical thought since Aristotle. It has been interpreted in various ways, often acquiring a negative connotation as something that is best to neutralize. My working hypothesis is that in our times, indebtedness has reached a global scale and has become an extreme form of compulsion to enjoy: unexpectedly, it has turned into the condition that characterizes the potentiality of action. In its various forms, debt has become the premise of current modes of subjectivation and, as such, needs to be reproduced rather than repaid.

Foucault's research is one of the most fertile for an assessment of the extent to which this indebtedness, this condition of "lacking," can constitute the privileged precedent for the pursuit of profit today. In this framework, it is necessary to underline the problematic connection between "Christian pastoral power" and "economic-governmental power" (Foucault, 1983, 2010a).

One of the greatest merits of Foucault's research is that it has not limited economic analysis to questions of work, ownership, interest, the accumulation of money, or the definition of the instrumental rationality that underlines them. Foucault speaks of economy in terms of "government," precisely to turn around the classical opposition between Christian charity and commercial rationality, thus identifying a different and meaningful link between Christianity and the economy.

Following the same path, Giorgio Agamben has recently undertaken an investigation on the Christian roots of the economy and modern "governmentality" that is of particular relevance to my work here (Agamben, 2011). At the origin of the current economic government of human beings and the world Agamben sees the theological paradigm of trinity and the Patristic development of an "economy of salvation." His analysis tries to integrate the shift, which in his view Foucault did not describe convincingly enough, from ecclesiastical pastorate to political government; however, in the process, in a sort of inversion of Foucault's work, he tends to abstract the theological *dispositif* (apparatus) from its practices, whereas Foucault consistently followed the development of both government and techniques of subjectivation simultaneously, because he saw them as constitutively linked.

Foucault's intention was undoubtedly to present a thorough study of "biopolitics." In my view, the most relevant aspect of his research is the assertion that the naturalization of politics and its transformation into biopolitics are not only an effect of the politicization of life as it is increasingly deprived of its forms and qualities and reduced to simple biological life. While this is the aspect of it that has received the most attention in recent years, in my view the debate on biopolitics today needs to take into account the mechanisms of subjectivation applied to the capacity of human living beings to shape and value their lives starting from the purposiveness without end that characterizes it. This, I believe, is the most urgent question arising from Foucault's work, and it is worth pursuing.

In order to recover the problem of the economy at the heart of Foucault's theory of governmentality while keeping within the confines of an analysis that does not lose sight of the practices through which power constitutes itself in economic terms and produces its own pathologies, this work starts with a return to Max Weber's seemingly outdated thesis on the origin of capitalism. Despite its limits, an element of Weber's position that is often left at the margins of its analysis works with one of the main aspects of my investigation. In my view, something that is currently not being discussed can in fact be of great use to our reading of the present. This is the argument that the main driver of the capitalist machine is the auto-finality implicit in the search for profit. What sets the mechanism in motion, for Weber, is not an acquisitive drive or an interest geared toward accumulation, but rather the illogical logic of "profit for profit's sake."

This implicit auto-finality of the search for profit as a main driver of capitalist economies that emerges from Weber's thesis, prior to pointing to the possibility of an internal critique of the developments of Weber's theory, opens up a wider question concerning the ability of human beings to relate to themselves in the absence of a predetermined goal. The fact that when separated from the interest in a specific acquisition profit still exists as an end in itself presupposes the experience inherent to human living beings of something beyond the situations they individually respond to, and points to a potential that cannot be exhausted in individual realizations. Every goal achieved, for men and women, exists only on the basis of that intrinsic auto-finality of their action, something Aristotle was the first reflect on.

An analysis of the uses of Weber's thesis for our reading of the present is called for because the path of self-destruction that contemporary life has embarked on is an end in itself, and the psychopathologies of this malaise of contemporary civilization are only tips of a much larger iceberg. Nurturing psychopathologies is largely part of this course and of its various manifestations, from democratic policies, the precarization of work in the economy, private indebtedness in financialization, migrant forms of production in the global labor market, the image of consumption in the commodified society of the spectacle, as well as the reduction of women's bodies to mere "accompanying" tools of new forms of power. These are not special phenomena: they constitute the ability of human living beings to relate to themselves in an autotelic way. In the path we have just described, this potential is split into different gradations, in the form of a freely produced dependency, and subjected to an exercise that involves singular lives in its realization.

1. A reinterpretation of Weber's thesis along these lines is offered at the end of the book. First, my work follows a path that takes into account the opposition to this interpretation of Weber.

At the beginning of the 1980s in France we witnessed the emergence of an anti-utilitarian movement linked to the journal *MAUSS* (*Mouvement anti-utilitariste dans les sciences sociales*), which has considerable influence on contemporary debates. Suffice it to mention the latest works of Serge Latouche, one of the best known members of MAUSS, much followed recently also by global movements engaged in a critique of unlimited growth. Whether on the course traced by Marcel Mauss and Karl Polanyi, or following the work of Georges Bataille, the anti-utilitarian movement has often confronted Weber's thesis without ever taking into serious consideration his notion of the profit of capitalist enterprise as an end in itself. Instead, in Weber's theory, it has regarded utilitarian reason as the single ailment of the mechanisms of the capitalist economy and its power. Given its importance and reach, a preliminary confrontation with this thread of research was deemed appropriate. The principal purpose of my work in this initial phase is to reveal the potential and limits of a framework that, in pursuing a critique of the capitalist economy, tends to separate the dimension of the gift and disinterestedness from that of utility and instrumentality.

In Weber's theory, irrespective of the satisfaction it might procure or of the utility or interest that drives it, in order to coincide with the effective gain of the enterprise, profit must be an end in itself. Auto-finality underlies, in this sense, any search for the means to achieve the ends identified by interests and geared to realizing the useful: this surplus inheres in it intimately. Consequently, a reconstruction of the political formulation of "interest" between the seventeenth and the eighteenth century is summarily presented, which against the anti-utilitarian reading identifies the mechanisms "interest" adopts, as a vector of utility and freedom, to functionally coincide with the power it is founded upon and with what exceeds personal utility in a convergence toward the "common good." In the political formulation of interest here presented, I find the development of a discourse aimed at the constant production of a freely construed dependency. What makes it possible is the internal neutralization of the disinterested auto-finality that characterizes human action. Weber regards the autotelic dimension as something exceeding instrumental reason, a main driver of capitalist enterprise. In the political notion of interest, this is translated in the terms of a spontaneous convergence of individual freedoms into a sort of "disinterested interest" that belongs at once to each one and everyone; in this, a new properly economic formulation of power is created. The intrinsic opacity of interest is due to the fact that despite their irreducible multiplicity, the convergence of points of view is guaranteed. Opaque is also the rationality that governs this process: the maximization of the interest of each individual coincides with something that, by exceeding it, is no longer it and only becomes realized through the full satisfaction of goals that are clearly outlined in the abstract form of consensus and, above all, become a common good with an end in itself.

In a path that is internal to the economy and calls this rationality back into question, the shift carried out by the main exponents of neoliberalism in the twentieth century might appear as a radicalization of the foundations of the classical liberalism that emerged from the political formulation of interest in the seventeenth century. Friedrich August von Hayek offers an indicative example of this: while searching for an economic legitimation of the political institution, Hayek speaks of a "spontaneous order" that produces itself on the basis of a "discipline of freedom." In his work, he outlines the growth of liberty in modes of discipline as an indirect form of political intervention that manifests itself as a self-managed order coinciding with that of the market. Hence the reduction of various classical figures of *homo oeconomicus*—the producer who owns the means of production, the wage laborer, the man of exchange, and the consumer—to the entrepreneur, in particular the self-entrepreneur. This implicitly radicalizes Weber's theory, in a shift from capitalist enterprise to the self-managed order of the market.

Hayek opens up a series of questions that were later developed by some of the most notorious members of the Chicago School, Theodore Schultz and Gary Becker, whom I also discuss. Their theories of "human capital" have found huge applications in contemporary forms of production, to the point of giving a new life to the use of the word "capitalism." Investment in human capital is the primary mode of the current economy and even working activities come to coincide with an entrepreneurial practice that is an end in itself. Thus, Weber's notion that the real driver of the capitalist enterprise is the ability to capitalize on what has no end but its own self becomes fully realized. The capitalization of the work each makes on oneself entails a form of self-discipline, a discipline of freedom in Hayek's sense, or, in keeping with my intention to revive Weber's theory I would speak of a sort of renewed asceticism. This exercise takes on forms that are very different from those Weber was thinking of when he wrote of the forms of life of the entrepreneur at the beginning of the last century. However, the connection between asceticism and the economy is central to his thesis and needs to be rethought, in an analysis where asceticism is not limited to the practice of renunciation as a means to achieve an extrinsic goal, but as something that is at the heart of human conduct. This is, after all, what emerges from Weber's own framework.

2. Past works on Weber have privileged the paradigm of secularization, underlining how goals shifted from a transcendent to an immanent finality in the debate on the origins of capitalism. For Weber, the secular translation of inner-worldly ascetic conduct carried out by Calvinism allowed for a separation of the rationality of praxis from the extrinsic finality of the transcendental ethical reward of Christian ascendance. Starting from his intuition and moving beyond it, rather than question the "origin" of capitalism my work posits the problem of the meaning of a mechanism that, despite this shift of finality onto a plane of immanence, seems to keep its inner workings unchanged while producing effects that profoundly differ with the conditions of its functioning. Weber's thesis on asceticism can thus be considered under new light.

It was thus deemed useful to carry out an analysis of Christian asceticism, on which Weber's thesis is premised, too. But rather than presupposing *what* asceticism is in Christianity, my work seeks to see *how* a form of life *in* Christ was constituted. This investigation claims neither to be exhaustive on this issue nor to outline a general interpretation of Christianity from the origins. Instead, I try to focus on a particular aspect that is extremely relevant to the overall discussion: the fact that in early Christianity a properly "economic" mode of life emerges and precedes the accomplished formation of asceticism in it. Through Weber and beyond Weber, it is possible to see how Christian ascesis and economy have been a fertile ground for the comprehension of Western economic discourse, especially considering that the "economy" is the form of expression of the experience of life in Christ since its origins, even before asceticism became a Christian problem as such. Starting from the link Weber identifies between Christian asceticism and capitalist economy, an economic mode of Christianity is identified that has emerged time and again in the development of economic discourse until it found its own radical actualization. Rather than outline an evolution of the link between the Christian notion of the economy and Western economic discourse, or underline a single root of economic discourse in the West, my intention is to find the possible and different historical actualizations of a mode that seems to have found its peculiar expression in Christian discourse.

The notion of economy formulated in early Christianity refers to the experience of freedom from the *nómos* of faith. It is the expression of the rule of law in the antinormative form of its accomplishment whereby life and law, *oîkos* and *nómos*, coincide. This is the first time the life of everyone so clearly takes on the semblance of an investment. The experience of sin at the basis of Christian existence becomes the experience of a *debt* that, thanks to the gift of grace, does not need to be repaid but can, as such, be administered in the form of an investment. Unstinting gratuity and economic administration, disinterest and interest, are not opposed to one another, they are connected at the outset. Making life fruitful in these terms seems an investment for no return. Whoever makes this investment, on the one hand, faces the impossibility of realizing in his "works" the commandments of the *nómos*, on the other hand, in seeking to profit from his actions, becomes separated from the goal it was turned toward in his "works" and can only resort to the auto-finality implicit in human praxis. However, in the Christian perspective, gain resides in this loss. The dimension of the gift and of disinterest in grace acts upon human conduct and allows it to suspend the goal orientation that characterizes it as "deed." Keeping the tension toward the future alive, however, creates a peculiar mode of investment on what in action has no other end but itself and according to the knowledge (*sophía*) of this world appears to be meaningless. In the perspective outlined in my investigation, this mode of experience finds its peculiar expression in Christian life: the possibility to invest not on deeds and their effects, but on the very praxis whose goals seem fundamentally purposeless.

In this respect, some have spoken of disinterested "inoperosity" as what inheres in early Christianity and made it possible to identify the "purity" in its origin that was allegedly betrayed. The singling out of an uncontaminated side of Christian history within the history of its power has always been a difficult task. The Christian community is immediately exposed to the management of gratuity and this consigns it to an unknown dimension of freedom. This freedom, which consists of the possibility of emancipation from an extrinsic norm and exemption from a relation of obligation aimed at the productive realization of an external command, is at the foundation of the institution of the Christian community but immediately ends up identifying itself with obedience, in the form of an absolute adherence of life to the law, of *oîkos* to *nómos*. Since its beginning, the practice of Christian life measures up with an unknown form of political institution, an autonomous production of subjectivation realized through faith. This experience has had an enormous influence on the modern development of a political and economic discourse fundamentally geared to the production of a freely construed dependence, since Kant, and especially after Hegel. However, it seems reductive to ascribe these moments to a single course of evolution or degeneration of Western rationality, as has been the case until Weber and in some ways also to our days. It seems more useful to reconstruct the different practices where an experience of life has found, historically, its realization and radical expression in Christianity since its origins.

In the history of Christianity, the clear recovery of an extrinsic finality that transcends human action can be traced back to the beginning of a transformation of the economic experience of life. This shift occurs at a time when asceticism was being clearly formulated as a Christian problem. The *oikonomía* becomes developed as an abstract plane of salvation, the divine plan of a history that one needs to conform to. Asceticism is here constituted as a technique functional and subjected to power: theology never ceased to provide the instruments for the survival of asceticism in centuries of its history.

In the Patristic perspective, the "economy of salvation" becomes a veritable economy of divine life and its incarnation in trinity theology and in Christology, and the divine order of the world in theology and history. This development privileged the formulation of a properly economic discourse as attested by recent threads of research on medieval history. This research has been of particular interest to my analysis here because it starts from a movement internal to ascetic literature. These studies demonstrate how the discourse on the economy, in the medieval period, is not only concerned with questions of accumulation, as the debate on usury seems to suggest. Instead, great attention is given to the texts produced in monastic institutions: these are taken literally as political and economic reflections. The paradigm of the commerce of salvation between God and man is the key to reading this monastic literature. However, when inspected closely, the production of an economic lexicon is evidenced by means of a detailed analysis of the ascetic experience. Asceticism thus becomes separated from the meritorious orientation whose goal is heavenly salvation; it becomes seen as a form of investment in itself, not on what can be securely acquired, but on what can be used on the basis of one's ability to renounce it. The ability of doing without nurtures ascetic life and gives "value" to things: this is the origin of Western economic discourse. What matters is neither the definitive possession of something, nor the capacity to do without it in view of an extrinsic goal. Instead, it is the possibility of investing in something that cannot be definitively owned, and refers to something that has no other end but itself in praxis. The form of "common good" becomes a fundamental device in the political mechanism of inclusion and exclusion for a community made up of those who act in conformity with the modes of profit implicit in renunciation, where renunciation becomes the only precondition for the circulation of wealth within said community.

Beyond possible ideas of a "spirit" of capitalism in Catholicism retraceable to these studies, and beyond the limits of such suggestion that also pertain to Weber's hypothesis, these two positions, while different, seem to agree on one important point, which is rather implicit in their respective works, and yet crucial to the study presented here. Although it is inscribed in the logic of a finalistic orientation of the commerce of salvation, my work examines asceticism in economic terms not so much as a functional technique of the economy of salvation, but as a fundamentally evaluative aspect of praxis and its intimate ability to invest in something that leads to the auto-finality implicit in it. Similarly, while in Weber inner-worldly asceticism is a praxis that allows for the separation of rationality from the extrinsic finality of a transcendent remuneration, this does not entail that economic action becomes thus exclusively entrusted to a formal rationality singularly geared to the calculation of the means necessary to the achievement of finally predetermined and solely immanent goals. In Weber, the planned exclusion of transcendent finality and the immanent orientation that result from it, in fact, allow for the emergence of an auto-finality to which human conduct is consigned preventively, and which in capitalism becomes "irrational," the enterprise as an end in itself. In other words, in both cases profit and the ability to invest are connected to something that is its own end, more than relating to an extrinsic finality.

3. While this is the framework of my outline of the connection between asceticism and the economy, as per Weber's contribution, it is worth reflecting again on the religious experience, which ascetic practice originates from. Among human experiences, the religious one most puts to fruition its being autotelic and this is attested by some of the most important studies in the sciences of religion between the nineteenth and the twentieth century. In this period, the social dimension of religious experience was given predominance in the work of Marcel Mauss, Émile Durkheim, and the members of the Collège de Sociologie; while others such as Rudolf Otto, Gerardus Van der Leeuw, or Mircea Eliade concentrated on its ontological and existential dimension. Religious experience in its various forms is such that the auto-finality implicit in human action reveals itself as a power with an end separate from man, and because of this it is also capable of constraining his conduct.

It is necessary to investigate the sense in which it is possible to claim that an investment in the auto-finality of praxis finds is final historical realization in the capitalist economy. Its separation seems to coincide, here with the practices through which it reproduces itself. One might say that capitalism, today, seems to be the self-referential religion of human life.

At this point, my investigation turns to a fragment written by a young Walter Benjamin on "capitalism as religion." Despite its rhapsodic character, this text opens up new paths for understanding the phenomenon. Karl Marx's work, too, is a privileged element of this confrontation with Benjamin's critique of capitalist society. The question of "real abstractions," so central to Marx's analysis of the processes of capitalist self-reproduction, is further illuminated if one considers the techniques of abstraction of life inherent to religious experience, which in Benjamin's short text takes on the character of a religious cult.

The parasitical derivation of the capitalist economy from Christian religion is underlined by Marx in several of his works, and taken on by Benjamin, for whom it becomes a permanent cult of man as "being in debt" through a perpetual form of indebtedness that reproduces the ways human life becomes subjected in Christianity. On these premises, in the rest of the work I try to show how, in so far as man is a living being without biologically determined extrinsic goals, and thus an end in itself, he has definitely become, in capitalism, a "being in debt": his existence is turned into a lack, a void that cannot be filled, and because of this it is constantly reproduced rather than filled. This is the presupposition for the subjectivation that is realized through it.

Alongside Marx, Benjamin names three other figures of modernity in his short text as the high priests of the capitalist cult: Friedrich Nietzsche, Sigmund Freud, and Max Weber. Aside from the criticisms that can be leveled against their work, what is relevant to my study is that they all identify, albeit in different ways, a problematic and constitutive link between asceticism and the economy, and this is the focus of the last part of my investigation. They see the mechanism that regulates ascetic practice as an anthropological device; they all similarly identify it, although they describe it differently: for all of them, ascetic practice involves a technique of abstraction that is not reduced to the mere negation of the living. Human life, without biologically predetermined ends, finds through this practice the forms of its self-sustenance. In Nietzsche this is "resentment," in Freud it is "removal," and in Weber the process of "rationalization": they explore the same mechanism in these different ways. In all their analysis, however, it is possible to detect an excess that is not exhausted in the practice it originates from. The will to nothingness linked to the will to power, in Nietzsche, the economic problem of masochism in Freud, and the meaninglessness of the rational and self-reflexive logic of profit in Weber are the three forms of this excess. On the basis of the Christian frame of reference it is possible to speak of debt and guilt to describe this remainder, this surplus. In any case, it concerns the state of lacking that emerges as a void to fill but above all the lack is a surplus that is constitutive of human beings and as such is reproduced while being simultaneously neutralized. Not only do these three thinkers see the finality without a predetermined goal, this determining characteristic of human beings, as being incorporated in the need for self-preservation and acquiring definitive goals that men and women are prepared to strive toward for their entire lives. Above all, what becomes clear is the manner in which this finality without goal is tuned into an abstract end in itself that neutralizes the potential that belongs to it and orients the movement it is caught up in toward something that is irreversible.

What seems to be the task today is finding an exercise capable of reconquering, time and again, the reversibility of this motion. The activation of counter-conducts that move in a different direction or the attempt to find points of resistance to the power that governs us as in the framework opened up by Foucault's research can still be insufficient. But one should not call into question, on this issue, the whole deactivation of the governmental dispositif, as Agamben proposes, because this seems more impracticable. The deactivated "inoperosity" within the machine of government comes to be almost limited to a lifeless sphere. Instead, what is at stake is not so much the possibility of deactivating, but rather that of reactivating, in ever changing ways, the finality without end which inheres in human praxis and coincides with its power to innovate and to change. This opportunity is given to men and women, and linked to the difficult task of radically questioning its current separation in the self-destructive form of the global enterprise that is its own end.

*Chapter 1*

# The End in Itself of the Economic Enterprise

In the first chapter of *The Protestant Ethic*, Max Weber cites a long quote from Benjamin Franklin. In his view, the quote is an exemplary description of the mechanism that grounds capitalist economies, which he notably terms "the spirit of capitalism." Commenting on the quote, Weber writes: "all Franklin's moral attitudes are colored with utilitarianism." Soon after, he adds: "but in fact the matter is not by any means so simple"; a closer look reveals that "something more than mere garnishing for purely egocentric motives is involved." Indeed, for Weber the main question is that "the *summum bonum* of this ethic, the earning of more and more money, [. . .] is thought of so purely as an end in itself, that from the point of view of the happiness of, or utility to, the single individual, it appears entirely transcendental and absolutely irrational." In the mechanism Franklin describes, "economic acquisition is no longer subordinated to man as the means for the satisfaction of his material needs. This reversal of what we should call the natural relationship, so irrational from a naïve point of view, is evidently as definitely a leading principle of capitalism as it is foreign to all peoples not under capitalistic influence. At the same time, it expresses a type of feeling which is closely connected with certain religious ideas" (Weber, 2001:18). This is the question we problematize here.

As anachronistic as it might seem, a return to Weber's thesis on the origin of capitalism for the purpose of reading this book helps define the idea of profit as the end in itself of capitalist enterprise, and to do so not merely in the terms of an instrumental and utilitarian logic of the satisfaction of personal interests. Returning to Weber's framework can cast a different light on the self-destructive enterprise that confronts us globally, one where, no matter how strong, even the notion of personal interest loses its explanatory power when dealing with a phenomenon that is clearly marked by a general lack of meaning. Today, the whole planet faces collapse, a point of no return, and even the people who from this mechanism would have only drawn advantage now have to deal with the direct and self-damaging consequences of their trust in its functioning. A notion of instrumental reason as the ailment of accumulation and unlimited growth striving to realize personal utility is by itself inadequate to explain the mechanisms behind such phenomenon and its imminent and catastrophic effects.

Despite its potential relevance to our present, this aspect of Weber's argument has never been given due consideration in the critical literature, which has mainly offered interpretations that go in the opposite direction to the one outlined here. The critical literature presents utilitarianism and the satisfaction of personal interests as one of the unquestionable foundations of the capitalist economy, and opposed to this view an "anti-utilitarian" notion of human beings and the world has emerged.

In this context, starting from my different reading of Weber's thesis, it is useful to question, first and foremost, the sharp separation between what is gratuitous and disinterested and what is instrumental. According to anti-utilitarianism, the former is constitutive of human beings and their social realm, while what is instrumental and linked to the logic of utility allows for the emergence of the capitalist enterprise as a deviation and denaturalization of it. To identify the mechanisms that feed this enterprise, I believe it makes sense, instead, to radically rethink the role played by that which has no other end but itself.

## On the General Economy and Its Excess

At the end of the 1940s, in collaboration with the nuclear physicist Georges Ambrosino, Georges Bataille began work on the project of an "economy on a universal scale," which called into question the issue of the energy necessary to life. His aim was to work out a notion of the energy that concerns the living as such. Similarly, to the sun "that gives without ever receiving," this force always seems to be in excess of the mere survival it guarantees nonetheless (Bataille, 1991:28). An exuberance of useless energy is typical of living beings, so much so that the "energy produced" is "superior to that needed for its production" (Bataille, 1991:469). This *surplus* permeates life not in the form of an advantageous accumulation, but in that of a gratuitous unproductive expenditure, as in the case of the "expenditure" of solar energy.

In his 1933 essay entitled "La Notion de dépense" (The Notion of Expenditure) Bataille had already presented this view of *dépense*, of an unproductive expenditure at the origin of life. But around twenty years later he returned to the question in the framework of a "general economy." "General" mainly means that the question cannot be addressed as a mere technicality; its object cannot be treated as a "thing." For Bataille, "The economy is man himself who is not reducible to things" (Bataille, 1991:472). Bataille's anthropological approach to the economy grounds his notion of a general management of life wherein a surplus is its permanent and constitutive reality. Rather than the striving for a productive satisfaction of primary needs, human activity is characterized by unproductive expenditure. Contrary to the dominant capitalist economy, Bataille presents this surplus gratuity as the main driver of the general economy. Known are the elements of ambiguity present in his work, and the openings they have permitted (Esposito, 2015). Bataille's work is largely relevant to our argument, not only because he qualifies human life in economic terms, but also, and especially, because in his approach human beings are ontologically marked by a constitutive excess, and their actions cannot be reduced to the productive activities of their self-sustenance.

The fundamentally social dimension of the surplus gratuity at the origin of human life is also confirmed by Marcel Mauss in his essay on *The Gift*, which Bataille cites. Bataille not only underlines the connection between religious and economic behavior that emerges in the practice of the *potlatch*, he also emphasizes that "it would be futile, as a matter of fact, to consider economic aspects of potlatch without first having formulated the viewpoint defined by *general economy*" (Bataille, 1998:68). In his view, "there would be no potlatch if, in a general sense, the ultimate problem concerned the acquisition and not the dissipation of useful wealth" (Bataille, 1998:68). For Bataille, what happens in the social practice of the gift exchange of the potlatch is a constitutive human fact concerning the power of uselessly and aimlessly squandering what is given, rather than the possibility of acquiring means useful to one's survival. This power gives way to an obligation to reciprocate that becomes itself a form of power. For Bataille, the squandering of the gift, an acquired prestige turns this power into a mode of appropriation; yet this takes nothing away from the fact that the potlatch is still the opposite of calculated and profitable exchange and of the appropriation and accumulation of things. Despite clear ambiguities and contradictions, what matters in his view is that this practice realizes above all "the useless squandering of oneself and one's goods;" in other words, the possibility, for man, to "*use* that whose *utility* it denied" (Bataille, 1998:73), which is to say, something that has no end other than itself.

The practice of the potlatch expresses the excess gratuitousness at the foundation of Bataille's general economy and resurfaces time and again in different forms (for instance, where he writes of its role in the glorious economy of the Church during the Renaissance), but as he makes to coincide the moment it was definitively excluded from it with the advent of the capitalist economy. Its survival was made impossible by the full realization of instrumental reason and the "rule of utility" imposed by capitalism. Determinant to this turn, in Bataille's argument, is Weber's thesis that the origin of capitalist modes of production is to be found in inner-worldly Protestant ascesis: "Weber deserves the credit for having rigorously analyzed the connection between a religious crisis and the economic turnover that gave rise to the modern world" (Bataille, 1991:116).

For Bataille, who takes to heart Mauss's lesson and is an active participant to the *Collège de Sociologie*,

> This religious determination of the economy is not surprising; it even defines religion. [. . .] Religion is the satisfaction that a society gives to the use of excess resources, or rather to their destruction (at least insofar as they are useful). [. . .] The only point is the absence of utility, the gratuitousness of these collective determinations. They do render a service, true, in that men attribute to these gratuitous activities consequences in the realm of supernatural efficacy; but they are useful on that plane precisely insofar as they are gratuitous, insofar as they are needless consumptions of resources first and foremost. (Bataille, 1991:120)

According to Bataille, Weber's greatest insight was that he demonstrated the fundamental shift in Christian religion, first with Luther, and then, especially, with Calvin. The element of the gift, generally implicit in the realm of religion, with Christianity acquired a special valence in relation to the role of "deeds" with respect to "grace." Protestantism established a clear distinction between gratuity and instrumental reason; thus utilitarianism could be established as the dominant logic of the capitalist economy.

Weber's greatness, for Bataille, was evident in his appreciation of the legacy left by Calvin that was taken up and continued by English and American Puritanism. Calvin, no less than Luther, rejected merits and deeds, but his principles were different and of greater effect: "for Calvinism, with all its repudiation of personal merit, is intensely practical. Good works are not a way of attaining salvation, but they are indispensable as a proof that salvation has been attained" (Bataille, 1991:123). In this sense, for Bataille, Calvinism "carried the overturning of values affected by Luther to its extreme consequence." Calvin did more than deny that forms of expenditure were deserving of redemption, as already evidenced in the aspirations of the Catholic Church of the Renaissance, he also limited the possibility of useful deeds: "what he offered man as a means of glorifying God was the negation of his own glory." For Bataille, "the sanctification of God was thus linked to the desacralization of human life," thus sanctioning "the relegation of mankind to gloryless activity" (Bataille, 1991:124).

> The revolution affected by the Reformation has, as Weber saw, a profound significance: it marked the passage to a new form of economy. Referring back to the spirit of the great reformers, one can even say that by accepting the extreme consequences of a demand for religious purity it destroyed the sacred world, the world of nonproductive consumption, and handed the earth over to the men of production, to the bourgeois. (Bataille, 1991:127)

The lucidity with which Bataille charts the emergence of the unproductive expenditure of human energy does not exempt him from criticism of his reading of Weber and the way he uses his thesis to lend support to a "limited" view of the capitalist economy as based on a utilitarian logic and on the satisfaction of personal interests. It is now necessary to question the adequacy of this interpretation of capitalism, one that is common in recent literature, while taking into account the recent transformations of the capitalist mode of production. Aside from Bataille's reading, what remains relevant in Weber's thesis and the fecundity of related research will soon be demonstrated. Despite the limitations of his argument and of those that

followed in its footsteps, there remains a great unexplored potential in it
for our reading of the present.


## Utility Is Not Enough

Contrary to "the tradition of the classical economists, who attempted to
base the law of the market on the alleged propensities of man in the state
of nature," and who also abandoned "all interest in the cultures of 'uncivilized' man as irrelevant to an understanding of the problems of our age"
(Polanyi, 2001:128), Karl Polanyi is one of the first scholars who used
anthropology and ethnology and the research of Bronislav Malinowski
and Richard Thurnwald on the economic comportment of primitive people in an attempt to confute, in line with Bataille's position, the idea of
a "timeless economic man" as interpreted by the utilitarian logic of the
market. In *The Great Transformation*, Polanyi claims that "if one conclusion stands out more clearly than another from the recent study of early
societies, it is the changelessness of man as a social being." In his view, "the
outstanding discovery of recent historical and anthropological research is
that man's economy, as a rule, is submerged in his social relationships"
(Polanyi, 2001:128). For him, "so-called economic motives spring from
the context of social life" to the extent that "the economic system is, in
effect, a mere function of social organization" (Polanyi, 2001:134). Polanyi
observes that in primitive societies man "does not act so as to safeguard
his individual interest in the possession of material goods; he acts so as to
safeguard his social standing, his social claims, his social assets" (Polanyi,
2001:130). "The human passions, good or bad, are merely directed toward
noneconomic ends" and all acts of exchange do not primarily take the
form of barter, but occur "by way of free gifts that are expected to be recip-
rocated" (Polanyi, 2001:131). The economy *sensu stricto* is thus reduced to
the expression of a determinate economic system marked by a generalization of market relations and their becoming autonomous from the fabric
of social relations. The peculiarity of Western society, for Polanyi, is that
it does without the meaning of social community and substitutes it with
individualistic utilitarianism.

> The true criticism of market society is not that it was based on eco-
> nomics—in a sense, every and any society must be based on it—but

that its economy was based on self-interest. Such an organization of economic life is entirely unnatural, in the strictly empirical sense of exceptional. (Polanyi, 2001:414)

Polanyi, though he does cite Malinowski and Thurnwald, unlike Bataille, never explicitly refers to Mauss in his works; and yet the essay on *The Gift* seems to work implicitly as a premise of his argument. Common to both Mauss and Polanyi is clearly the presupposition that personal interest and the notion of "utility" are the foundations of a market economy. They both criticize the "naturalness" of utilitarian economics; the notion, according to the logic of the market, that it is natural for human beings to equate interest with an individual search for utility. Mauss writes that "the word 'interest' is recent in origin and can be traced back to the Latin *interest* written on account books opposite rents to be recovered" (Mauss, 1966:131). To the claim that "the victory of rationalism and mercantilism was required before the notions of profit and the individual were given currency and raised to the level of principles," he adds that "one can date roughly—after Mandeville and his *Fable des Abeilles*—the triumph of the notion of individual interest" (Mauss, 1966:74).

In his study of archaic societies, Mauss charts the functional relationship between gift and exchange. The working premise of his argument is the conviction that the market economy is a recent historical phenomenon that calls into being characteristics that are entirely artificial and opposed to man's originally social nature. In the archaic societies he analyzes, the phenomenon of the gift is a system of reciprocal relations at the origin of what he defines "total social facts"; it results from deeds that are at once free and constrictive, where the freedom of the gift obliges the recipient to reciprocate, and it is precisely this that makes social cohesion possible (Fimiani, 1984).

Mauss writes that "much of our everyday morality is concerned with the question of obligation and spontaneity in the gift," that "it is our good fortune that all is not yet couched in terms of purchase and sale," because "our morality is not solely commercial," but "we still have people and classes who uphold past customs and we bow to them on special occasions and at certain periods of the year" (Mauss, 1966:63). Nonetheless, the system of total performance manifested in the phenomenon of the gift, "towards which we are striving to have our own society—on its own scale—directed" (Mauss, 1966:66) is almost completely confined to archaic societies; so much so that, in his text, Mauss calls for a "return to the old and elemental" (Mauss, 1966:67). For Mauss, the logic of the gift is reactivated in contemporary societies in the welfare systems of social democratic countries; these are desirable ways in which society and the fundamental sociality of man are defended, and for which the market logic is compensated.

Compared to Mauss, Polanyi underlines the plurality of forms of exchange behind social cohesion (reciprocity, redistribution, market), and believes that "forms of integration did not represent 'stages' of development, [. . .] they did not entail any temporal sequence" (Polanyi, 2001:313), as implied in Mauss's analysis. Mauss charts the gradual development and transformation of archaic societies (where we find "total performances") to ancient societies (founded on the "principle of gift-exchange"), followed by a shift to modern societies where the market is predominant. Similarly, for Polanyi the market economy is an "exceptional" phenomenon in the history of human societies and the elements of the gift are still present in it only as marginal residues, perhaps represented by the exchange of presents at Christmas. As he claims in the closing lines of *The Great Transformation*, even the path of social democracies toward redistribution does not exclude the market, a view he shares with Mauss. Finally, for both, whether as an archaic form of exchange or as something other, the gift is definitively excluded from the theoretical framework of modernity.

At the beginning of the 1980s in France, the anti-utilitarian move-ment in the social sciences formed a research group under the acronym MAUSS (Mouvement anti-utilitariste dans les sciences sociales), to inves-tigate the questions opened up by Mauss himself and later taken up by Polanyi. Unsurprisingly perhaps, despite the indications left by Mauss's legacy, the group was confronted with the need of reintegrating the gift within a framework of postmodernity, or of at least questioning its sup-posed exclusion from modernity. What led the anti-utilitarian movement to question its theoretical premises was that at the beginning of the 1990s they witnessed a profound change in the classical modes of production: with their ingenious ability to put to work precisely what was "useless," new modes of production were now relying on flexibility, creative facul-ties, and skills developed in the realm of communication and personal investment for work. In all of these, real practices of "self-giving" could be discerned: a "great transformation" was taking place, and its effects were only just coming to light.

Issue twelve of the *Revue du MAUSS* of 1991, for instance, featured an article by Ahmet Insel on the theory of efficiency wages outlined by the recent Economics Nobel PrizeP winner George Arthur Akerlof, where the labor contract is recast as a "partial gift exchange" (Insel, 1991). In 1993, Bernard Cova published an article on the gift in management theory. A similar resurgence of interest can be discerned in recent research involving members of the anti-utilitarianism group where the gift is discussed in the framework of environmental studies. After the creation of the World Business Council for Sustainable Development in 1992, which saw the participation of large corporations such as Nestlé, Fiat, Total-Fina, as Western governments and enterprises initiated discussions, in terms of environmental sustainability, of the problems arising from the exploitation of the ecosystem, Serge Latouche, one of the main exponents of MAUSS whose work has been closely followed by global movements critical of unlimited growth, determined that it was no longer possible to speak in terms of "sustainable development," as he had done initially, and thus introduced the term "de-growth" to redefine a life style that is alternative to the one dominant in the so-called developed world (Latouche, 2009).

Parallel to this clear and somewhat unexpected recuperation of the notion of gift by the utilitarian camp, and its subsequent redefinition by MAUSS researchers, was also what Alain Caillé, one of the founders of the anti-utilitarian movement, has termed a philosophical "rehabilitation" of Mauss himself (Caillé, 1989). The reference is to Mauss rehabilitation in philosophy by Emmanuel Lévinas and by Luc Boltanski in sociology, but especially to Jacque Derrida, who writes, in an anonymous text published in the *Revue du Mauss*. In his introduction to the issue of the *Revue* prior to the publication of Derrida's text, Caillé also outlined his philosophical interpretation of the gift and explained the peculiar situation MAUSS found itself in, one where "from spending the first ten years critiquing, amongst other things, utilitarianism and the axiomatic of interest that permeated the social sciences, we had to start fighting a notion of the gift that was too disembodied and spiritualized [. . .] in order to demonstrate how it was, in fact, full of very real interests" (Caillé, 1989).

Derrida's *Given Time* sums up ten years of reflection on the meaning of the gift. In this work, Derrida writes of his relation to Mauss's though by means of a reading of a short but unsettling text by Baudelaire, *La Fausse Monnaie*. In this reading, the story of the gift of a false currency indicates both the impossibility of a gift, and, due to its implicit incalculability, also the unique reality of it. Derrida presents a distinction between gift and exchange to then situate Mauss's work within the domain of the latter. Derrida reduces the circulation of goods, products, monetary signs, and commodities that move exchange and when the economy originates, to the inner dynamism of life and, with reference to the "circularity of time," to human life itself, or, in other words, to the constitution of the subject, the "movement of subjectivation" (Derrida, 2005:24).

On the one hand, Derrida concedes that human beings "never give anything without calculating, consciously or unconsciously, its re-appropriation, its exchange, or its circular return-and by definition this means re-appropriation with surplus-value, a certain capitalization"; here, he writes, "the very definition of the subject as such" is under question, because "one cannot discern the subject except as the subject of this operation of capital" (Derrida, 1992:101, 2005). On the other hand,

> Throughout and despite this circulation and this production of surplus-value, despite this labor of the subject, there where there is trace and dissemination [...] a gift can take place, along with the excessive forgetting or the forgetful excess that [...] is radically implicated in the gift. The death of the donor agency [...] is not a natural accident external to the donor agency; it is only thinkable on the basis of, setting out from the gift. This does not mean simply that only death [...] can give. No, only a "life" can give, but a life in which this economy of death presents itself and lets itself be exceeded. Neither death nor immortal life can ever give anything, only a singular *surviving* can give. This is the *element* of this problematic. (Derrida, 2005:101–102)

The gift, for Derrida, is fundamentally *uneconomic* and "impossible" (Derrida, 1992:7, 2005) because it is the condition of possibility of giving life as well as of its oblivion. The main reference point for his argument is Heidegger's notion of *Ereignis*, the *giving oneself* of being in its oblivious concealment. Derrida's argument has the merit of following Bataille and leading the question of the gift—and of exchange—back into the properly philosophical terrain of the self-production of human life. However, the emergence of an unproductivity internal to capitalization leads him, and Heidegger, to the obscure presupposition of an impossible possibility of the event of a gift that is "different" and "separate," its vital economic movement being nothing but a "trace." Here the need of what Caillé defined as "fighting a notion of the gift that was too disembodied and spiritualized" that the anti-utilitarian movement faced when confronted with the philosophical reworking of the questions opened up by Mauss's essay, though rather generic, does not seem unjustified. And perhaps it should not come as a surprise that Derrida's perspective also had resonance in the field of theology, in support of a stance on charity as opposed to the material logic of the market economy.

## In Defense of Society: Society State and/or Market?

The first reaction to the devastating economic crisis we are experiencing, motivated by the clear change of course in U.S. policy, was to conjure up the old alternative between state and market. This alternative presupposes a separation between the realm of human giving and disinterestedness and that of the instrumental and calculating logic of the market driven by human interest. In Europe, even before the effects of the crisis were fully manifest, even the proponents of the policies of neoliberalism had readied themselves for the eventuality of such an alternative and, in some instances, went as far as developing a critique of a sort of "market-based" view of the market. Although state intervention is an efficient remedy to the most recent deleterious effects of the disastrous management of the world economy, identifying state management as a clear alternative to the market, as a plan, seems too facile an option: today, the state that ought to represent such an alternative lacks all the prerequisites that would allow it to play the role of antagonist to the market, leaving open all the difficulties implicit in this contraposition and the separation it presupposes.

Furthermore, a comparison between the current situation and that of the crash of 1929 keeps being made. On this, it is worth remembering that even in1944 Polanyi had recognized the dubiousness of the argument that contrasts state and market and identified it as one of the major causes of the fall of Wall Street and the subsequent victory of National Socialism in Germany. According to Polanyi, on the one hand, the economic logic of the market professes that an intrinsic harmony governs economic principles, yet unless society had protected itself with recourse to the intervention of the social state, the harmonious self-regulation behind these principles would have led to the destruction of the very society they purported to defend. On the other hand, the obstacles to the self-regulation of the market did nothing but put society in a different danger. For Polanyi, this inner crisis led to the affirmation of National Socialism as the most "efficient" form of "protection."

> In the half-century 1879–1929, Western societies developed into close-knit units, in which powerful disruptive strains were latent. The more immediate source of this development was the impaired self-regulation of market economy. Since society was made to conform to the needs of the market mechanism, imperfections in the functioning of that mechanism created cumulative strains in the body social. (Polanyi, 2001:355)

On the one hand, the state protection of the social realm arises from a need of self-preservation that is internal to society; on the other, the promoters of economic liberalism and of the self-regulation of the market did not refrain from demanding "the intervention of the state in order to establish it, and once established, in order to maintain it" (Polanyi, 2001:270). "The stubbornness with which economic liberals [. . .] had supported authoritarian interventionism, merely resulted in a decisive weakening of the democratic forces which might otherwise have averted the fascist catastrophe" (Polanyi, 2001:391).

> The fascist solution of the *impasse* reached by liberal capitalism can be described as a reform of market economy achieved at the price of the extirpation of all democratic institutions [. . .]. The economic system which was in peril of disruption would thus be revitalized, while the people themselves were subjected to a re-education designed to denaturalize the individual and make him unable to function as the responsible unit of the body politic. (Polanyi, 2001:397)

During World War II, this thesis was supported by others such as, for instance, Franz Neumann in his work *Behemoth*, published in 1942. The purpose of this book, as the subtitle reads, was to identify the "structure and practice of National Socialism" in economic terms, as it emerged from the crisis of the Weimar Republic and the coming together of state and market in the form of a "totalitarian monopolistic economy," presented as what was declared to be the government of mass democracy. The debate between Neumann and the Frankfurt School is well known (Marramao, 1981). The "social" character of National Socialism and its economic matrix, which Neumann and Polanyi analyze and see as being related to its totalitarian form, is the extreme manifestation of a misunderstood conflict between state and market. This leads to questioning a mode of defending society implicit in both the form of state power and its bond with the logic of liberalism, and in the self-regulation of the market guaranteed by the intervention of the state even during the last stages of Hitler's regime.

A similar and equally pressing question arises from the terms of current comparisons between the recent economic crisis and that of 1929. A marked difference from the debate that continued up until the end of the last century is that as an interpretative category of the phenomenon of Nazism and the expression of an extreme phase of the domination of Western abstract, repressive, instrumental, and sacrificial reason, the notion of totalitarianism has now lost its efficacy. Underlining this notion was also a critique of the modern mass democracies that succeeded National Socialism. Despite the persistence of mass and totalitarian forms of power, and despite the recognition of a deep link between totalitarianisms and mass democracies, this interpretation appears inadequate when merely equated to an application of the sacrificial paradigm. More poignant is the argument found between the lines of the economic interpretation of Nazism offered by Neumann and Polanyi. For them, liberalism, state power, and, in its extreme form, the regime of National Socialism, are driven not so much by repression, as by the need to defend society, though the latter invariably results in the annihilation of what was meant to be protected.

From such a standpoint, the "evolution of the market model" supposed to precede this process remains unclear. Polanyi offers a critique of the classical notion of *homo oeconomicus* and charts this evolution without clarifying some important passages. On the one hand, he claims that the mechanism of the market has led to the erroneous belief that economic determinism was a law valid for all human societies, thus legitimizing the predominance of Western society over "uncivilized" countries and communities. On the other hand, Polanyi leaves the relationship between the economy and society partly unexplained. His argument betrays a homogeneous vision of the economy that recalls the Aristotelian distinction between economy and chrematistics: one the one hand, a "natural" economy intertwined with society; on the other hand, an "unnatural" one driven by personal interest. What remains unclear are the mechanisms and modalities of this "exceptional" shift to the unnatural, especially if the instance of defense intrinsic to social reality is taken into account, a defense that though not explicitly admitted to, is particularly applied to the market society.

The free self-constitution of the social is somewhat implicit in the logic of the market as discussed by Polanyi and this also emerges from more recent interpretations. For instance, the late studies of Michel Foucault have left a strong mark on contemporary philosophy. Society Must Be Defended is the title of his 1976 course at the Collège de France and inaugurated his research on biopolitics, which is still debated not only for its relatively recent publication but also for its relevance to an analysis of the present. The standpoint of the defense of society, previously outlined as an element implicit in Polanyi and Neumann's works but never followed up to its logical conclusions, in Foucault's analysis clearly emerges from the need of making politics independent from the juridical state model of sovereignty and of thinking of power in terms of relations of forces, "power relations" that are plural and mobile, and in terms of their dynamism, even in the form of the "care" implicit in social reality that ultimately coincides with the modes of "care of the self" on which it is based.

Foucault felt the need to investigate the "unpolitical" aspects of forms of power that were contemporaneous to him, the fact that power had fundamentally become biopower, the defense and care for mere biological life, and Nazism, with its destructiveness, represented the premise for as well as the most extreme expression of this. Thus Foucault's research moves from a standpoint that is, in a way, external to politics in order to approach the intrinsic heterogeneity and inner dynamics that animate the drive to defend society. In the lecture series of 1977–1978 that immediately followed Society Must Be Defended, Foucault introduces "governmentality" and its "security" devices as techniques of protecting society, now specifically identified as "population." These notions are key for an interpretation of both the history of modern states in their liberal and social democratic guises, and of the politico-economic logic of the market in its neoliberal version. In this context, the state is one way of governing, and not the essence of power; yet its stability depends precisely on the fact that it only exists in the articulate and complex web of the governmental practices from which it results. Its political character is not a given but the effect of a series of complex structures of government; its originally nonpolitical character makes it impossible to see them merely as its efficient cause. Instead, government is the means through which politics historically unfolds in the

forms of instituted power, and its political-economic configuration represents the most extreme version of neoliberalism and thus fully exposes its
implicit heterogeneity, and its undeniable intrinsic ungovernability.

Foucault essentially plumbs the depths of the different ways of drawing together what is heterogeneous in the actual historical figures of governmentality. Informing his work is the conviction that government is
essentially "the government of men," in the sense that men are both beings
that must be governed and a matter/substance that needs governing. In
this framework, the individual and social plane are intrinsically joined so
as to both appear as the result of "processes of subjectivation" where an
ungovernable element is constantly and necessarily caught in the web of
governmental activity. Unsurprisingly, Foucault spent much of his final
years studying the ancient techniques of constitution of the subject and
the ascetic practices of subjectivation; there, though not always straight-
forwardly, he identified in Christian religion a turning point of the history of governmentality, which caused the emergence of an unprecedented
form of constitution of the subject as a "field of generalized obedience"
(Foucault, 2010a:177). On this course, liberalism becomes a stratagem of
Christian religion.

One of the aims of our work is to make Foucault's intuition on the
Christian origin of liberal governmentality explicit and to try to investigate
the practices through which this shift occurred more closely. Therefore,
our work cannot be exempt from a preliminary inquiry on the presumed
utilitarian matrix of liberal governmentality; this should not limit itself to
a critique of the "interested nature" abstractly presupposed in the *homo
oeconomicus* (as offered by the anti-utilitarian developments of Mauss's and
Polanyi's analyses, though these are still worth our consideration). Instead,
against the grain of such approach, it will be necessary to reconstruct
the mechanisms and practices that made it possible, without recourse to
the alleged separation of human gratuitous and social character from his
merely instrumental dimension.

## Passions and Interests

The most complex aspect of Weber's thesis on the "spirit" of capitalism,
as we have seen in Bataille and will explore in more detail in our analysis
of Weber's works, is the shift from inner-worldly Protestant ascesis to the

instrumental action pertaining to the economic domain. In Weber's view, the Reformation operates a religious legitimation of capitalism and functioned as a vector for the valorization of mundane activity. Luther's notion of grace as the motor of inner-worldly ascesis frees human agency from all transcendent finality, to the extent that, according to the anti-utilitarian argument, a sharp distinction is made between the donative and transcendent dimension of social relations on the one hand, and on the other, an instrumental reason at the origin of capitalism that definitively excludes any logic that is not strictly selfish (Caillé, 1989).

However, Weber's argument is more complex than this, not only because for him in the shift from inner-worldly transcendence to instrumental action human agency becomes valued only at the price of a radical devaluation of its condition, seen as being corrupted by the debt of sin. More importantly, the instrumentality of action, aimed at identifying means for ends dictated by interests and geared toward the search for individual utility, presupposes an autotelic condition: its profiting results from an end in itself, independently of the satisfaction that it may give, or any one individual's utility and interest. This is so that, paradoxically, in Weber's view, the "acquisitive drive and rationalism of utilitarianism still have nothing to do with modern capitalism" (Weber, 2001:517).

The antecedent of the capitalist economy is not the *homo oeconomicus*, but the figure of the inner-worldly ascetic, whence profit is not merely seen as a response to the logic of individual interest. On the one hand, according to Weber, the "acquisitive drive," as a sign of grace, has an intrinsic and self-reflexive purpose that is mysteriously at the origin of the "irrationality" implicit in Western dominant rationality, and this aspect of the argument is the most questionable. On the other hand, the search for profit is a form of "accounting for existence" rooted in life "conduct," where life itself is a "commercial enterprise," and this aspect of Weber's argument throws light on the complexity of human action as an auto-finalized praxis and presents affinities with Foucault's studies on the nexus between economic and governmental power and ascetic practices of subjectivation. In any case, it is important here to underline that the constitution of interest as a driver of action is linked to questions that emerge from praxis.

From this standpoint, it is worth approaching the origin of utilitarianism with a different outlook, to verify how and why interest comes to acquire such predominance, and to reconstruct thus the modes of identification of what is useful to its satisfaction. With all probability from such an investigation a very different picture from that offered by the anti-utilitarian movement would emerge. Unable to take on such an onerous task in detail, here I simply point out that while during the Classical period and Late Antiquity, the discourse on passions, which we dwell on later, was formulated as *áskesis*, as a constant exercise on the self, in Christian ascetism it became explicitly appreciated in economic terms, and proliferated, again, in the moral treatises of the 1600s. This discourse became a determining factor in the formulation of interest as the primary drive of human action. The elaboration of interest as a search for the means to achieve predetermined ends, as oriented toward the realization of utility, presupposes a practice of auto-finality that is intrinsic to human praxis. Its presence is dependent on man's ability to relate to himself without extrinsic ends; it is based on the experience, well represented in the debates on ascetism within Christianity and Paganism, of a potential that is in excess of the individual situations it responds to, a potential that is never exhausted in each determined realization, and that in fact exposes how every accomplished end exists only thanks to an auto-finality that is implicit in the actions of men and women.

At a closer glance, then, one could put forward the hypothesis that, in this context, utilitarianism does not emerge as a mere confutation and subsequent separation of Christian morality, but represents an accomplished radicalization of it (Laval, 2007:126). Indicative in this sense is, for instance, the fact that in the work of Bernard de Mandeville a clear application of the Christian notion of divine grace can be detected (Laval, 2007:107–126). Unsurprisingly, the Dutch doctor, author of the *Fable of the Bees*, the manifesto of utilitarianism, was educated in a rigorously Calvinist milieu. In fact, Mandeville's idea stems from his reflection on the struggle of the passions and on the possibility of finding a government of concupiscence in opposition to desires as put forward by the most radical Christianity of the seventeenth century; his reflection results in the claim that such government is not only possible, but also in conformity with the "corrupted" nature of human beings.

Albert O. Hirschman demonstrates how and to what extent, between the end of the 1500s and the beginning of the 1600s, the debate on man's opposing passions contributed to the formulation of the new paradigm of interest, of which he tries to chart the history. According to Hirschman, once passion was deemed destructive and reason ineffectual, the view that human action could be exhaustively described by attribution to either one or the other meant an exceedingly somber outlook for humanity. A message of hope was therefore conveyed by the wedging of interest in between the two traditional categories of human motivation. Interest was seen to partake in effect of the better nature of each, as the passion of self-love upgraded and contained by reason, and as reason given direction and force by that passion. The resulting hybrid form of human action was considered exempt from both the destructiveness of passion and the ineffectuality of reason. No wonder that the doctrine of interest was received at the time as a veritable message of salvation! (Hirschman, 1977:43–44)

In this framework, interest is understood as a "compensatory passion," as a "counterweight" to the damaging and destructive egotistical passions, and furnishes a justification of capitalism "before its triumph." This prompts our investigation of the intrinsically political-economic function of the notion of interest.

## Maximization of Power: Interest between Freedom and Common Good

Although a properly "political" understanding of the term "interest" can be documented since the first half of the sixteenth century, its origins are still "cloaked in an aura of mystery" (Ornaghi, 1984:3). The question is complicated by the philological and semantic vicissitudes of this ambiguous lexeme (Devoto, 1967). The Italian word *interesse* is the substantive form of the Latin infinitive *inter-esse* that properly indicates "to be amongst," "to be part of," "to participate"; the impersonal form also means "there being a difference between," from which derives "to be of importance," "to matter." This semanteme is ambivalent at the outset: the term is not only employed in the sense of a "result of money," but also to signify "damage," "detriment," "disadvantage" (for instance, in Boccaccio and Ariosto). A similar situation concerns the French term *intérêt*, the English *interest*, and the German *Interesse* (Ornaghi, 1984:3–6). In effect, the ambivalent nature of interest only fully comes to light once the Latin word, used in the substantive form since the thirteenth century, becomes a key concept to identify a repayment obligation: while an interest entails a price to pay for the debtor, and thus a "disadvantage," for the creditor it represents something to receive, thus an "advantage." The majority of scholars believe that this semantic ambivalence lays at the roots of the dualism typical of the whole modern vicissitudes of interest, so much so that as soon as one shifts from its philological and semantic analysis to a reconstruction of its use in political discourse, "this congenital ambivalence [. . .] runs the risk of turning into a sort of 'schizophrenic' dualism" (Ornaghi, 1984:7).

The political use of the word interest is undoubtedly linked to the history of the modern state. Interest and "raison d'état" are intrinsically connected, as demonstrated in Friedrich Meineke's studies of the "idea" of the raison d'état in modern history. As the raison d'étaté impregnated the modern state, making it entirely similar to a "rationally organized large enterprise," so did the "doctrine of state interests," stemming directly from the raison d'étaté, constitute the origins of that "auxiliary practical science" on which the whole state order was built and consolidated (Meneicke, 1924:149–196). Despite the original intertwinement between the constitution of the modern state and the idea of interest, the political understanding of this word reveals from its very outset a schizophrenic relation to state discourse, because it implicitly contains the greatest impediment to the transfiguration of the concrete interest of the individual into the abstract political interest of the state. While the "personification" of the unity of the state seemed facilitated by conferring to it an autonomous interest different and distinct from that of single individuals and yet still as objective as that of any other "person," in fact, this "state interest" inevitably ended up bringing to light, beyond the "abstract" figure of this new entity, the very thing that the process of abstraction was meant to "conceal": the interests of those who exercise power.

For a reconstruction of the political use of this term, it is also important to note that from the outset what flows into the concept of interest is the whole inheritance of the medieval notion of *utilitas*. This notion had progressively come to mean, under the guise of *utilitas omnium civium*, *necessitas communis*, and *necessitates et utilitates civitatis*, the *bonum commune* that would later become a determinant in the medieval development of economic language. Rather than attenuating the schizophrenia implicit in the political understanding of interest, this development reinforced it because it not only brought to light the fundamentally unpolitical nature of interest in relation to the juridical construction of the state, but also because it allowed for the emergence of its convergence with what exceeds personal utility, in the immediate merging of it with the common good functional to the power it was founded on.

The juridical-political use of the concept of interest related to the logic of the state identifies it as an irreducible element of human action that is unconditionally referred to the individual as its subject, and as something engaged in the building of a structure or mechanism that is able to unify in a "general interest" all particular ones. Though aimed, as in Jean Jacques Rousseau, to accomplishing an extension of the politics of state sovereignty over the generality of private interests, this mechanism always functions thanks to the contractual technique of renunciation and the handing of single interests over to the general one. This movement establishes the law and various forms of prohibitions of individual actions; the only center of the state, the exclusive holder of the general interest, turns into what construes the subjects of right. Although it both legitimately "represents" and "governs" the totality of fractioned interests, the state is constantly ridden with this antagonism between the general sovereign interest and the plurality of interests in society, thus revealing how the subject of interest is never completely eradicated and instead continues to exist even after the establishment of a juridical structure meant to incorporate it. The subject of interests is thus irreducible to the subject of law. From the standpoint of juridical power, the making autonomous of a so-called civil society validates the correlative making autonomous of the state and its identity with political power *tout court*, reducing and recasting the fundamentally regulative element that propelled associative modern life as based on social pacts to the rank of "economic," and thus unpolitical, interest. This irreducibility of the subject of interest to the subject of law does not exhaust its implicit tensions with common interest and reveals, nonetheless, a political side different from the state but still internal to it and thus more effective.

In this respect, it is worth recalling David Hume's claim that the motivation for respecting the political covenant ought not to be sought in the presence of the contract, but rather in the interest that one has in it: if there is no interest, nothing can oblige one to obey the pact (Hume, 1994:99–101). The juridical constitution of the contract, in itself, is always vulnerable to its transgression. In the sixteenth chapter of the *Theologico-Political Treatise,* Baruch Spinoza affirmed much the same: "a compact is only made valid by its utility (*ratio utilitatis*), without which it becomes null and void" (Spinoza, 1951:113). For Spinoza, *utilitas* is the real application of the desire that founds all human actions/passions, as the affective carrier of an individual interest intertwined, freely and necessarily, with the multiplicity of all individual interests. *Utilitas* is the function of preservation proper to every mode of being as it participates (*inter-esse*) to the multiple modalities of existence. In Spinoza's terms, by amplifying its affective and primarily social attitude, utility nourishes the auto-finalization implicit in the modal being of human life.

On the one hand, Spinoza presented the constitution of a common life that eluded the juridical transferal of each one to a sovereign and opened up the question of democracy as a common reason of utility and, in this sense, as constituent of social life itself. On the other hand, for Hume, interest holds society together because it is the only thing that, by means of "consent," can be translated into public utility (Hume, 1994:99–100). This issue is fundamental to understanding how the freedom from which the interested character of action stems can also aliment a form of economic, rather than juridical, power. Here what matters is not so much a preventive obedience to the law, but rather the free conformity with the internal rule of its maximal economy. This is to say: at stake is not the maximization of the effects of the institution of power that, as derived from the sacrificial paradigm at the basis of the juridical constitution of the state, reduces its costs to a minimum by handing over and renouncing individual interests. What matters, instead, is the optimization of individual interests that, in the form of each individual's self-domination, results in a constant mode of domination that implicitly coincides with the *common good*, consensually undertaken as what is publicly useful. The continuous and constant production of a critique of any instituted form of government thus gives rise to a stable form of power: the freer one is to satisfy one's own interest and from an extrinsic bond of obligation, the more one is obedient, so to speak, and governable, on the basis of an absolutely adequate relation between single interest and common utility, one that is constantly manifested in the modes of a general "consensus" and a concomitant critique of instituted government in the legal form of the contractual pact.

In this sense, the political-economic use of interest derives from the thought on the passions, most present in the treatises of the 1600s, alimented by a practice of decodification of desires that emerged in Christian ascetism as an activity predisposed not only to the renunciation of the passions, but also, and especially, as we shall see, to their methodical activation. If the decoding of the element of the passions practiced in Christian ascesis unveils the possibility, for man, of relating to himself in the form of a government that can only emerge on the basis of a radical experience of the intrinsic auto-finality of human praxis, its politico-economic formulation makes it possible to conceive of interest, an invariant aspect of the passions, as maximally governable. Man's self-reflexive ability to give form to a praxis that has no preventive end but itself comes to coincide, here, with interest, not so much as the individual drive of human action, but rather as its specific character, as a universal and abstract aspect of it. From this standpoint, as Hume claims, the preservation of the human species would not be possible without the motive of interest. This naturalness, this invariability of interest has to be maintained, it has to be *left free*, free to express its specific homogeneity; because the more it remains unchanged, the more it is penetrable and manageable. The game of passions and desires, which is at once spontaneous and regulated and managed, gives rise in each person to the production of an interest and constitutes, at the same time, the aliment of a collective one. Thanks to this universal and abstract character, human nature is not only something on which and against which the sovereign must impose just laws. There is no human nature over and above which stands a sovereign to whom one is connected in a relation of obedience/transgression that fundamentally entails a negation of one's drives. The identification of interest as a biological invariant specific to the human species that has to be kept unchanged in view of its penetrability and political management, characterizes the properly economic form of the power at play here. In other words, one might say that politics grasps human nature as such, not as something separate and presupposed that is to be subsequently reintegrated; this is a strategy of anticipation that, though in completely different terms, both Hobbes' *Leviathan* and the Greek *polis* have in common. At play is another strategy of power still internal to the logic of the state that sees acting in the order of politics as acting in the order of nature, a naturalness of man that is more politically penetrable the more he is left free to express his biological invariance, which he merely needs to look after.

In the mechanism that immediately multiplies interests, one that is managed by the market as its own field of realization, the free will of each spontaneously and almost involuntarily agrees with the freedom and interests of all. Due to its opaque, untotalizable nature and despite the convergence it eventually spontaneously ensures, the economic realm is definitely and originally constituted by points of view whose multiplicity is irreducible. Its rationality is that described by Adam Smith with the metaphor of the "invisible hand." As if following a plan of providence, the hand is a sort of immanent translation of the economy of salvation formulated by the Patristic of the first centuries of the Christian era. Its invisibility emerges from its intrinsic opacity, an inevitable unknowability of the totality of the process that exposes it to a state of permanent crisis; this condition is essentially inherent to the economic realm rather than being a mere stage of its development.

The political formulation of interest coincides, in the end, with the development of a discourse on the production of a freely established dependency. Its realization becomes possible thanks to the internal neutralization of the disinterested auto-finality that is inherent to human action. This political formulation of interest gives rise to an element of excess in the form of a spontaneous convergence of individual freedoms. The autotelic dimension recognized by Weber as the transcendent aspect of instrumental reason and as the main driver of the capitalist enterprise, in the politico-economic use of interest manifests itself as a sort of "disinterested interest," both of each one and of all, where each one naturally ends up converging together, and whereby a properly economic form of power can develop. The maximization of individual interest coincides with that which, by exceeding it, is no longer individual; not only is it realized through the full satisfaction of clearly defined ends, more importantly, it also becomes a common good that finds its end in itself in the abstract form of consensus.

## The Spontaneous Order of *Homo Oeconomicus*

The freedom of interest, as a constituent mechanism of the economic form of power, is brought to bear on the discourse on passions and the intrinsic opacity of the economic realm. This development, internal to the economy, questions its rationality. In this framework, the major exponents of neoliberalism in the twentieth century carry out a determinant shift: they radicalize the founding elements of classical liberalism and the political formulation of interest on which this was largely based. The most representative figure in this respect was undoubtedly Friedrich August von Hayek, whose thought is a sort of grafting of different neoliberal currents, as demonstrated, topographically, by his varied academic posts: first in Vienna, with Ludwig von Mises, then in London at the London School of Economics, and from 1950 in Chicago among the activists of the Chicago School, to finally end up, from 1962, in Freiburg, where he frequents the main exponents of Ordoliberalism.

According to Hayek, the new liberalism is fundamentally different from classical liberalism because it exposes the connection between economic and political institutions, to the extent that the original dialectical relation between state and market is translated, in neoliberal practice, into a total economic legitimation of the political institution. Of particular note in this respect is the notion of "spontaneous order" wherein the market, a "game of catallaxy," constitutes the very basis of the political institution. The explicit reference to cybernetics, information and system theory allows Hayek to use the expressions "self-generating order" or "self-organizing structures" as synonyms to describe what he sees unfold in the market as the self-constituting process of a political institution (Hayek, 1982:xix). In this passage, he identifies a relation of reciprocal influence between the economy and the law. Hayek leads the juridical discourse on the state back to the economic question of the search for a noningenious naturalness of the rational order. In this sense, in his view the distinction between "natural" and "artificial" is reductive. Rather, the point is to do without the idea of order as the product of an intentional design, the result of an artifice of abstraction that is rational and fully comprehensible. The spontaneous and self-generating social and political order produced through the market is, according to him, abstract in an entirely different sense. The "primacy of abstraction" expressed by the market inheres the properly human experience of the limits of conscious reason and the advantages man can draw from processes of which he is not fully aware.

From an explicitly evolutionist standpoint, Hayek criticizes the idea of a "logic" of abstraction typical of what he defines as the "constructivist rationalism" represented by Descartes. This views abstractness as "a property confined to conscious thought or concepts, while actually it is a characteristic possessed by all the processes which determine action long before they appear in conscious thought or are expressed in language" (Hayek, 1982:30). "Abstractness," for Hayek, is "not only a property possessed to a greater or lesser degree by all (conscious or unconscious) mental processes, but the basis of man's capacity to move successfully in a world very imperfectly known to him—an adaptation to his ignorance of most of the particular facts of his surroundings" (Hayek, 1982:30). From this stand-point, all rules governing human actions relate to this "primacy of abstract-ness" not as the construction of an artificial order "directed from above" that would only require obedience, but as "the outcome of a process of evolution whose results nobody foresaw or designed" (Hayek 1982:37), a spontaneous, self-organized order. Hayek writes that "its degree of complexity is not limited to what a human mind can master" (Hayek, 1982:38); because "not having been made it cannot legitimately be said to have a particular purpose, although our awareness of its existence may be extremely important for our successful pursuit of a great variety of dif-ferent purposes" (Hayek, 1982:38). For Hayek, what ensures the sponta-neous maintenance of said order is the regularity of the comportment that its elements acquire within it when following rules in response to their surroundings.

Rather than "rules" one ought to speak of "regularities," because the social structures they originate from "are neither natural in the sense of being genetically determined, nor artificial in the sense of being the prod-uct of intelligent design, but [. . .] directed by the differential advantages gained by groups from practices adopted for some unknown and perhaps purely accidental reasons" (Hayek, 1982:155). These practices that are evolutionarily selected become, for Hayek, "systems of rules of conduct" that presuppose forms of discipline. Hayek attempts to identify, in evolu-tionist terms, the provenance of abstraction from praxis and its intrinsic auto-finality by presupposing discipline as a condition of possibility of the rules of life; and yet he does not refrain from operating an inversion in favor of the former, one that allows him to defend, in a transcendental way, the "primacy of abstractness."

The observance of determined rules aims to restrain "natural instincts which do not fit into the order of the open society" (Hayek, 1982:160). But cultural evolution does not merely amount to the establishment of pro-hibitions that take on the form of positive laws that can be either observed or transgressed. Taking into account "the succession of the different eco-nomic orders through which civilization as passed in terms of changes in the rules of conduct," one can see how they "made that evolution possi-ble mostly by relaxations of prohibitions: an evolution of individual free-dom and a development of rules which protected the individual rather than commanded it to do particular things" (Hayek, 1982:161). In this perspective, "freedom" is a characteristic aspect of human beings and an "artefact of civilization" (Hayek, 1982:163). Hayek believes that "freedom was made possible by the gradual evolution of the discipline of civilization which is at the same time the discipline of freedom" (Hayek, 1982:163). Each social order and democratic legislative power presupposes a *nómos* that is defined as the "law of freedom." At the heart of his argument is a need to construe a freely produced subordination.

Hayek writes,

> a policy making use of the spontaneously ordering forces therefore cannot aim at a known maximum of particular results, but must aim at increasing, for any person picked out at random, the prospects that the overall effect of all changes required by that order will be to increase his chances of attaining his ends. [. . .] The common good in this sense is not a particular state of things but consists in an abstract order which in a free society must leave undetermined the degree to which the several particular needs will be met. The aim will have to be an order which will increase everybody's chances as much as possible. (Hayek, 1982:114)

Competition, for Hayek, is a constant "discovery procedure" that does not presuppose a rational comportment, but construes it as the condition of possibility of this order (Hayek, 1982:117). Competition is a "method for breeding certain types of mind," so that "the very cast of thinking of the great entrepreneurs would not exist but for the environment in which they developed their gifts" (Hayek, 1982:76).

Order is produced, for Hayek, through a sort of indirect form of intervention that, through the creation of an entrepreneurial competitive *environment*, augments the freedom to act within it. The classical figures of *homo oeconomicus*, the producer who owns the means of production, the waged laborer, the man of exchange and the consumer, are all referred back to the figure of the entrepreneur as a "self-entrepreneur," and every one's action becomes, in itself, entrepreneurial (Bröckling, 2007). The neoliberal vision realized in the shift from capitalist enterprise to the self-organized order of the market is, in this sense, a radicalization of Weber's argument. In so far as praxis is made to coincide with this naturalness of adaptation to one's environment that is spontaneously "functional" to the abstract order of self-preservation, any element of innovation, no matter how inherent to an entrepreneurial comportment, as Joseph A. Schumpeter claims, is totally squashed within it and thus neutralized; all creativity is ruled out a priori and exclusively conceived of in the terms of a faculty that is presumed and only proper to a fully aware and rational subject.

## Lifelong Rents

One of the most delicate moments in Hayek's line of reasoning concerns the definition of the "primacy of abstractness" in relation to the "spontaneous" constitution of a sort of self-organizing order. His argument here appears to be rather sophisticated: on the one hand, it incorporates some of the main aspects of the critique of classical liberalism; on the other hand, it also puts forward, again, the extreme vision of neoliberalism.

The most radical critique of the "primacy of abstractness" found in classical liberalism is undoubtedly offered by Karl Marx. For Marx, in capitalist modes of production this primacy is materialized in the value of commodities and founded on the *quantity* of labor time expended for their production. As soon as labor is sold as a commodity that is abstractly measurable by money on the market, the quality of labor power becomes an abstract quantity. Therefore, it becomes manifested as a separate form that takes on the role of an a priori category and the very condition of possibility of the process of accumulation of capital. In this shift, according to Marx, political economy managed to operate an inversion whereby the prominence of the abstract derives from the praxis of production, and this is pregnant with consequences for economic science and beyond.

Marx speaks of *real* "abstractions"; the "reality" of their manifestation is the mark of a truth that the capitalist process of production has mastered though perversely, because it is praxis that qualifies, for human beings, the forms and modalities of abstraction. Of relevance to our argument is that the undeserved appropriation of this truth emerges in Hayek's perspective with greater force than in the classical political economy surveyed by Marx.

The point, for Marx, is to identify a characteristic trait of human life in the formation of real abstractions, one that the capitalist mode of production has come to own, thus neutralizing its creative potential (Virno, 2004:111–139). In this sense, for Marx, the capitalist process of abstraction of life is not merely resolved in a sort of invasion of social reality from the outside. A critique of the capitalist mode of production cannot entail an idyllic return to the "concrete," to the primary and donative dimension of society, because the formation of real abstractions coincides with man's activity and cannot do without it. In capitalism, real abstractions are fetishes through which social relations become expressed as things, thus neutralizing the implicit questionability of the relation itself. On the other hand, the reality of abstraction pertains to human praxis and its inherent capacity to relate to itself without a predetermined end, it concerns the relation as such that traverses human life.

Marx's critique of the real abstractions of capitalist modes of production might have influenced the formation of neoliberal theories, especially those found in Hayek. Although the radical force of this possibility is yet to be fully recognized, it is of great significance especially to the current configuration of the economy. Some of the main exponents of the Chicago School, such as Theodore Schultz and Gary Becker, since the 1960s have critiqued the classical notion of labor as an activity that is separate from the rest of human reality and its qualitative variables; their critique appears in many ways very close to that developed by Marx. For Marx, the main problem with the buying and selling of labor power, its object being "the simple expenditure of psycho-physical energy," is that it reduces the generic potential to produce (i.e., the "labor in general" that can become a commodity as such only when separated from its activities) to a commodity and to a historically determinate form. Similarly, for the main exponents of the Chicago School, the most problematic element of the classical view of labor is its automatic pairing with the wage as the means of exchange of an abstract activity. Instead, theorists of the Chicago School claim that the activity of work cannot be reduced to simple wage labor, but needs to be conceived of as a rent, a lifelong rent that involves the most intimate aspects of those who carry it. For Marx, the critical question with the purchase and selling of labor power was that unlike all other commodities it fundamentally had no autonomous existence and did not materialize in a product because it did not exist outside of the body of the worker and his life. In many ways, the critique of abstract labor offered by the Chicago School can be interpreted as a radicalization of Marx's position, in so far as the activity of work is introduced into a process of investment that involves life itself in its entirety, whereby man as such becomes a form of capital: "human capital."

For Becker, "investment in human capital" means dealing with "activities in order to maximize money income" (Becker, 1976:94) in the future, not only the income corresponding to the work done in a determined time.

Therefore, the "real income," everything that is earned through work activity as a whole, is not reduced to the income perceived in the present, time and again, but crucially includes future compensations linked to personal investment. In this sense, contrary to the belief that the term "investment in human capital" ought to be restricted to monetary costs and revenues, Becker claims that his analysis is "applicable independently of the division of real income in monetary or psychic components" (Becker, 1964:94).

Economic theories of human capital radicalize Hayek's position but also implicitly incorporate Marx's critique of labor, without ever entering a direct confrontation with Marx's argument. In line with Marx's approach, Hayek identified the abstraction from praxis, and yet he operated an inversion in favor of the former. In the footsteps of classical political economy, this inversion allowed him to defend a "primacy of abstractness" that is functional to the order he aimed to outline. In the same direction, the Chicago School theorists did not limit abstraction to the only measurable quantity of labor time, but extended it over its quality, to the point that life itself, as a whole, became the privileged form of capital. This move resulted in much more than a simple extrinsic application of the economy to realms that are normally considered noneconomic, such as education, training, family, health, and security. In many of the branches of economic science itself, such as the analysis of economic growth, studies of labor markets or migration flows, investment in human capital somewhat became configured as a need internal to collective well-being, as a condition that could be constantly realized through constant individual application (Bazzicalupo, 2006). The economic rationality of *self-interest* as an explanation of human comportment coincides here, as in classical economics, with the tendency of individuals to maximize their own utility function. The maximization of utility is seen as a personal investment that in itself translates into capital, and not only does its accumulation exponentially grow over time, its effects are also irreducible to individual benefits: they automatically involve the common good. In this perspective, not only is labor "freed" from the passivity it was constrained in, in the classical version; consumption, too, is no longer simply a reconstitution of lost energies, it becomes itself a productive factor of investment. More than to a primitive accumulation, at stake here is a constant accumulation now disconnected from specific working activities, and increasingly related to the potential intrinsic in "labor-power" itself (Virno, 2004); the latter is able to keep reproducing value the very moment it is produced. Had there been no danger of overusing Foucault's neologism biopolitics and contributing to its excessive proliferation in the semantic field, here one might employ the notion of "biovalue," introduced by Kauchik Sunder Rajan, to describe the economic power constantly expressed by life (Rajan, 2006).

In any case, perhaps this is not only a question of power over the bare natural life of man deprived of its qualities and reduced to a biological element among others—as, following Foucault, biopolitics has been understood in recent years (Agamben, 1998; Esposito, 2008); rather, this device applies to the human ability—albeit biological—of giving form and value to one's life. After all, Foucault explored something similar in his archaeologies of the intimate links between governmental techniques of power and technologies of the self as ascetic practices. The ways power subjugates appear to be intrinsically linked to the modes through which subjects constitute themselves as such by giving form to life.

Of note are, in this respect, the current trends in theories of human capital in the biomedical field. Not only is knowledge in this field radically placed at the service of the optimization that human life carries out on itself in order to better itself, to the extent that in its "postgenomic" form, according to Nikolas Rose, it is possible to speak of a "molecolarization of forms of life" (Rose, 2007:98). The criterion of individual rather than national or population health is also made functional to the logic of profit that underscores the contemporary multiple forms of capitalization of vitality today. Now, each citizen must become an active partner in the pursuing of health and accept the fact that the responsibility for his own overall well-being not only coincides with a personal investment, but also involves the well-being of the whole community. In the complex web of forces that is sewn thus, aspirations related to health and the conduct of individuals can be governed indirectly by constantly adapting the ways in which people freely express themselves in their own lives.

The huge success enjoyed by theories of human capital in the recent developments of global economics is under everyone's eyes. Understanding this phenomenon merely in terms of an "end of work," as has been done, is reductive to say the least. Instead, the spread of these forms of capitalization of life coincide with the full extension of the time of work to all moments of existence, and with more flexible and precarious ways of working from a contractual point of view. Contrary to the predictions of the Chicago School, this phenomenon has not resulted in a general rise of incomes; in fact, the gap between rich and poor has notably widened.

More importantly, what has grown is an impression that despite the intention of creating new meaningfulness by bringing about an identification of life with work, the current mode of production is deeply nonsensical and self-destructive.

In this sense, the activity of work coincides with an auto-finalized self-entrepreneurial practice. This fully realizes Weber's vision that the real motor of the capitalist enterprise is its ability to invest on what has no other end but itself. By reviving Weber's argument, it is possible to discern a renewed asceticism, an "economic conduct of life," in contemporary individualizing modes of production. This is why Hayek speaks of a "discipline of freedom" underlying the "spontaneous order" of the market. An intrinsic ascetic constitution of capital seems to be at stake. Inner-worldly ascetism is not, as Weber thought, the premise of capitalism but the way capital reproduces itself, though in ways that are far from the actual forms of conduct of ascetic life of the Weberian entrepreneur of the beginning of the last century. The nexus between ascesis and the economy, so central to Weber's thesis, must thus be newly investigated in this framework, and its relevance needs to be reassessed for a reading of the present.

## Financialization of the Market and Private Indebtedness

Before embarking on an investigation of the link between ascetism and the economy on the premises outlined so far, it is worth returning, briefly, to the world crisis we confront. This crisis was allegedly caused by turmoil internal to the financial world and independent of the development of the processes of production. First, we need to ask how a financial economy supposedly extraneous from the processes of the real economy could possibly set into motion a global mechanism on such an enormous scale. But people still speak of the need to return to the real economy and the fall of the financial markets is interpreted by most as a deviation or a perversion of real capitals affected by a stock market, which, instead of investing in the real economy, supposedly continued to aliment only "unproductive" rents.

However, the financial economy has been pervasive and involved the whole economic cycle for several years. Each credit card payment, for instance, is part of the world of finance. The functioning of the car industry, too, is entirely based on mechanisms of credit (*leasing*, etc.). But finance is not only cosubstantial with the production of goods and services, and thus with the world of work in the classical sense. The total subsumption of individual life under the world of finance was accomplished thanks to a considerable derailing of private household savings into the stock market: this made it possible to transfigure private indebtedness and turn it into the motor of the world economy.

Private debt has become the new form of investment and revenue of the global economy; this unknown fact is worth considering, as the economist Michael Hudson has recently done. Having identified in public debt the main cause of the U.S. world domination in the past twenty years, Hudson focused on "a new psychology of private debt" that the Obama administration ought to give careful consideration to, given its relevance to the global economy.

Since the 1980s, the great processes of financialization were alimented in increasingly sophisticated and efficient ways by the channeling of private savings into the stock market. In the 1990s the investment of private savings in the stock market generated additional revenues linked to new forms of production based on innovative cooperation known as the *new economy*; and this was the most explicit realization of the economic theories of human capital. In this phase, different forms of income were developed and linked to the revenues of the enterprise, such as *stock options* for managers and pension funds or investment funds for others. In the two years that followed the turn of the millennium, the Fed lowering of interest rates from 6 to 1 percent finally created the incentive for indebtedness in a way never seen before, so that the crisis of the new economy would not result in a depression similar to the one that followed the crisis of 1929. American families could obtain a practically unlimited credit from the banking system, using their house as guarantee.

The flow of private savings into the stock market made it possible for individual risk to be channeled into capital risk. In other words, the ventures of capital were no longer separate in the form of entrepreneurial risk for innovation; they were individualized and made to coincide with the risks of savers themselves. Financialization, thus, properly entered the realm of the lives of individuals, not only in the guise of savings, future earnings, and pensions; as the subsumption of life under finance was underway, so did social relations change to facilitate the concentration of financial risks among the weakest, including those who had no savings. The fact that financial risk became concentrated in the poorest strata of the population demonstrates that the financialization of the economy can function on the basis of the inclusion of life itself in the creation of value. This highly unstable model feeds on its own instability. Several financial crises have occurred in recent years, to the extent that the crisis has been said to have become permanent today (despite the claim that an economic recovery is underway). Its duration coincides with its efficacy. At stake is a form of power over individual conducts and life practices wagered, time and again, in the increasingly precarious forms of its/their administration.

The organization of finance consists of moving from one "bubble" to the next, making individuals intimately dependent on the trends of the financial markets. This mechanism is fed by a process of valorization in the financial community that depends on the trust of its participants, a sort of "faith" that, from the outset, is at the heart of this economic form of power (Berti, 2006:22). Single investors do not react merely to legitimate information, but to what they believe to be the actions of other investors confronted with given information. The shares on the stock market are thus self-referential; they refer to the independently acquired beliefs on the real economic value that underlies them. A form of performativity is implicit in this trust in the stock market; its self-referentiality is functional to its own inner movement.

Financialization is the *modus operandi* of new economic processes (Fumagalli and Mezzadra, 2009), and this is linked to the fact that the realization of profits depends, today, on a form of consumption derived from financial revenues that originate in diffuse modes of indebtedness, in the creation of an added demand fueled by private debt and fed by trust in the financial markets. These are the effects of a virtual wealth that favors consumption in the absence of real liquidity. At stake in this process is not only the becoming rent of income, but the transformation into rent of life itself,, into a rent that is nonrepayable. In the subsumption of life under finance, debt finds new forms of investment that radically expose its implicit default and the need for it to be constantly reproduced. New modes of accumulation of value discover a privileged mechanism of self-feeding in this debt that cannot and should not be repaid. Global indebtedness is thus revealed to be at the foundation of the engine of the world economy and of the power based on it.

## Chapter 2

# Oikonomía and Asceticism

In the preceding chapter, we tried to demonstrate the contemporary relevance of Weber's thesis on the origin of capitalism. It is now time to verify the foundation of this thesis: the Christian matrix. In Weber's argument, the paradigm of secularization represents a shift in objectives affected by the emergence of capitalism: at the origin of the capitalist economy lies a shift onto the plane of immanence. But given the level of complexity of a phenomenon of such global dimensions, this explanation seems unsatisfactory.

Michel Foucault's writings on pastoral power and liberal governmentality seem more convincing. For the purpose of this work, one of their main merits is that they sidestep the classical antithesis between the economy and Christianity usually found in studies on this issue—including, to an extent, Weber's.

The aim of this work is to radicalize Weber's thesis that capitalism originates in inner-worldly Protestant asceticism and, following his insights, to try and offer a genealogical reconstruction of Christian asceticism that does not assume *what* ascesis was during the rise of Christianity, but rather investigates *how* it became a form of life with Christ. To this purpose, it is first necessary to ascertain that a properly "economic" mode of life did in fact emerge during early Christianity. This would have meant that human beings could invest not in their "works" and their effects, but in a practice that fundamentally appeared to have no purpose. It was not until the second century, when the *oikonomía* became an abstract plane of salvation one had to conform to by means of practices that were functional to its organization, that a complete formulation of asceticism could explicitly be developed as a Christian problem in Christian literature.

I now explore the extent to which an analysis of this phenomenon can throw light on the mechanisms underlying the contemporary economic power that, on the surface, appears to be completely immune to any form of ascetic logic. However, I do not do this by tracing, on Weber's trajectory, a further and single evolutionary or degenerative tendency in Western history; instead, I reconstruct how, time and again, the economic experience of life expressed so radically in early Christianity was actualized in history.

## Christianity and the Economic Form of Power

Karl Löwith wrote a study on the theological presuppositions of historical philosophy several years after Weber's work on this question, to which he owes its framework. He wrote it in order to demonstrate that throughout modernity the search for the meaning of human action is marked by an eschatological view of Christian derivation, even after the modern notion of progress comes to substitute the theological notion of providence. In his view, by developing an ultimate goal to strive toward, they both arise from a common and primary aspiration to dominate a process of time that would otherwise be meaningless (Löwith, 1949). In this sense, the orientation of Christian theology and the modern vision of *homo faber* share a teleological matrix explicitly directed toward the domination of the world. The shift from one realm to the other was made possible by secularization (Lübbe, 1965), which caused a definite turn in the orientation of human action, from a transcendent to an immanent finality, as also described by Weber.

Löwith's work is part of a known debate unfolding in Germany around the middle of the last century (Marramao, 1985, 1994; Monod, 2002). Several contributors to this debate often characterized Christian religion as being, from the outset, intimately connected with the process of secularization, thus casting doubts on all attempts to identify a different Christianity.

In recent years, thanks to the philosophical return to early Christianity—especially that of Paul of Tarsus—conversations have moved on a path other than that indicated in the debate on secularization. The discussion has also been spurred by the publication of the sixtieth volume of Martin Heidegger's *Gesamtausgabe*, entitled *Einleitung in die Phänomenologie der Religion*, which collects several lectures from 1920 to 1921 largely dedicated to a phenomenological analysis of Paul's epistles (Heidegger, 2010).

This recent debate arises out of a powerful reawakening of movements of religious fundamentalism and identity, the growing affirmation of a homologizing process of globalization, and the irreversible decline of the political categories of modernity. In this context, it "deconstructs Christianity" in order to identify its relevance to the present and redeem it from the binary logic that had characterized it in the previous German debate. The German debate that took place in the middle of the last century primarily focused on the existing nexus between secularization and modernity. There were those who believed that modernity only consummated its Christian premises (Löwith, 1949), and those who claimed that, on the contrary, Western modernity affirmed itself against Christianity (Blumenberg, 1966; Marquard, 1981). In 1995, Jacques Derrida and Gianni Vattimo's edited collection, *Religion*, marked the first step toward a different framing of the problem and questioned the German debate (Derrida and Vattimo, 1998).

This volume set out to provide a new definition of Christianity for the present: despite their differences all contributors tried to identify a "pure" side of Christianity as the bearer of a betrayed truth that they wished to resurrect for the present. To recall some of the best known interventions, some sought in Christianity a nonconciliatory nucleus, "without redemption" (Vitiello, 1995); others searched for an "ultimate" side of Christianity that could be an opening to "freedom" (Cacciari, 2004); others attempted to highlight the "dis-enclosure" of its closure (Nancy, 2008); to reconstruct the declaration of a "universal singularity" of the event in its implicit truth (Badiou, 2008); to seek its "perverse and revolutionary core" (Žižek, 2003).

Giorgio Agamben's frequent readings of Paul also belong to this thread (Agamben, 2005); his most recent studies are particularly relevant to my research. There Agamben seeks to define a "theological genealogy of economy and government" (Agamben, 2011). On Foucault's footsteps, he turns to early Christianity and tries to offer a genealogical study of modern governmentality. Valuable to this debate, Agamben offers an illuminating analysis that starts with the use of the word *oikonomía* in the New Testament, where an "entirely economic" discourse can be discerned (Agamben, 2011:38). Based on an examination of Paul's writings, Agamben contests the view—frequent in theology—that the word *oikonomía* takes on a theological meaning for the first time in these texts (Agamben, 2011:35).

Despite the fact that in the semantic constellation of the term *oikonomía*, which includes the verb *oikonomeo* and the noun *oikonomos*, the meaning of these words as they appear in the New Testament might in some sense seem nonspecific and to always result from its context, the way these terms are used is identical to that of the Greek and Roman world. On both cases oikonomía refers to an activity concerning things at one's disposal. This is different from the theological meaning of "divine plan of salvation" that Löwith also refers to. As Agamben often points out, the meaning concerns an activity, a task entrusted upon someone that has to be given credence and realized. In his view, even when oikonomía is related to a *mysterion,* as in Col 1:24–25 and Eph 1:9–10, it always means "administration," "execution," or "actualization" of the mystery of redemption that was once hidden and has now come to completion; it never means a plan of salvation (Agamben, 2011:36–39).

Agamben's interpretation moves from a need to keep a distance from the majority of the studies on this issue, where Paul's use of the Greek term *oikonomía* is thought to be nothing more than a recovery of the version accepted in Hebraic Hellenistic literature, where the term is used in a way similar to the Stoics': oikonomía in their sense concerns the role of Jahvè in nature and history, just as for the Stoics it referred to the order of the universe guided by Pronoia. In support of Agamben's thesis, one could mention that the Greek translation of the Septuagint uses the term *dioíke-sis* to indicate divine action (only in Is 22:19 and 21 do we find the use of oikonomía with reference to God). In any case, not all studies of this theme interpret the term *oikonomía* in the theological way as a "key word" that could open a "perspective on God's life before time," thus providing "the basis and climate for a further evolution of the economy of salvation" (Duchatelez, 1970:277–279). Agamben mainly refers to the work of Gerard Richter, who offers an important overview of the issue (Richter, 2005). But, before Richter, the most decisive proponent of this thesis was John Reumann who, while distinguishing between Paul's view and Lucan's, sought to highlight the peculiar "administrative function" implicit in Paul's term. Reumann claimed that with this term "one did not simply and abstractly have to think of the divine plan, but rather of 'administration,' of the 'actualization' of the mystery" (Reumann, 1966:165).

In any case, most of the literature on this issue, despite the efforts of Reumann, Richter, and a few others, does not recognize Paul's use of the term *oikonomía* as other than what, up until the German theology of the 1900s, was defined as *Heilsgeschichte*, "salvation history" (Reumann, 1966:161), and fails to register that the absorption of the problem of the economy into the history of theology was subsequent to Paul and only dates back to the second or third century. Deprived of the meaning acquired in the perspective of "salvation history," which according to Löwith is the premise of modern philosophy of history, the "economy of mystery" proposed by Paul (Eph 3:9) seems to lose theological power and disorient as to the meaning of such an "administration."

Paul used the term most systematically: seven uses are traceable in the texts collected in the New Testament, three in Luke 16:2–4 and Paul 4 (1 Cor 9:17; Eph 1:10, 3:2; Col 1:25; 1 Tim 1:4). However, an understanding of the meaning of this term in early Christian literature needs to take into account the large number of references to the economy present in the texts of the New Testament (unfortunately this analysis is missing from Agamben's otherwise comprehensive work). In the Synoptic Gospels, many of the parables on the Kingdom of God refer to a domestic situation in need of administering: from the parable of the sower in Mt 13:1–23, Mk 4:1–25, and Lk 8:4–18; to that on talents in Mt 25:14–30 and Lk 19:12–27; or the one on the loyal administrator in Mt 24:42–50 and Lk 12:42–48. Although it involves profit, the economy prospected in these texts does not entail the possession of goods, nor is it simply exhausted in an exchange of good deeds for salvation. Suffice it to mention, in this respect, Jesus' words on the uselessness of the accumulation of earthly treasures compared to the "real treasure" of the heavens (reported in Mt 6:19–24 and Lk 12:33–34); or the comparison between the Kingdom of Heaven and the "hidden treasure" or "precious pearl" (in Mt 13:44–45); or the parable of the rich young man (in Mt 19:16–26, Mk 10:17–27, and Lk 18:18–27); or the episode where Jesus chases the merchants out of the temple, in Jn 2:16 and the Synoptics (Mt 21:12–22; Mk 11:15–17; Lk 19:45–47); or, finally, the parable of talents recounted earlier. Neither money nor the skill to accumulate it have anything to do with the economic activity under question, as demonstrated by the parable on the dishonest administrator (Lk 16:1–8); the episode of the rich fool (Lk 12:18); or as can be deduced from Jesus' own words in Lk 16:9–13. Under question is profitable administration, where gain and loss are not ruled out but concomitant, as evident, for instance, in the parable of the generous father who welcomes back his son who had spent all of his wealth (Lk 15:11–31). The economy presented here does care about life but, like the "birds of the air" and the "lilies of the field," it is not "anxious" about survival and does not demand the toil of labor, as can be read in Mt 6:25–34 and in Lk 12:22–31.

The vocabulary that describes the experience of early Christian life is eminently economic: through it, the new Christian community seeks to define itself, and the theological perspective of sacred history that would later be developed is not prominent at all in this vocabulary. In this respect, one might define it as an economic translation of the Judaic juridical vocabulary it originates from. Like in Hebraism, at stake is the constitution of the community, and yet, the lexicon of Christian *ekklesía*, as Agamben writes, is "economic" and not "political"; Christians are the first wholly "economic men" (Agamben, 2011:38). And he later adds: "from the outset, the Messianic community is represented in the terms of an *oikonomía*, and not in those of a politics. The implications of this for the history of western politics are yet to be established" (Agamben, 2011:39).

In an attempt to add to the shift Foucault describes from pastoral power to political government, despite identifying the fundamentally economic status of the Christian community, Agamben regards the paradigm of the trinity and the Patristic declination of the "economy of salvation" as the origins of the idea of economic government of men and things that became predominant during modernity in the West. He reiterates, in a different version, the same framework of the debate on secularization that he criticizes; more importantly, he isolates Paul's Messianic experience because in his view it involved a practice of inoperativeness that would later be betrayed. If, as Agamben claims, in order to deactivate the governmental *dispositif* that has devoured it, this "inoperativeness" would now need to be practiced, at the heart of such experience lies the notion of an "ungovernable [. . .] that can never take on the form of an *oikonomía*" (Agamben, 2011:80). Because of this, his entire economic definition of the Messianic Pauline community becomes problematic. After all, if, as it seems to be the case, due to the constitutive incompatibility of inoperativeness and forms of government, all attempts at reactivating different practices of government were at risk of being curtailed, it would be difficult to pursue the deactivation of the mechanism of government attributed to it, and this relegates inoperativeness to an opaque and sterile corner.

To understand the economic situation of the Christian community entails first and foremost a reference to its relationship with the law, as Agamben frequently showed in his work on St. Paul's Messianism. The question of the accomplishment of the law and its antinomies is inherent to the Messianic experience of life in Christ, and at stake is a critique of the juridical form of government. But this critique does not merely entail the transfer to a different plane of something that retains its power, as it would if one was simply dealing with a process analogous to that of secularization. This is unlike the modern form of sovereignty that was interpreted, in these terms, as a secularized version of divine sovereignty while still retaining the logic of its power. It is also unlike any attempt to substitute the *Torah* with a different law that can replace it or its ordering, as was the case in the second century when, as we shall see, the term *oikonomía* of the New Testament was invested with a meaning different from that used by the first Christian generation.

The Torah's critique of the juridical form of power in early Christianity seems motivated by the search for an administration of life that does not exhaust the possibilities inherent to human life into a fixed condition of domination that separates off that which cannot be governed, nor does it seem to be realized by orienting itself toward an ultimate goal on which human action exclusively depends. In fact, it is more like an unknown experimentation of different strategies of change of what, as such, eludes a stable government and an ultimate meaning, and thus necessitates a peculiar activity of administration, an oikonomía, as such.

Perhaps, as Agamben's theory suggests, this is really the first time in Western history that life is not neatly separated off for the purpose of being governed. Instead, this was the case in the order of the Torah, which is sacred because it is separate from the profane order of nature, and in the classical distinction between *oîkos* and *nómos*, between a private and natural realm linked to the *zoé*, and the public and political realm of the *pólis* as the field of development of *bíos*. The experience of Christian life, while deeply confronted both with the precariousness of the life it intends to govern and with its constitutively ungovernable and meaningless character, does not renounce some form of government, nor does it simply strategize to deactivate the existing one. Instead, it inaugurates an *economic mode of power* that defines itself as such because it shares and develops from the same assumptions of the legal structure of the political and social pact of the alliance between God and the people of Israel, while critiquing them and taking them in a different direction.

Therefore, it would be entirely reductive to univocally ascribe this experience to a process of secularization that incorporates it in a single path of evolution or degeneration of Western rationalization, as some did in Weber's footsteps. But it would be just as reductive to isolate an uncontaminated aspect of Christian history from the history of its power, and to find in Christianity the origins of a "purity" that would later be betrayed, or ascribing the current paradigm of governmental power to the economy of salvation or the dispositif of the trinity. In my view, it seems more fruitful to try to reconstruct, as far as possible, the singularity of the experience of early Christianity, to outline the peculiarity of its economic formulation of life. This can contribute to understanding specifically economic phenomena as well as a different reactivation of them.

## Norm and Transgression: The Experience of Debt

In early Christian texts, the Hebrew term *torah* is translated in Greek as a technical term of Hellenistic jurisprudence: *nómos* or *didaskalía*. This confirms that the text that was sacred to the Jews is received not only as a religious text, but also, and above all, as a juridical code. In this sense, an intimate correspondence between law and life is definitively introduced into Western thought, with a peculiar character: the commandment presents itself as a form of control over human life that, while enforcing its observance, supposes its infraction. In this respect, the Jewish experience of the relation of man to the law is the most radical because it essentially contains the possibility of its transgression.

In the Jewish world, nature is freely created by God, a good deed and a source of joy and well-being. What irreparably changes the natural course of things is Adam's act of disobedience, but the only reason Adam the man can disobey is that since his creation he is ruled by a commandment. According to the Bible, there is only disobedience where there is a commandment; Adam's gesture opens up an anthropological realm marked by the obligation to command. In Western history, thanks to this biblical tale, human nature became marked, irretrievably, by its relation to an original commandment. Adam's disobedience shows that a changed relation to the law can bear consequences that touch upon the being of man. Adam's transgression of divine command gives rise to a substantial transformation of not only the status, condition, and being in the world of the transgressor, but also of his nature. As Adam, man appears to be naturally inclined to transgress the law, in conflict with it, and thus fundamentally dangerous, wicked, and sinful, and this is the description of an established tradition in theology (Coccia, 2008).

Adam's disobedience is at the origin of a historical and contingent view of human nature. After Adam, though man becomes a "slave to sin," he also comes to occupy an exceptional position within the order of nature. What is particular about man is the relation he establishes with the law, wherein lies the possibility, for him, of *not* doing what he is ordered to do. Thus, one might say that man does not obey divine law *naturally*. The mere recognition that he *could* follow it, and is *free* to do so, is founded on the possibility that he might transgress it, on the fact that man is capable not only of accomplishing this or that action in compliance with an order, but that he is also, and more importantly, capable of *not* doing so. This inability of *naturally* obeying the law lies at the origin of his transgressive power and coincides with the possibility of his *freedom*—a freedom that entrenches human action in a more essential self-reference than its being oriented toward a specific actualization.

Arguably, all St. Paul's reflection on the law does is radicalize this experience. By exposing the tension between "commandments," "works of the law," and "faith," Paul identifies the prescriptive and normative aspect of the law as that which, by itself, gives rise to transgression, to the extent that speaking of sin would make no sense without the law. The relationship between law and sin is not one of simple identification; it is more complex because the law has the power to expose sin, hyperbolically (*kath'hyperbolén*), and thus reveals the fundamental unenforceability of the precept (Rom 7:13). According to Paul, this *possibility of not* executing a given order that is inherent to human action and constantly exposes one to punishment and condemnation is at one with the impossibility of immediately translating commandments into "works." This condition lies at the very origin of the nature of action where the latter cannot find its accomplishment in the form of "works."

Christian life deeply transforms the juridical configuration of transgression expressed in the Torah and man, defective at origin, here experiences a "debt" that, through the *gift* of grace, does not need to be filled, but to be simply administered as an investment. The margin between the law and sin is the space where the "law of Christ" is situated. As "grace," this law suspends all judgment and works pertaining to it; its suspension knows no appeal; it is the realization of a justice adequate to the law of faith and exceeds all works and obligations that link them to the precept. Thus, the Jewish experience of the law is translated into an "economic" experience of life, by means of which everyone's existence takes on the form of an investment on oneself and on one's being in debt.

In these terms, making the most of life is an investment with no return: the investor has to, on the one hand, deal with the impossibility of realizing the commandments of the *nómos* in the "works," while trying, on the other hand, to gain from his actions in a way that, detached from the aim of his works, shows weakness. But in Paul's words, in Christ's life "power (*dýnamis*) is made perfect (*teleîtai*) in weakness" (2 Cor 12:9); so, in the Christian perspective, human action emerges from a lack characterized by a potentiality that is not realized in the form of force or works but, instead, in "weakness." Gain lies in the loss that this weakness entails. The aspects of gift and disinterestedness that characterize grace cause human action to suspend the goal-orientation that characterizes it as work, and by maintaining its tension, this allows for a peculiar mode of investment in something that, in praxis, only knows its own end, something that appears meaningless in "the *sophía* of this world" that is always geared toward finding an ultimate goal to realize.

At work in this experience is an economic relation of the self to the self: the fact of not belonging to oneself and to have been "bought at a price" (1 Cor 6:20). The price paid by Christ turns the guilt and sin identified by the law into a debt that, as such, cannot be repaid. Of relevance to this discussion, in the early Christian texts, the death and resurrection of Christ are literally defined as "paying a debt," the "price of redemption" (*apolýtrosis*). Sacrifice, normally the cause attributed to this event, is not exhaustive as an explanation. At stake here is an integrally economic translation of the juridical management of justice, to the extent that Paul eventually speaks of justice "apart from the law" (*chorìs nómou*) (Rom 3:22). This form of justice neither defers the sentence to the future, nor does it execute it. Instead, it is a justice of the time of the now, the "now-time" (*ho nŷn kairós*) that becomes operative in action by justification through faith. According to Paul, this justification operates through the faith in Christ. The gift of grace outstrips all due service and, in faith, identifies a productive kind of administration of life that deactivates all extrinsic obligations and thus all effective chances of compensation. On these premises rests the possibility of a charitable economy where gratuity is not opposed to economic administration.

On the one hand, the fact that through the price of the ransom paid Christ's gesture freely justifies the faithful cannot be understood with mere reference to sacrifice, where sacrifice is the only compensation for the sin of all, and the fruit of an exchange that applies the logic of retributive justice. Nor, on the other hand, could it be said that the gesture simply eliminates all calculations in favor of a gratuity that is always an excess. Instead, Christ's death and resurrection seem to inaugurate an economic management of the gift that rather than requiring a duty of compensation in the form of exchange or counter-gift entails the possibility for man of investing in praxis instead of works, and this praxis appears to be fundamentally aimless.

In this scenario, it comes as no surprise that the theories of the gift explored earlier do not specifically mention Christian grace, apart from a very few exceptions (Tarot, 2008) where our hypothesis is confirmed. Grace does not presuppose an obligation in the form of a counter-gift, in fact, grace deactivates obligation by means of an economic administration of the faith in Christ; and for this reason it cannot belong to the logic presented by Mauss in his famous essay. It only seems possible to apply the theory of Mauss to the Christian paradigm where, in the history of Christianity, an extrinsic and transcendent finality is clearly reinstated, where human action is univocally directed, and praxis can be conceived of as a counter-gift that corresponds to the gift of grace. In any case, the constitutive antithesis between the economy and Christianity that is usually outlined in studies on the subject and that even Pope Benedict XVI referred to in the Encyclical *Caritas in veritate*, is in crisis and this gives way to the possibility of rethinking the Christian matrix of economic power that Weber's thesis on the origin of capitalism is concerned with. In this perspective, it is important to keep in mind this unknown coexistence between gratuity and economic management of life that can be retraced to the beginning of Christian discourse.

## Faith as a Political Institution

The majority of the formulations available from the early confessions of faith in the life of Christ can be found in Paul's letters, such as the *Epistle to the Philippians*, where he writes: "every tongue acknowledges (*exomologése-tai*) that Jesus Christ is Lord (*Kýrios Iesoûs Christós*)" (Phil 2:11). In the language of theology, the majority of confessions included in the texts of the New Testament are said to present formulae that are purely "Christological," where, in other words, the only faith professed is that in *Kýrios Christós*, such as the one just quoted. One hypothesis was that the formula

*Kýrios Christós* was created during the persecution in contraposition to *Kýrios Kaîsar* (Cullmann, 1948:25–28). However, like the confession in the *Epistle to the Philippians*, the formula refers to a more ancient practice internal to Judaism that does not concern only the communities of Hellenized Christians (Hurtado, 2003).

The Greek term *kýrios* used in these professions of faith is derived from the Indo-European root *\*kleu*, from which come, in several languages, a series of words linked to natural prosperity, profit, and advantage and, thus, to force and power that can also be divine. In Greek, the same root links the verb *kyeîn*, "being pregnant, carrying a child," the noun *kŷma*, "swelling (of waves)," as well as *kŷros*, "force, sovereignty," and *kŷrios*, "lord, sovereign" (Benveniste, 1969:422–423). In Greek *kýrios* also means "lord" in the sense of "landlord," "tutor," "curator," "custodian," whence the Latin version of *dominus*, from *domus*, "house." When transposed in this semantic context, the sovereignty of God and its Messianic royalty, typical of Judaism, which Paul's use of *kýrios* makes reference to, are critiqued in a manner that questions the activity of government itself. The sacred-juridical side seems to be replaced here by a natural overabundance pertaining to the domestic realm. With Christ, this administrative view of existence deeply transforms the juridical model of divine sovereignty of Judaism from within.

In faith it is possible to recognize the propelling mechanism that allows for this operation, which is constitutive of the Christian community. This mechanism has been defined as "politico-theological" precisely because of its dialectical relation with the *nómos*, which "transcends the juridical relation of subjection *nolens volens* to a sovereign" (Sandri, 2007:11). When it comes to this question, rather than "political theology" it would be more appropriate to speak of its accomplished "elimination," given that faith in Christ emerges from what intrinsically exceeds the juridical order given in the Torah. In any case, faith touches on a crucial element of the experience of Christianity. From the outset, the novelty of this experience lies in its making its political, rather than juridical, effects explicit; in doing so even before Eusebius, Augustine, and Thomas Aquinas and finally Luther defined the Christian community as *congregation fidelium*, a political unity whose orbit once also attracted the empire. Therefore, faith is foundational for the Christian community, right from the beginning. The difference from "Judaic faith" is not that, as some claim, the Christian experience is merely individual (Buber, 1950); rather, the fundamental difference is the rigid structure of obligation to the law that underlies it and tends to turn faith into fear, fear of the wrath of God (*orgè Theoû*) and fear of punishment (Assmann, 2000:48–56).

In order to understand the meaning and political power of Christian faith, it is important to note that in his study on the linguistic roots of Indo-European institutions, precisely in the chapters dedicated to the economy, Emile Benveniste links the Greek word *pístis* and the Latin word *fides* to the transmission, developed over centuries, of an ancient structure described as a "relation of personal loyalty." In this sense, in the various linguistic and institutional forms through which it found expression, "faith" is the credit one enjoys from someone as a result of having trustingly abandoned oneself to them and having thus established with them a relationship of loyalty. This means that faith entails the trust that is accorded—that which is given—as much as that which is enjoyed from someone, the credit one has. At the same time, faith also has an active and a passive, an objective and a subjective meaning: that of "given guarantee" and that of "inspired confidence." On the one hand, as Benveniste claims, the "partners of this 'trust' do not enjoy an equal status" because "the one who detains the *fides* someone else has placed in him, has this someone in their power," so much so that "this relation entails on one side the power to oblige and on the other an obligation" (Benveniste, 1969:88). The institution that is being reconstructed through language here is one where "a link is established between a man who has authority and one who is subjected to him because of a personal commitment" (Benveniste, 1969:76). For the discussion presented here, it is indicative that the terms considered explicitly refer to a "pact" or an "alliance." Of importance is also the fact that the obliging power called into question here does not entail force or the violence of command as much as persuasion. Benveniste also reminds us here that, for instance, in Greek the verb *peíthomai* has the same root as *pístis*, "faith," means "I obey" in the sense of "I let myself be persuaded." In this institution, a complete adherence to one's object of trust is at stake. "Christian faith" is the development of this adherence where, as Benveniste also claims with reference to the work of Antoine Meillet, "the ancient relation between *fides* and *credo* is revived." Here "*fides*, a profane term, evolved towards the meaning of 'religious faith' and *credence*"; what originally meant "to give *\*kred*," that is, to put one's faith in someone and expect protection from them thus connecting with them in faith, comes to take on the meaning of "confessing one's *fides*" (Benveniste, 1969:90).

However, rather than the sacralization of a profane element, the Christian faith seems to push to its extreme consequences an institution that already exists, thus inaugurating a new form of power: economic power.

Through Christianity it is possible to see the emergence of a form of obliging power that is not extrinsically constrictive; on the contrary, individuals are involved in it in so far as they are free. One might say that through faith in Christ the law is accomplished as oikonomía because it presents itself both as freedom from the *nómos* and full loyalty to it. In a way, in the experience of life in Christ, the more one is *free* and liberated from the definitively extrinsic obligation to the law, the greater his *obedience* on the basis of a relationship of absolute adjustment of life to the law. If the law is in force because it is Messianically already accomplished, there is an exact conformity between forms of life and forms of law, between *oîkos* and *nómos*. Faith becomes the main insurance operator of the form of power inaugurated here, that even assumes the expression of "love."

It is not so surprising, then, that the community of the faithful in Christ, though conceived of as a global social body, is articulated in small local units, each, in turn, *ekklesía kath'oîkon* (1 Cor 16:19; Rom 15:5; Col 4:15), where the expression *kath'oîkon* indicates not only the physical place where meetings are held. Even though it seems reasonable to presume that the first Christian groups met in private households, in its classical meaning *oîkos* appears to be the model on which *ekklesía* was to be structured. Of significance is that in the letters attributed to Paul's circle, the hierarchical bone structure of the classical *oîkos* is the point of reference of what Luther would later call the *Haustafel* of Christian communities: that is to say, starting from the fact that in the experience of the life of Christ distinctions "are nothing" (1 Cor)—there no longer is man, woman, freeman and slave—wives ought to be faithful and obey their husbands as house lords, and so should children and slaves (Col 3:18–41; Eph 5:21–6, 9; 1 Pet 2:13–3, 7). But in the hierarchy of episcopates and deacons told in the early Christian texts, *oîkos* is not the expression of a power that manifests itself as law; instead, it is an economic and administrative power (Ti 1:7), to the extent that Paul himself, as an apostle, claims to be "bursar" of Christ and of the mystery of God.

The constitution of economic power originates in a form that is not that of legitimation, though there certainly is a question of recognition of authority. Paul keeps facing the need to be recognized as the principal referent of the community he addresses in his writings; the conflicts emerging from his letters largely revolve around the determination of who is to be followed and for what reasons. But authority does not derive from the recognition of its legitimacy once and for all. Rather, the recognition is dependent on the way power is exercised, executed, actualized, and administered, time and again, and as such approved because believed to be just. It is not admitted to be true *una tantum* by force of law; it is constantly confirmed in the way it is administered, which the life of everyone fully adheres to through the manifestation of one's faith.

The form of power inaugurated here is decisive not only for the institution of modern politics, but above all because it remains effective even after the state structures on which it rests enter into crisis and fully reveal the essential contingency of their juridical order. In this sense, it is worth mentioning Carl Schmitt's notorious definition of modern sovereignty, as the extreme synthesis of the phenomenon and implicit manifestation of its very crisis. For Schmitt, sovereign is not the one who institutes the rule, but the one who has the right to suspend it. Although this definition does not throw much light on the contingency of the law but underlines, instead, the threshold of its legitimacy, it still points to the most critical aspect of the law. The connections between Schmitt's thought and Weber's political theory are well charted. But Weber goes further than pointing out the symptoms of a crisis of the juridical form of modern power, as Schmitt did (though admittedly in the attempt of turning them into strengths); Weber also identifies in "faith" the fundamental operator of the legitimacy of power, not only or not so much because of its legal structure, but rather in terms of the economic configuration it assumes under capitalism.

## The Spirit, or How to Experience the Flesh

There is one highly problematic question in the early Christian texts that was to arise again, especially in the interpretations of monks, and play a determining role in the history of Western thought, that is, the relation between *sárx*, "flesh," and *pneûma*, "spirit." Some claim this was in fact an invention of Paul (Sand, 1967; Gnilka, 1997:261); although the term *pneûma* is widely used in Stoic literature, its coexistence with *sárx* can first be discerned in Paul. *Sárx* and *pneûma* are not the Christian correlative of the classical distinction between *sôma*, the "body," and *psyché*, the "soul"; instead, they are two modes of being that seem to correspond to "life" (*zoé*) and "death" (*thánatos*). Living, in this sense, corresponds to a spiritual, "pneumatic" condition that, rather than preexisting it, is concomitant and alternative to "death." The question of "how" (*pôs*) it is constituted (1 Cor 3:10) is more important than *what* it brings. So one might say that one the one hand, the "spirit" (*pneûma*) that, with the "flesh" (*sárx*), characterizes the anthropology of Paul, does not refer to something specific to individual psychology; on the other hand, *sárx* is not indistinctly identified with biological substance or natural life. Instead, they both lie at the origin of human ways of living, of the modalities through which human life is formed.

Of note, in this sense is that the Western tradition has received these two polarities so as to relegate the relationship between *sôma* and *psyché* to the realm of individual psychology, reconnecting, instead, the spiritual realm that was opposed to *sárx* to the public sphere, which in the German language was semantically reabsorbed in the term *Geist*. It is emblematic that this operation, as carried out by Hegel, had such influence on the definition of the disciplines that spiritual sciences (*Geisteswissenschaften*) came to be named in opposition to the "natural sciences" (*Naturwissenschaften*). At stake in this discussion is an excess of the individual and psychological as opposed to the impersonal and collective dimension that characterizes the experience of Christianity from the start, a "spiritual" experience of not belonging to oneself, an experience of freedom (1 Cor 6:19).

In Paul's text there is an essential discontinuity between *sárx* and *pneûma*. It would be inappropriate to read into his words a linear relationship between the two where a shift to a definitively spiritual subject is possible. According to Paul, access to spirituality is not given in the progressive repression of the impulsive element of the "flesh." As evident in the seventh chapter of the *Letter to the Romans*, there is no homogeneity between will and reason: one does exactly what one does not want to do (Rom 7:15), not merely because one does not know what is good. In Paul's vocabulary, the "involuntary" essentially pertains to all that is "carnal" (Rom 7:14); it is a way of being that goes through the spirit and divides it, turning the impersonal and common experience of truth into something singular. It is not easy then to univocally identify in the first experience of Christian life the sacrificial instance of a definitive transfiguration of the singularity of the flesh into a solely spiritual body. From the outset, the element of the flesh presents an ambiguity that would in fact never really be resolved, even in later and more conciliatory interpretations.

If in Paul's terms the "flesh" (*sárx*) is the deadly mode of man's being in constant tension with the "spirit" (*pneûma*) that gives life, it is also through the flesh that death and resurrection are accomplished, as freedom not from the flesh but from the law of sin. The Christian experience of the flesh, on the one hand, refers to sin and death; on the other hand to the possibility of its resurrection. This ambivalence also refers to the Patristic development of Christ's *incarnation* as a means of universal salvation. But the universality of the Patristic dispositif tends to definitively negate the element of singularity in the lack of distinctiveness of the species realized in the incarnation. Instead, in the first experience of Christian life, singularity is not negated; it seems to be what constantly escapes all univocal forms of appropriation.

The difficulties of the first Christian communities to find a stable form of government seem to originate from this. The enfranchisement from an extrinsic link of obligation to command that is realized in the economic form of existence experimented here call into question, on the one hand, the possibility of transgression implicit in the law, and on the other hand, the very condition of freedom that pertains to it. The instance of nongovernment that characterizes early Christian communities takes the form of an experimentation of what is ungovernable in man's life: not to order chaos, but to turn the nongovernability of life into an experience of government, an "economy of mystery" (Eph 1:10). The participation of the "body (*sôma*) of Christ" (Rom 12:5) can lead, according to Paul, to the unity of members otherwise dispersed, and thus try to neutralize the complexity at play. But the form of the "law of the spirit of life" in Christ does not turn the "psychic (*psychikós*) body," or natural body, into a "spiritual (*pneumatikós*) body" through a univocal and irreversible process of spiritualization where the dispersion can definitively become uniform; it does so because it is vivified in the "flesh" that inhabits it and that constantly exposes it to alterity and reversibility, to its ungovernable plurality.[1]

Therefore, the "economy" as management of life in Christ reveals the possibility of a concomitance between the ungovernable element and what can be governed, between what can be lost and what can be possessed, which calls for further consideration. On this issue, one needs to recall Jesus' words as reported in Mark's testament, usually cited as an example of the sacrificial paradigm of Christianity, according to which salvation presupposes a renunciation that is later repaid:

Whoever wants to be my disciple must deny (*aparnesástho*) themselves and take up their cross and follow me (*akoloutheíto*). For whoever wants to save their life will lose it (*apolései*), but whoever loses
their life for me and for the gospel will save it (*sôsei*). (Mk 8:34–35)

Negation and the loss of oneself in the experience of the life of Christ
is not a mere moment in the evolutionary process of salvation; as evident
in this passage, through it, it is possible to experience the coexistence of
loss and possession, of dominion and indomitability, and this cannot be
negated.

The process of canonization of the ascetic practice, or *Regula Vitae*,
was inspired by the words reported by Mark, practiced by the medieval
monastic orders and codified in the expressions *Sequela* or *Imitatio Christi*.
However, the word *áskesis* does not feature in the texts gathered in the
New Testament (the verb *askéo* does, but only once in *The Acts of the Apos-
tles* 24:16; see the term *askéo* in the *Grande Lessico del Nuovo Testamento*,
1963:1314–1318). In any case, it is not easy to detect an effectively ascetic
soul in the first Christian generation; in fact, this issue has been much
debated and the object of many different and often divergent interpretations in theology. One of the major difficulties is perhaps the implicit
bipolarity of the experience of the "flesh" in the life of Christ, worth considering also in the context of this work.

## Áskesis: An Exercise of Possibility or an Action Conforming to an End?

In the West, to speak of asceticism it is not necessary to wait for Christianity to catch on in late Antiquity. It is not true that a Christian ascetic
ethics was opposed to the laxity of Pagan sexual morality (Foucault, 2005;
Brown, 1988). The question is more complex than it might seem from a
superficial analysis, and can certainly not be dealt with in its complexity
here. I will simply point out the significance of the presence of a discourse
on asceticism in classical and late Antiquity, so important that ascetic practices end up seeming, here no less than in the Christian world, something
other than secondary or marginal. A plausible explanation for this phenomenon must be sought in the existing connection between asceticism
and philosophy (Hadot, 1995; Rabbow, 1954).

From the beginning, the philosophical act was not only situated in the order of an abstract knowledge, but consisted in a fundamental conversion that upsets the whole of life, that changes the being of whoever carries it out. At one time, philosophy was understood as a discourse and mode of life. In the classical era and later in Hellenism, the practice of life—*téchne toû bíou* or *ars vivendi*—was not something other than philosophical discourse or external to it. If philosophy is a form of life and thought through which one questions the modes of accessing truth, the life of the philosopher is research: a practice, an exercise and an experience of transformation that totally involves him or her. On the philosophical path, truth is never presented as the object of logical reasoning. Rather, logical reasoning is none other than the constitution of the subject, and the subject who possesses it is not already preventively constituted as such. Truth is given to the subject at the price of some modifications in his or her own being. Love, the passion that in the Platonic sense is inherent to this movement, takes the form of an áskesis, a practice of transformation of those it involves. Suffice it to recall the famous passage in *The Republic* where the contemplation of the intelligible world is linked to *paideía*. The conversion (*epistrophé*) of the soul that is accomplished through it entails an exercise, an áskesis that does not merely involve the activity of contemplation, but the very possibility of contemplating, the power (*dýnamis*) of truth that exceeds all acts of knowledge (Plato, *Republic*, 2007:518b–e). In the philosophical ascetic practice, one experiences the fact that knowledge and rational comportments are not simply goals achieved in exchange of a renunciation of the self. The point, instead, is what one comes to know about oneself in order to be open to give up some of one's self. The price the subjects pay to access truth is intimately connected to the effect produced in them by the very fact that they tell or are able to tell the truth.

The hierarchical relation between the rational plane and that of drives, in the most naive reading, constitutes the main goal of ancient philosophical asceticism, and yet here loses priority and is thrown under a different light. There is a tension between the two planes. However, áskesis is never presented as a practice where reason subordinates instincts, but rather as a technique of accessing truth. Philosophy, as "life according to the *logos*," is placed in the realm of excellence and the most elevated of human virtues, though freed from the inconveniences that active life entails, it is never understood as a mere abstract theory.

Even for Aristotle, who strongly affirms that the highest knowledge is that one chooses for oneself, thus apparently unrelated to the way of life of the knower, *theoría* is contemplative life not opposed to practical life but a particular form of practice itself, a theoretical *práxis* that, as such, is an end in itself. It comes as no surprise, then, that Heidegger, in his plan for an ontology of "factual" life experience, where he declares the end of metaphysics, though critiquing Aristotle, also returns to the fundamentally practical dimension of Aristotelian philosophy, paving the way for a radical rethinking of the classical distinction between theoría and praxis.

The "practical" nature of contemplation in Aristotle is based on a distinction between real action (*práxis*) and technical-productive activity (*poíesis*). While the sole aim of production is a product distinct from the activity that generates it, the aim of praxis is, instead, inherent to the activity itself, which in this sense is a *eupraxía*, a good action (Aristotle, *Ethics* 6.1140b). The full circularity of the action that contains its own aim and principle is fundamental to Aristotle's argument for a definition of praxis as an exclusively human feature that is structurally distinct from all other animalist abilities to move when provoked by an external stimulus, which the animal responds to with a reaction rather than an action (Aristotle, *Ethics* 1139a). According to Aristotle, each extrinsic finality of human action is founded on the fact that praxis is implicitly an end in itself, and this is because of the fundamentally potential character of human action. While natural potential is, strictly speaking, determined prior to its enactment, the power (*dýnamis*) at play in the ethical sphere is detached from predeterminations and abandoned to itself. Its existence is only due to "exercise" (*áskesis*) and "habit" (*ethos*) (Aristotle, *Ethics* 1103a); these transform the ontological status of power from within, making it somewhat autonomous, that is, in possession of its own end without having to deduce it from external elements as is the case with merely natural power. This situation exposes human action to the complexity of contingency, of what can or cannot be; to what, unlike the animal world, is not univocally tied to its immediate realization. Unsurprisingly, in this context, although he had tried to present an exhaustive development and peculiar definition of *dýnamis*, Aristotle still wishes to allow for a dangerous, unsettling element to emerge from within the potentiality of action, something that is to be eluded.

Though radically different in the way it is articulated, a similar idea is the Biblical concept of "sin." Here, the "freedom" of the contingent nature of man is fundamentally related to *nómos*, whereas in the ethos we find in Aristotle it was related to *phýsis*. The leap from the animal state Aristotle identifies is always structured in an intimate and constant relation with "nature." Biblical narrative, instead, refers to the "law."

The intimate relationship between freedom and *nómos* that so essentially characterizes the Biblical framework is precisely what, in Christian faith and the "economic" experience of Christ, turns "sin" into "debt." The "defect" that prevents the potential nature of human action from finding its realization in "works" that conform to the precept, is exactly what in Christian discourse turns into a peculiar form of investment; an investment in the "power (*dýnamis*)" that, as Paul wrote, "is made perfect in weakness" (2 *Corinthians* 12:9) and whose results coincide with the loss from which it originates.

Aristotle's attempt to neutralize the potential being of human nature is evident in the way he managed to turn thought, which he previously described as essentially something potential, into a "pure act," "thought about thought," something fundamentally identical to itself and separated from any possible change and movement, inhabiting the realm of the "necessary" rather than the "possible." This separation leaves an indelible mark on the rational practice of philosophical ascesis: the latter starts being presented as belonging to a model of instrumental rationality and goal-oriented action, and this, in many respects, would remain the case for centuries (it is detectable even in Weber's work). Therefore, praxis becomes reduced to the status of mere *means* for the attainment of established *goals* and the *logos* that, in the Aristotelian model of the "pure act," was fundamentally powerless, becomes linked to praxis only in a relation of ends/ means; it becomes an abstract power that is *an end in itself*, toward which each actualizations, like a stage, is uniquely oriented.

Despite the sharp separation Aristotle posits between *poíesis* and *práxis* and from which the intrinsically practical nature of contemplation— another end in itself—derives, the difference between the two spheres is less straightforward than it might appear at first. The meaning and the outcome of an action cannot easily be separated in his argument, to the extent that he uses the same word for both: *télos* (end) (Aristotle, *Ethics* 1139b). I do not intend to dwell here on all of the aspects of Aristotle's argument on praxis, the peculiar relation between means and ends and the influences it came to have on more advanced technological developments (De Carolis, 2004:38–44). What matters for now is to highlight the inevitability of the teleological framework that affects, from the outset, the concept of action and that, even in the autotelic perspective of philosophical-aesthetic praxis can be detected and is inherited by Aristotle.

On this basis, the reason why ascesis becomes an explicitly "Christian" problem precisely at a time when worldly elements become univocally oriented toward an ultimate goal that determines whether they have meaning within a progressive and irreversible development becomes clearer. This is the time when the "economy of mystery," as the governing of life in Christ, becomes an "economy of salvation," an abstract and divine plane to which history seems oriented. Human praxis becomes, then, inscribed in a plan to which it moves. In the Aristotelian model mentioned, it becomes almost definitively turned into an action conformed to an end.

"Man" as generic being is an integral part of this, where everyone and the species, individual and universal history are identified through sin. Because of the degree of responsibility for the existence of evil attributed to him, man comes to establish an "ascetic" relation with the world that ranges from absolute devaluation to the possibility of "using" it differently. The "negative" that originates in sin, through various degrees and modes of renunciation, becomes inserted in a process of redeeming self-subsistence. Thus begins a more minute and complex codification of ascetic life, one that reveals an ambiguity right from the outset. Ascetic life derives from the first generation of Christians' critique of a mode of praxis aimed at the realization of "works" that conform to the law; it comes from a radical experience of human action and its fundamentally potential nature (Filoramo, 2007:257).

Despite this, from the outset, appears to be a perfecting activity and technique functional to a plan of salvation, an abstract order to conform to. This shift confers to ascetic praxis an irreversibility whose purpose is future redemption; but it also turns it into a privileged technique that the subject can use to become subject and as such shape his or her life, open to a mode of external subjectivation that is not aggressive but rather aims to coincide with it in capillary ways.

Retracing the ways ascetic practice became affirmed in the history of Christianity is all the more urgent if one observes the development of the power inaugurated through it: a dispositif that feeds on the ability of human living beings to shape and value their lives as a "being in debt." In this sense, it is possible to see how it is only very slowly that ascesis becomes explicitly debated in Christianity. The first signs of an actual debate are only discernible at the beginning of the second century. The main protagonist of the debate is undoubtedly the Gnostic movement that despite its multiple and varied manifestations converges on a radical demand of devaluation of all that is carnal and worldly and a rejection of history. This position originates from the idea that creation is the result of a secondary divinity, usually identified with the Jewish God to whom the cause of all evil is attributed.[2] The opponents of Gnosticism contributed to the constitution of what would later be defined as "true discourse" and converge into the formulation of the Christian dogma. The operation whereby human action and history become recuperated into a perspective of a stable government of the world was carried out precisely thanks to the Gnostic devaluation of the worldly element, as we later argue.

## The Abstaining Body: Form of Freedom and Exercise of Power

Early Christian communities were constantly exposed to states of crisis, so much so that the very survival of the *ekklesía* was in danger. Because of this, its immunity system had to be progressively strengthened and move towards a "self-definition of Christianity" (Hafner, 2003) that consolidated the elements of reaction for the sake of stabilizing its power. Those who radicalize the antinomy of its direction believe that it is necessary to find a substitute for the *Torah*; because, as Justin claims, a "law placed against law (*nómos dè katà nómou*) has abrogated that which is before it" (Justin, 2015:78). And if "an eternal and final law—namely, Christ—has been given to us, and the covenant is trustworthy (*diathéke pisté*), after which there shall be no law (*nómoi*), no commandment (*entolé*)," there needs to be a conduct that does not result into chaos (Justin, 2015:80). The element of the flesh in its original bipolarity is at once a mortifying aspect of human life and the vehicle of its resurrection; it becomes the center stage where freedom from *nómos* can find a new way of being and the form of a new kind of power. In its element as flesh, the body is regarded as the primary agent of this freedom and self-government becomes a form of domination.

The abstaining body is the best way of critiquing action that conforms blindly to the law. Abstinence is conceived of as the fundamental principle of reversibility of the works of the law, the possibility of investing the prevailing order, even by stalling the direction of reproduction. The deactivation of the praxis that conforms to the law, which for some is for the purpose of mere survival, turns the abstaining body into a free body. Marcion is probably the most extreme example of this path of gnosis. The separation of the lazy, good, and unknowable God from the active, creative, and legislative God, the noncoincidence of the pneumatic with the carnal Christ, elements that all gnostic systems have in common, radicalize this devaluation of action: their roots trace back to Paul's critique of the "law of the works." For the Gnostics, salvation is not dependent on that peculiar form of praxis that is faith, but rather on a knowledge purified of all practical elements, a knowledge that is divine *gnosis*. The Greek distinction between theoría and praxis that originated from the experience of an intimate connection between the two planes here becomes pushed to its extreme, resulting into an almost total indifference toward human action. In several Gnostic currents, the most radical forms of asceticism thus become juxtaposed to an unbridled libertinism, so as to demonstrate that no action leads to salvation; or, rather, that every action is equally redemptive because, in itself, it is deprived of value (Jonas, 1958:283–305).

This is why Irenaeus of Lyons, opposing the critical position of the Gnostics on praxis, tried to trace the origin of human action to a definition of divine action. In doing so he uses the word *oikonomía*, which he adopts to outline the particular activity of salvation at stake in Christian life. With oikonomía one does not generally refer to Christian practice. Rather, it describes a particular *order*, a *direction*, a *disposition* (whence the correlative Latin words *dispositio* and *dispensatio* that are used to translate the Greek term). Irenaeus is the first to refer only to Christ or God when speaking of ordering economic activity, never to man or to *ekklesia*, as instead is the case with Ignatius or Justin who see the church as the earthly economy of God. For Irenaeus oikonomía basically means divine disposition or government, and he refers it to God's creation and Christ's incarnation. His criticism of the Gnostics concerns the problem of the resurrection of the flesh. As he writes in book five of *Against Heresies*, the Gnostics "despise the entire dispensation (*tèn pâsan oikonomían*) of God, and disallow the salvation of the flesh (*tèn tês sarkòs soterían*)" (Irenaeuse, 2012:338). For him, the economy of God is accomplished in Christ, and it is a "dispensation [by which the Lord became] an actual man (*katà tòn alethinòn ánthropon oikonomías*), consisting of flesh, and nerves, and bones" (Irenaeuse, 2012:339). This order is realized for the sake of the humanity (*tèn oikonomían toù Theoû tèn epí tê anthropóteti genoménen*) that every individual and as a totality, the individual identified in the species, must conform to the divine plan of salvation accomplished in conformity with the "real man" Christ. For the first time, in Irenaeus, incarnation becomes the fulcrum of the divine economy: "dispositio incarnationis" (Uhrig, 2004:114–188); it is a device that abstracts and dominates human life, the element of the flesh being its main form of ailment.

The Gnostic economy of divine pleroma, compared to numerology (Irenaeus, 2012:356) finally comes to coincide with the eternal regularity of nature because it does not entail a progressive and temporal form. For Irenaeus divine government is temporalized and, although it does not yet properly coincide with a history of salvation as it would later be the case, it is still configured as a process with a purpose. "God thus determining all things beforehand for the bringing of man to perfection (*teleîosis*), for his edification, and for the revelation of His dispensations" (Irenaeus, 2012:280).

Therefore, Irenaeus is careful to save monotheism, as he is convinced that Gnostic dualism, which separates a God that is good from one that judges and creates, destroys the divine economy, the unity of creation, and the unity between the terrestrial and carnal element and the divine and spiritual one, as well as denying the meaning of human action, which ought to be recovered through the orientation toward a finalized plan that it must adequate itself to. Irenaeus looks for a typological interpretation of the scripture rather than a historical reconstruction of the divine plan of salvation (Richter, 2005:116–141); but he also opposes to Gnostic systems an "economy" that becomes a secularized divine government as a finalistic and irreversible process. As he writes in book one of his *Against Heresies*,

> The Father made all things by Him, whether visible or invisible, objects of sense or of intelligence, temporal, on account of a certain character given them, or eternal (*temporalia propter quamdam dispositionem*) and [. . .] by His Word and Spirit, makes, and disposes, and governs all things. (Irenaeus, 2012:35)

Rather than teleology of the logos, one can speak of a "Christology," where the divine government is accomplished in the embodiment of Christ. Christ has "become incarnate in man for the sake of man, and fulfilling all the conditions of human nature (*tèn katà ánthropon oikonomían ekplerôsantos*)"

(Irenaeus, 2012:351). The economy of the father (*preorisméne oikonomía*) is accomplished with the Son, in his incarnation and the resurrection of the flesh that it makes possible. In this perspective, there is no notion of divine self-revelation implicit in a clearly Trinitarian discourse, such as that of Tatian; similarly, no idea of an actual "ascetic" participation of man to the government disposed by God can be detected. The economy takes on the meaning of a progressive education of mankind only with Clement of Alexandria. However, in Irenaeus we can already see how human praxis is essentially deprived of determined goals and only finds meaning in this framework thanks to its orientation toward divine dispositions.

Essential to this moment was the reception of *áskesis*, in the classical sense, in the Christian tradition. This occurs concomitantly with the presentation of Christianity as a "true" philosophy because while the Greek philosophers only possessed "particles" of the Logos, Christians were in fact in possession of the Logos embodied in Jesus Christ (Justin, 2015:80). According to Clement of Alexandria, who was the first to link Christian philosophy to *paideía* as education of mankind, Christianity is the full revelation of the Logos and the "doctrine that follows Christ" and "recognizes God as creator; and extends providence (*prónoia*) even to every particular fact [. . .] and teaches (*didáskei*) and lead (*politeùesthai*) us according to our capacity to resemble God and grasp the divine disposition (*oikonomía*) as the leading principle of all of our education (*paideía*)" (Clement, 2015:52). In order to conform to the economic disposition of salvation, a constant exercise on the self is necessary. In this framework, ascesis becomes a technique functional to the power underlying this leading principle.

Underscoring this perspective is the notion that human beings do not develop a sense of justice "naturally" (*phýsei*) but by acquisition and learning (*mathései*) (Clement, 2015:40). According to Clement, "God has created us naturally social and just; whence justice must not be said to take its rise from implantation alone (*ek mónes tès théseos*). But the good imparted by creation is to be conceived of as excited by the commandment (*entolés*); the soul being trained (*mathései paideutheíses*) to be willing to select what is noblest" (Clement, 2015:8). So far so that "God shares everything amongst everyone according to merit (*kat'axían*): his economy (*oikonomía*) is just—the differences of virtue according to merit, and the noble rewards, He indicated the equality of justice" (Clement, 2015:45).

Clement was confronted with the crisis of the early Christian generation and the problems intrinsic to Paul's perspective concerning the justification of faith and the "economic" management of the gift of grace, which can even lead to a radical devaluation of human action, as it did in some factions of Gnosticism. In this context, Clement proposes to recover the notion of praxis in terms of *paideía*, exercise, and discipline, as an "economy of the soul (*oikonomía tês psychês*)" (Clement, 2015:42) that conforms to a divine economy. An ascetic practice economically oriented towards salvation must correspond to the gift of grace, almost as a counter-gift. Ascetic action acquires the *value* of redemption in the unstinting exchange inscribed in the divine plan.

Abstaining from evil deeds means diminishing evil, because "one's energy (*enérgeis*) diminishes (*kataíro*) with inaction (*apraxía*)" (Clement, 2015:62). Ascesis then becomes a peculiar form of praxis, a constant exercise of deactivation of action that tends, as its ultimate goal, toward contemplation. One only arrives at this after a long process of perfecting in Christ. In agreement with the classical distinction, for Clement, theoría and praxis, contemplation and action are separate. There are two kinds of instruction (*paideíai*): "there are assigned two kinds of correction (*paideíai*): knowledge (*gnôsis*) and the training according to the Word (*katá lógon áskesis*), which is regulated by the discipline of faith and fear (*ek písteos te kaí phóbou paidagogouméne*)" (Clement, 2015:62). Clement claims that "the end of the Gnostic here is, in my judgment, twofold,—partly scientific contemplation, partly action *he theoría he epistemoniké*" (Clement, 2015:102). Though separate, these two realms interact and manifest their intrinsic correlation, already recognized in classical discourse. According to Clement, "true instruction (*alethinè paideía*) is desire for knowledge (*epithumía tìs gnôseos*); and the practical exercise of instruction (*áskesis paideías*) produces love of knowledge (*agápe gnôseos*)" (Clement, 2015:63). Hence the notion of a "Christian" gnosis that is distinct from other forms of Gnosticism.

Because of its orientation toward contemplation and knowledge, for Clement ascesis entails a detachment from the body: "in fine, the Lord's discipline (he kyriakè áskesis) draws the soul (*psyché*) away gladly from the body (*sómatos*)" and it does so by means of a conversion (*metáthesis*) (Clement, 2015:89). Contrary to the Gnostics who followed Valentin and especially Marcion, Clement aims to identify a redeeming feature in the flesh, and thus tries to redeem the notion of reproduction. In his view, not only is generation "saintly"; "without the body (*áneu toû sómatos*), how could the divine plan for us in the Church (*he katá tèn ekklésian kath'emàs oikonomía*) achieve its end (*télos*)? [. . .] Lord himself, the head of the Church, came in the flesh (*en sarkì*), though without form and beauty" (Clement, 2015:103). The element of the flesh is recuperated through the possibility of its negotiation. The negative that originates in the flesh is thus included in a process of redemption where life becomes the end that is obtained by going through death, the mortification of the flesh.

In the attempt to translate pagan ascesis into Christian terms, Clement presents áskesis in a classical form, as a natural conformity of will and intellect difficult to reconcile with the perspective outlined in chapter seven of the *Letter to the Romans*. This agreement, however, is here an exercise on the desire of the flesh, so that, like in Paul, the flesh begins to emerge also in its involuntary elements. On the one hand, "volition takes the precedence of all; for the intellectual powers (*hai logikaí dynámeis*) are ministers of the Will (*boúlesthai*), and Will (*boúlesis*), Judgment (*krísis*), and Exertion (*áskesis*) are identical" (Clement, 2015:77). On the other hand, he also writes:

> The human ideal of continence (*enkráteia*), I mean that which is set forth by Greek philosophers, teaches that one should fight desire and not be subservient to it so as to bring it to practical effect. But our ideal is not to experience desire at all. Our aim is not that while a man feels desire he should get the better of it, but that he should be continent even respecting desire itself. (Clement, 2015:57)

In the Christian perspective opened by Clement of Alexandria, the domination of desire does not entail an absolute sovereign control over it, although, occasionally, this is achieved, contingently, as in Aristotle, or in the pagan ascetic practices of late Antiquity. In Christian áskesis, desire invests the modality of domination itself in different ways. Its negation does not tend to fight its object once and for all; on the contrary, it opens up the possibility of deciphering the faculty of desire in all of its details, and with it, the possibility of enjoying it, too.


## A Struggle with the Flesh

Many are the differences separating pagan and Christian ascesis. The áskesis of late Antiquity is usually interpreted as a freely chosen life practice, aimed at self-mastery; Christian ascesis, on the other hand, is normally

identified with a coercive practice of self-renunciation. During the apol-
ogetic phase of Christianity in the second century and its translation into
a "true" philosophy, however, an interesting affinity can be discerned: in
both late Antiquity and Christian áskesis, action and contemplation interact to the extent that, though separate, theoría and praxis converge into
a single activity. Both cases involve modes of self-mastery. In Christianity
these end up turning into an accomplished form of renunciation aimed at
divine disposition. In the Greco-Roman and the Christian áskesis alike,
this practice of self-mastery, which is both a contemplative and a practical
activity, becomes the premise for the domination of others. But while in
pagan asceticism natural life (zoé) linked to survival and reproduction is
excluded and circumscribed to the realm of the oíkos, which is the only
place where an "economic" form of administration of the private dominion as separate from the pólis can be found; in Christian ascesis, the natural realm depends on the very freedom of action and thus is the realm
through which salvation is possible, while the oikonomía becomes the
public and common management of the "mystery" of life itself. The "flesh"
is not only an object of sin, and thus of renunciation, but also the means of
the "economy of incarnation" of Christ: the divine plan of world order that
one must conform to through a progressive process where one becomes
adequate to a divine disposition that abstractly posited.

After Clement, Origen is perhaps the one who most clearly conceived
of the divine government of the world as an oikonomía (Origen, 1885:64).
Origen radicalizes Clement's perspective and claims that God's economic
leadership is inscribed in the life of each person and becomes the "government of the souls" (theòs gàr oikonomeín tàs psychás), a process aimed at
eternity (Origen, 1885:65). Like Clement, Origen believes that the "contemplative" and "gnostic" (theoretiké) life of the soul is different from practical life (praktiké) in so far as it is the contemplation of divine "economic"
nature and the activity of self-revelation of the Trinity and of the plan of
the government of the world. Although practical life is a sort of prelude
to contemplative life, the knowledge one acquires in it conforms to divine
activity and preserves the characters of praxis.

Origen's distinction between contemplative and active life left a mark on
the Monasticism of later centuries and was largely influential on the discussions of the Anchorites, who had opted for a solitary life, and the Cenobites,
who were connected to the common life of the monastery. Evagrius Ponticus,
also called Evagrius the Solitary, begins his guide to ascetic life, the *Praktikos*,

by introducing this distinction. According to him, active life is ascetic life, and "gnostic" life, or the life of "knowledge," is the direct science of God in Trinity arrived at through *apátheia*. If in ascetic life the monk is constantly struggling with the passions and desires of the body, the achievement of a condition of impassiveness does not entail their mere elimination; on the contrary, one must "contemplate the reasons for the war" and recognize "the maneuvers of one's enemies" (Evagrius, 1970:83), to identify their tactics.

Evagrius is describing an actual battle. The enemies are the "demons" who take over the body in the eight negative thoughts (Evagrius, 1970:6) at the basis of the eight capital sins. In order to win this war one needs to be able to "identify the differences between the demons and distinguish the circumstances of their coming" (Evagrius, 1970:43). It is necessary to constantly analyze oneself because the "index of the affections that hide in our soul can be a word we say or a movement of our body" (Evagrius, 1970:47). He proposes an ascetic exercise where one does not have to "separate the body from the soul," but rather "the soul from the body"; the impassiveness that characterizes the contemplation of the true nature of things is not so much a final stage where the corporeal element is finally eliminated; rather, through a labor intrinsic to it, it is possible to accomplish the overcoming of its badly posed exigencies. "Those who take a misunderstood care of their flesh (*sárx*) and those who give it the attentions that provoke its desires must blame themselves, rather than the flesh. Those who know the grace of the Creator know this well, and it is those who, by means of this body (*sómatos*) have achieved the imperturbability of the soul and secured themselves, in some way, the contemplation (*theoría*) of things created" (Evagrius, 1970:53).

Evagrius was an Anchorite in the Egyptian desert of Nitria. Cassian moved to Egypt in 385 with the resolve to personally witness the lives of the most famous monks of his times. His encounter with Evagrius was decisive for Monasticism. When Cassian returned to the Provence around 399 with the intention of establishing institutions for Cenobites somewhere with a strong tradition of monasteries, he wrote the *Conlationes*, a diary of his spiritual journey in Egypt, twenty-four conferences for monks that reproduce his dialogues with the most prominent Egyptian Anchorites, and document the shift from Anchoritism to Cenobitism, from ascetic solitude of contemplation to the communal life of the monastery.

Cassian regards Evagrius as his master and agrees with his distinction between theoretical and active life. In the fourteenth conference paper, on the matters of spiritual science, Cassian differentiates between active science, or *praktiké*, and contemplative science, or *theoretiké*, and claims that "practical knowledge can be acquired without theoretical, but theoretical cannot possibly be gained without practical" (Cassian, 2012:158). Cassian radicalizes the active nature of contemplation by explicitly rooting it in ascetic practice.

The *fuga mundi* of the contemplative ideal of Anchorites does not aim, as Evagrius suggests, to the "separation of the body from the soul," but to a detailed deciphering of the exigencies of the body, which are normally misinterpreted. In Cassian, the constant regulation of every hour of the day becomes the premise for a definition of the rules of monastic life and makes it possible for monks to live in common as a coenobium. The monastic rule taking shape in the coenobium cannot be configured as law or an external command to which the individual is forced to submit. It is, rather, a meticulous codification of the techniques of self-discipline, where obedience is a form of life.

Self-discipline is at the foundation of Christian ascetic practice, and in Cassian and Evagrius becomes a struggle between the "flesh" and the "spirit." In the fourth conference paper, Cassian writes:

> Of the value of the conflict which the Apostle makes to consist in the strife between the flesh and the spirit. This conflict too we read in the Apostle has for our good been placed in our members: "For the flesh lusteth against the spirit: and the spirit against the flesh. But these two are opposed to each other so that ye should not do what ye would." You have here too a contest as it were implanted in our bodies, by the action and arrangement of the Lord. (Cassian, 2012:305)

The conflict Cassian describes is not fought between a subject, the ascetic, and the flesh as its object. The desiring subject is also the ascetic subject, object of its own practice. In the tenth chapter of the same conference paper, to demonstrate the complexity of the role of the flesh in the experience of Christian life, Cassian analyses the various meanings of the flesh in the Scriptures, the incarnation of the Word in John I, 14 and Luke's claim that "all flesh shall see the salvation of God" (Lk 3:6). In his interpretation of the passage in the *Epistle to the Galatians* (Galatians 6:16–17) that Cassian refers to in the citation above, he claims that for Paul the flesh is not a "substance," it is an "activity," a mode of being

(Cassian, 2012:187), and the ascetic subject is not solely identifiable with the spirit, that is, with whatever is left once the struggle for liberation is over; the ascetic subject is itself at stake in the battle. Flesh and spirit are at the origin of desires and will, they are modes of being of human freedom, of its self-reflexive nature.

The Christian asceticism Cassian describes gives rise to the paradox of a subject that is constituted as an object of his own practice. In this, there is a profound antinomy: the renunciation of the self is not the result of a mere negation of the carnal element; it is the path on which it becomes possible to decipher the most obscure and unmanageable aspects of the flesh. The subject of desire and its modes of pleasure are formed through this process of decoding, which also makes it possible to organize detailed mechanisms of control to govern what appears to be ungovernable.

The struggle between flesh and spirit, for Cassian, is the result of freedom and, starting with Adam's gesture, characterizes the human species and every individual belonging to it. It is not opposed to the divine plan: it is "useful" to salvation and part and parcel of the plan of salvation (*dispensation domini procurante*). It is "like some energetic schoolmaster (*diligentissimus paedagogus*) who never allows us to deviate from the line of strict discipline (*a districtionis et disciplinae linea numquam nos deviare concedens*)" (Cassian, 2012:89). Through the freedom he was granted, man is put to the test and does not remain idle (Cassian, 2012:95), but rather "must constantly endeavor to obtain the virtue of humility" (Cassian, 2012:111).

In defense of human freedom, Prosper of Aquitaine accuses Cassian of "semipelagianism" in his *Epigrammata* and *Liber contra Collatorem*. The disputes animated the monastery of Marseilles during the early fifth century, following the clash between Pelagius and Augustine on matters of grace and free will (Lettieri, 2001:307–380). Seen against the backdrop of the relationship between asceticism and the economy of salvation outlined here, these disputes highlight that despite diverging on important issues, their respective positions converge on a point that is highly significant for the influence of Christian culture on Western modernity. The semipelagian notion of *gratia subsequens* responds to the need of allowing human beings their autonomy of freedom and will, but the "merit" of their actions, in this framework, can be traced to their being functional to the plan of salvation, a sort of counter-gift for the original gift of grace. On the other hand, in the Augustinian perspective, grace is an absolute gift of freedom and ends up coinciding with the great power of *consenting* to this freedom as a need for an unconditional counteroffer. Both positions, though opposite, seem moved by the same intent: that of finding a stable form of domination of what is indomitable in human beings. This is not to diminish the importance of a discussion that deeply affected Western Christianity, nor is it intended to deny its diversity. However, it is evident that, though in different ways, freedom appears to be the principal operator of that form of power that coincides with the "economy" as a divine plan of government of the world and of history. If my hypothesis is correct, this mechanism is analogous to that in place in the economic power of our days.

The war on the flesh described by Cassian is testimony of an intrinsic ambivalence in asceticism that remains pertinent to the whole of the ascetic tradition in Christianity from then on. Though involving the most intimate fibers of our body, and though it is the only way to decipher the most obscure aspects of our being, this battle is in fact the result of a plan; the divine plane that, like an abstract economy of salvation, governs human beings down to the smallest detail, and is aimed at laying out a process of disciplining desires and a form of enjoyment that tries to make human beings conform to the preestablished order.

On the one hand, ascesis is a conduct functional to the power it is inscribed in, on the other, as an activity that constitutes the desiring subject, it is opposed to and in constant tension with it. In fact, in the fifth century, the monastic ascetic movement becomes marginal and keeps critical relations with the imperial Church after Constantine. The "meritorious" notion of asceticism that Luther would later oppose with his notion of justification *ex sola fide*, while feeding the marginal status of the monastic movement, is also intrinsically functional to the establishment of a government of the world that starts with each individual life.

# Chapter 3

# The Theological Construction
# of the Government of the World

Like all historical phenomena, the facts of the emergence of Christianity do not coincide with what has been passed on in written documents about them; moreover, not only is it impossible to pinpoint its manifestation to an origin, it is also not possible to access the source texts without a preliminary analysis of the manuscripts that have been handed down. Aware of these limitations, this research project aims to reconstruct the genealogy of Christian asceticism without presupposing *what* ascesis is to Christianity at the time of its emergence but rather asking *how* an ascetic way of life arises in Christ. In doing so, this study had to confront the development of an "economic" modulation of experience in early Christianity, which precedes the accomplished formulation of asceticism as a Christian problem.

The translation of the Judaic legal vocabulary into an economic perspective undertaken in the early Christian texts, together with the assertion that the "economy" is one of the prevalent forms of organization of early experiences of life in Christ, have evidenced how inseparable an economic mode of power is from this experience and how it consolidates through it.

On the one hand, the power inaugurated by Jewish Law has a juridical configuration, through its legal representation it manifests itself in the negative form of prohibition, and it is exercised by way of an act of obligation to which the possibility of transgression is connected; on the other, Christian faith, in the accomplishment of the law in Christ, presents itself as the wielder of a technique of power where the *nómos* is not a commandment extrinsic to one's existence but instead perfectly adheres to the life of each individual in the form of *oikonomía*. Thus, the plasticity of the Christian

faith comes to contrast with the rigidity of the juridical structure characteristic of the form of law found in the Jewish pact. The practice of faith is
the mechanism that grants Christ's gratuitous justification, thus it makes
it possible to build a web of power relations that are as efficient as mobile
and transformable. This freedom from the *nómos* that defines the "law of
faith" in Christ creates a complete juxtaposition between slave and master,
subjected and subject, losing and taking possession of oneself.

Freedom acts as the necessary condition for the existence of the mobil-
ity that characterizes the economic form of power here inaugurated. This
freedom is not, however, a voluntary submission to the force of the law, a
renouncing of transgression that resembles the obedience to a prohibition
extraneous to it. Instead, it is the full expression of the enforcement of the
law in its most accomplished form, where life and law, *oîkos* and *nómos*,
coincide. This entertains the possibility of a government that may not
even assume the role of a stable domination, unless it forces that which is
by nature nongovernable to become an element that is simply governed.

The difficulties inherent in this economic mode of power soon chal-
lenge the survival of the *ekklesía* and require changes that turn out to be
fundamental for its destiny. In the second century, the early Fathers of the
Church develop the oikonomía as an abstract plane of salvation, the divine
order of a history to which one must conform, and articulate it, for the
first time, as an explicitly Christian problem. The oikonomía is construed
as a technique functional to the power that underlies it; through it, the
"negative" is inserted into a process of salvation and self-sustenance. As an
exercise of the self on itself and as a practice of self-mastery, asceticism thus
becomes the most efficient form of domination for the system in which
it is inscribed: a meritorious practice aimed toward salvation. The critique
of the "works of the law" of the early Christian experience had made it
possible to suspend the orientation of action toward an extrinsic objective
and to invest in that which in human action has no other aim than the
one within itself. In relation to this critique, the human action that stems
from its own freedom and from the negativity that, in this new perspective, is part of it, takes on a new direction, one that will never be entirely
abandoned, not even in the Protestant condemnation of the "meritocracy"
of Catholic asceticism.

It is worth noting that in the most recent theological debate on the
issue of asceticism, research has mainly stemmed from an already formed,
almost presupposed, concept of Christian asceticism and then proceeded

to determine whether it is present in early Christianity (Padovese, 2002). The roots of this kind of approach may be found in the debate started between the end of the nineteenth and the first half of the twentieth century by the main advocates of Protestant and Catholic post-Hegelian theology. The existence of ascesis in early Christianity is often strongly denied or affirmed on the assumption that *what* is meant by Christian asceticism is sufficiently clear. With a few exceptions, to be dealt with later, what the different and sometimes opposing cases have in common, most importantly, is their veiled defense of a salvation government of the world through which theology, aware of the crisis that befalls it, endeavors to obtain the tools required for its own survival.

## Is There Ascesis in the "Good News"?

In 1900, a series of lectures held by the Protestant theologian, Adolf Harnack at Berlin University during the winter term of 1899–1900, were published by Hinrichs of Leipzig, under the title *Das Wesen des Christentums* (What Is Christianity). Although it was a minor work, completely eccentric compared to the author's usual writings, its influence was widespread: it met with much acclaim. In fact, it may be considered a key work on the subject of asceticism that helps situate an important part of post-Hegelian Protestant theological thinking.

The optimism professed toward a historical process that is seen as progress, capability of a prospective vision and critique, enables the most significant exponent of liberal theology to identify as "essential" to Christianity a plasticity, an innate predisposition for historical change, and a natural tendency toward evolution. For Harnack, the Christian religion is essentially flexible and must exercise this ability as a historical task. Hence, the concept of the gospel as a "social message, imbued with sacred rigor and enormous strength," "tied to the infinite value of the human soul," which "finds its place in preaching of the Kingdom of God" (Harnack, 1901:131). According to Harnack, "the tendency towards solidarity and towards brotherhood [. . .] [is] the essential element of its particularity."

> The gospel wishes to build a community amongst men, as vast as human life and as deep as man's need. [. . .] The eternal bursts onto the scene, the dimension of time becomes a means to an end, man

belongs to eternity. [. . .] By extending, without discontinuity, the idea of providence to the world and to man, reconnecting the ultimate roots to eternity, affirming the divine progeny as a gift and commitment, Christianity managed to give strength to the shy and uncertain attempts of religion and to bring them to their accomplishment. (Harnack, 1901:110)

In Harnack's work, the providential vision of events, rooted in the patristic notion of the economy of salvation and updated in post-Hegelian terms, becomes a theology of history from which the idea of an ideal community is born and to which the historical process must be directed homogeneously. It is in this framework that he situates "the problem of ascesis," which he treats separately as it is classed as one of the six core problems in the history of Christianity. He writes:

There is a widespread opinion, it is dominant in the Catholic churches and many Protestants share it nowadays, that in the last resort and in the most important things which it enjoins, the Gospel is a strictly world-shunning and ascetic creed. Some people proclaim this piece of intelligence with sympathy and admiration; nay, they magnify it into the contention that the whole value and meaning of genuine Christianity, as of Buddhism, lies in its world-denying character. Others emphasize the world-shunning doctrines of the Gospel in order thereby to expose its incompatibility with modern ethical principles and to prove its uselessness as a religion. (Harnack, 1901:79)

For Harnack it is not even worth discussing the way out of this that the Catholic church devised, where "authentic Christian life," which "finds true expression only in the monastic form" is juxtaposed with "an 'inferior' Christianity," without asceticism but "still sufficient" (Harnack, 1901:101). This is because he refuses to "see the gospel as a world-shunning doctrine." "The form of the union with God" proposed in the announcement of Christ "transcends," in his view, "the whole issue of the *fuga mundi* and of ascesis" (Harnack, 1901:120). The spoliation of the self it demands is not that of ascesis but that of "a fight against egoism" (Harnack, 1901:122). "The Gospel demands sacred self-examination, intense vigilance and the annihilation of the opponent within. There can be no doubt that Jesus requested a much higher degree of self-abnegation and spoliation than we would care to admit." However, for Harnack, "ascetic in the primary meaning of the word the Gospel is not; for it is a message of trust in God, of humility, of forgiveness of sin, and of mercy" (Harnack, 1901:93). The struggle the Gospel requires therefore coincides with "the love that serves and is self-sacrificing" (Harnack, 1901:95). "This struggle and this love are the kind of asceticism which the Gospel means, and whoever encumbers Jesus message with any other kind fails to understand it" (Harnack, 1901:95). Harnack categorically rules out the possibility that asceticism, seen as a threat to the "modernity" of the Christian religion and its success in the world, might be an original manifestation of Christianity. The Christian sacrifice of love, rather than being an escape from the world, is to be seen as the binding force of that "ideal community" that history must confidently move toward.

Notwithstanding, the crisis of Protestant theology in the wake of the Great War, Harnack's stance remains an important reference point also on the subject of asceticism. Besides differences, Harnack's influence can be detected, for instance, in the 1949 work of the Protestant theologian Hans Campenhausen, dedicated to Rudolf Bultmann: *Die Askese im Urchristentum*. The main view these scholars share is an explicit denial of the experience of an ascetic attitude in early Christianity. In addition to this they also share a critique of liberal theology. The whole debate centers on the problem of the "following" of Christ: *die Nachfolge Jesu*. For Campenhausen, "those who follow [Christ] are not imitating a model nor simply following an eternally valid law" (Campenhausen, 1949:11). In this perspective,

> The liberal and the ascetic interpretation both run the same risk. They both center the issue on fixed norms of Christian behavior which they try to practice both "internally," as an intimate disposition (*Gesinnung*), and "externally" through ascesis. In doing so they are actually missing the most significant point, that is, the unconditional personal bond with the Lord in whom trust is placed and the subsequent frankness with which any concrete form of reprimand or "calling" (*Berufung*) is received. (Campenhausen, 1949:11)

Campenhausen starts from an existential stance, akin to that of Bultmann, which is actually very distant from Harnack's view, and deals with the issue in several ways breaking it down according to property, wealth or poverty, food and sexuality. Differences aside, the conclusions are the same as Harnack's: "Early Christianity is unthinkable in ascetic terms" (Campenhausen, 1949:25); as "the ultimate sense of the Christian relationship with the world is not ascesis but 'freedom'—that is, the freedom of those who sacrifice 'their own lives' or, to quote Paul, are already 'dead' to the world" (Campenhausen, 1949:39). The optimistic attitude that Harnack shows toward history is replaced here with the tragic dimension of existence and the economy of salvation on which it is based, becomes unequivocally rooted to the incarnation. To the "scatological" foundations of Harnack's view, Campenhausen therefore juxtaposes a "Christological" standpoint (Campenhausen, 1949:37). Although it is far removed from the optimism of the liberal theologian for its individualistic and existential formulation, it is nevertheless akin to it regarding its aim of complete compliance with the divine plan of world government to which it is subjected.

The work of Campenhausen is cited under the entry *Askese*, in the third edition of *Die Religion in Geschichte und Gegenwart,* the dictionary compiled by Karl Georg Kuhn in 1957 that left its mark in the field of historical-critical theological research. Kuhn not only denies the existence of "ascetic tendencies and motives" in the annunciation and life of Christ but, like Campenhausen, also suggests a "Christological" foundation of the lives of the first Christians. The position inaugurated by Campenhausen and revisited by Kuhn influenced research in this field and is also shown by its inclusion in the *Askese* entry of the *Handbuch religionswissenschaftlicher Grundbegriffe* (see Schlatter, 1990).


## The "Merits" of an Ascetic Life: Governing History

The affirmation of an ascetic essence of primitive Christianity is characteristic of Catholic theology. A particularly interesting example of this is the work of the Benedictine, Anselm Stolz, a professor at the St. Anselm University of Rome during the 1920s and 1930s. In his posthumous book, published in 1943, entitled *L'ascesi cristiana*, he states that the heart of ascetic life in Christianity is the *Imitatio Christi* (Stolz, 1943). According to Stolz, the Christian ascetic is someone able to free himself from this world, as *extra mundum factus est*, who knows how to forgo his own will with humility to conform, in Christ, to the will of God. The sense of Christian ascesis is found in the "reproduction of the death of Christ." "To suffer for Christ is the necessary evolution of our status of immersion in his passion and his death; it is an essential part of Christian life" (Stolz, 1979:23).

Although Stolz subscribes to the "mortifying" view of Christian existence that held much ground throughout the history of Christianity, he sees the ascetic way as being accessible to all Christians and not only to the select few. In doing so he anticipates the position of the Second Vatican Council, his views isolating him from the stale atmosphere of the fundamentally "scholastic" framework of those same pontifical Roman universities in which he delivered his lectures. Therefore, it is not surprising that his work does not get mentioned under the entry *Askese*, even in the part dedicated to the Old and New Testament that appears in the first volume of the second edition of the *Lexikon für Theologie und Kirche*, published in 1957 (Schnackenburg, 1957) and later published as a complete work including the texts of the Second Vatican Council gathered in three additional volumes. However, it is maybe due to its critique both of the traditional view of Christian life and of modern devotion that the position of Stolz sheds much light on the Catholic conception of Christian ascesis, setting it apart from "modernist" criticism and "scholastic" rigidity. According to Stolz, asceticism is the practice through which each man may complete the "process of redemption, not entirely accomplished by the Incarnation." A meritorious view of human action underlies this sort of position; ascetic practice has functional value as it is an exercise that aligns the subject to the divine order that includes it.

A particularly interesting step in this direction is the position of Erik Peterson, emblematic of a certain kind of Catholic stance on the issue of asceticism. The text of his conference paper, held in Rome in 1948, was published later that year by Pontificia Universitas de Propaganda Fide, in the journal "Euntes docete" with the title *L'origine dell'ascesi cristiana*. It was subsequently included, together with other articles on the subject, in the 1959 book *Frühkirche, Judentum und Gnosis*. Dedicated entirely to several Christian testimonies from the Syrian area (the *Acts of Thomas* and the *Acts of Peter*, in particular), this book is important for our reconstruction of an important aspect of early Christian ascesis (Peterson, 1948:196).

What is at stake, according to Peterson, is the "contrast between two groups of Christian Jews over the issue of ascesis": one tied to the so-called pseudo-Clementine literature and a presumed radical "metaphysical dualism," and the other, documented in the Apocryphal Acts, that appears to present a more "truly" Christian version of the development of the text.

In Peterson's view, the metaphysical dualism, which is thought to find expression in pseudo-Clementine literature, does not lead "to real ascesis but only to that which the Protestant theologian Troeltsch describes as *innerweltliche Askese* (inner-worldly ascesis), considered a result of Lutheran dualism, that is, a reserved attitude towards the world that may not be called ascesis in the true sense of the word" (Peterson, 1948:201). Conversely, from his point of view, the issue is presented differently in the Apocryphal Acts. The problem of time appears to be the crux of the matter in determining a "truly" Christian experience aimed at an effective order and government of the history of human beings. Peterson writes:

> According to the Clementine homilies, the world of the future, that is, the Kingdom of God, is a reality completely belonging to the future that only actually begins after our death. Instead, the Apocryphal Acts see the Kingdom of God as something that is already present [. . .] Pseudo-Clementine eschatology is purely a thing of the future [. . .]. For this reason, the encounter of these two worlds, the present and the future one, does not find expression in an ascetic attitude. (Peterson, 1948:202)

"The ascesis of the Apocryphal Acts," on the other hand, has nothing to do with the "description of a future world, of an ideal Judaic millennium" but with the "reality in action" of the "Kingdom of God that is going to come" (Peterson, 1948:204). In the follow-up to the essay Peterson defines it as the "live reality of Christ who wants to become a worldly force, upturning the world as it stands in its current consistency and in its current duration" (Peterson, 1948:203).

From these premises a more general conclusion on Christian ascesis is deduced, one worth considering:

> It has been made clear how Christian ascesis in its original form has nothing do with either Greek philosophy or a metaphysical dualism: it is strictly related to the faith in the coming of the Kingdom of God drawing near. This Kingdom is not a completely future event, as in a paragraph of the treaty "de novissimis," but it is a present reality [. . .]. The historical research into the origins of ascesis in the Judaic-Christian world has not contradicted but confirmed the theory that Christian ascesis is inseparable from Christian faith itself. (Peterson, 1948:203)

Aside from the apparently neutral tone and the fundamentally philological nature of the discussion, in this brief essay Peterson does not withhold from a line of reasoning worthy of the opponent of Schmitt.

The scatological nature of Christian ascesis is defined as the "encounter of two worlds, the present one and the future one." The "reality in action" of the Kingdom of God in Christ, the accomplishment of which is not conceived as "a thing completely belonging to the future," eliminates all doubts, in his opinion, that there might be some inherent form of dualism in the most genuine Christian thinking. According to Peterson, this intimate tension between present and future seems to characterize the asceticism of early Christianity. Conversely, where the Kingdom is conceived of as a future "ideal Jewish millennium," it is only a metaphysical dualism that does not lead to real ascesis, if any, it only leads to what Ernst Troeltsch calls an "inner-worldly ascesis."

The apparently innocuous and hasty reference Peterson makes to Troeltsch regarding pseudo-Clementine literature perhaps points to a more complex debate that implicitly also involves Weber's theory of the origins of Capitalism. According to Peterson, Christian ascesis has nothing to do with the "inner-worldly" ascesis mentioned by Troeltsch and Weber. In his view, this type of ascesis is nothing but the extreme version of a form of radical dualism that enables (the logic of) modern finalism to be autonomous from any transcendental aim whatsoever. Instead, he holds Christian ascesis to be of an eschatological nature. Its salvational effectiveness is ensured by keeping the tension toward the future and thus, toward transcendence, alive. This implies the possibility that the Kingdom of God may be present as a "living reality" and may become a "worldly force" within the Catholic Church. This position is well known and has been articulated further and more explicitly with a clear reference to the Jewish people. The Jews, not having recognized the Christ incarnate and continuing to wait for his coming, are the "katechontic" element that prevents events from reaching their completion, but precisely for this reason, they also allow the Christian community to maintain, in the present, an effective relationship with the future.

The issue, treated in depth elsewhere, is also alluded to in this essay where the author refers to the "ideal Jewish millennium." A position normally applied to the Jews elsewhere is here ascribed to women. In the Acts of Peter and Thomas, the woman, according to his interpretation, is not only the one who gives birth but also the one on whom the consistency of the present and still unaccomplished world depends. "While women are still giving birth—writes Peterson—death reigns; the Kingdom of God shall come when the distinction between the sexes has been overcome" (Peterson, 1948:203). In regard to the question of Christian ascesis this means that "the ascesis of the apocryphal Acts is something more than an attempt to combat the concupiscence of the individual; it aims to stop births, and for this reason women hold an eminent position" (Peterson, 1948:203). The Marcionist tones that seem to emerge here do not hide the misogyny, directly connected to the anti-Semitism, of Peterson's Catholic stance and also reveals an equivocal position with regard to Christian asceticism. It is no coincidence that he only focuses his attention on the apocryphal Acts and does not refer to any other scriptures or passages from the New Testament. Through an apparently harmless philological method, Peterson seems to be trying to demonstrate how Christian ascesis is a technique in the hands of the power that governs it. Just like the position attributed to the Jewish people in regard to the existence of the Church, its present enforcement is efficient due to the ambiguity of its tension toward the future; that is, it directs the practice toward a future aim that renders its actions in the present operational.

## Converging Differences

From what we have seen so far, the Protestant and the Catholic position on ascesis appear to oppose one other. For the former, Christianity does not have ascetic roots; while, in the Catholic view, asceticism lies at the heart of Christian life. The opposition, at least in the authors examined here, is clear. However, at a closer look the similarities outweigh the differences. A key text to comprehend the evolution of the Catholic-Protestant debate over asceticism is the conference paper presented by Georg Kretschmar at the faculty of theology in Uppsala, on September 26, 1962, published in 1964 in the "Zeitschrift für Theologie und Kirche." Although he cites from the 1957 article, *"Askese"* published in *Die Religion in Geschichte und Gegenwart* and builds on the 1949 essay by Campenhausen, to whom, incidentally, his book is dedicated, Kretschmar's main intent is to directly confront the earlier mentioned position of Peterson. Kretschmar has issues with Peterson's foundation of Christian ascesis in eschatology, which construes the "live reality of Christ" as an imminent "worldly force" that can overturn "the world as it is in its consistency and its current duration." To such eschatology, as Peterson conceives it, Kretschmar contrasts "the personal bond with Jesus" as the nucleus of early Christian faith. If the main problem of the early Christian community is the meaning of the "imitation of Christ in post-paschal times, according to Kretschmar with this question we are also getting closer to the origins of ascesis in early Christianity" (Kretschmar, 1964:49).

The following of Christ is thus retraced back to the rabbinic idea of the "imitatio Dei" and the Jewish "way" inaugurated by the *Halacha*. However, Kretschmar adds that here "the problem was not the spiritualization of a concrete image"; rather, one must try to understand "in which direction" the following is to be undertaken (Kretschmar, 1964:50). In this respect he holds that the "perfection" within which the follower of Jesus resides, implies a close relationship with the "accomplishment" of the law of Jesus itself.

> Matthew does not interpret this overcoming the law in apocalyptic terms, in the sense that perfection is the criteria by which the end of time is defined, but as "accomplishment" (*Erfüllung*) in terms of salvation history (*heilsgeschichtlich*). This accomplishment is, however, connected to Jesus, as it can only be realized in following. In its essence, following is not to be traced back to a system. Although the followers are absolutely faithful to the law, there emerges a space for freedom. This is not obtained by way of a "backwards" overcoming (*Aufhebung*) of the law but by its "accomplishment" (*Erfüllung*), like a surpassing (*Überbietung*) "forwards." (Kretschmar, 1964:59)

According to Kretschmar, the "following" and the concept of perfection, theologically interpreted, imply an "eschatological and Christological foundation of ascesis" (Kretschmar, 1964:64). If ascesis is viewed, as in Peterson, as a fundamental element of Christian faith, its "eschatological foundation," however, "needs to be integrated with a Christological one" (Kretschmar, 1964:65). But this "Christological" integration of the Christian idea of "accomplishment," translated here into salvational-historical (*heilsgeschichtlich*) terms, in actual fact, does not contrast with the position held by Peterson, regardless of Kretschmar's clear criticism of his view of the Catholic Church. Here, too, ascesis does not escape the idea of a practice that conforms to a directional plan of governance of the world and of history.

When the differences between the various contributions that animated the twentieth-century theological debate between Catholics and Protestants on the theme of asceticism are put aside, the positions all appear to stem from the same implicit premise. A preconceived idea of Christian asceticism seems to be the undeclared premise from which the different interpretations are articulated. Asceticism is not analyzed in the modes in which it is actually organized, nor is there any trace of theological inquiry into the passage from the early "economic" experience of life in Christ toward the subsequently formulated economy of salvation as the divine plan of history. Eschatology and Christology are distinguished in order to underpin the different positions regarding Christian asceticism, but are, at the same time, presupposed and abstractly included in the readymade framework of salvation history (*Heilsgeschichte*).

There are at least two names that seem to stray from this route, that of Ernesto Bonaiuti and of Franz Overbeck. Their opposing positions on the subject in some ways contradict the direction of the debate considered so far: the Catholic Bonaiuti asserts that one may not speak of asceticism at the origins of Christianity; while for the Protestant Overbeck, asceticism is the deep core of Christianity at its birth. What these two positions have in common is also what distinguishes them from the rest of the debate.

In 1928 Bonaiuti published a book entirely dedicated to issue and aptly entitled, *The Origins of Christian Asceticism*. The influence of German liberal theology is clearly discernible. For Bonaiuti, as we have already seen in the main exponent of theological liberalism, "the message of Christ does not imply a system of ascetic precepts" (Bonaiuti, 1928:63).

As a convinced representative of the Italian Catholic movement known as "Modernism," Bonaiuti challenged the Catholic precept of "double consecration" and asserted that "the concept of a double form of ascesis, one reserved for the perfect and the privileged and the other conceded to the mass of believers, strayed from the outlook of Christ" (Bonaiuti, 1928:59). He therefore writes: "the small community that formed around Christ, thriving on its enthusiasm and its faith, wholeheartedly nurtures the certainty of the imminent triumph and at the same time enacts with such spontaneous automatism the laws of perfect renunciation and complete disinterest, having no need to entrust the purity of its ideal and uncontaminated severity of its plan to the ostentatious eccentricity of external practices" (Bonaiuti, 1928:59). After an initial clash with Gnosticism, "the transition and the mediation between Christianity, as an experience of individual perfecting" (Bonaiuti, 1928:108) comes about during the monastic organization of the fourth century, when the Christian religion had already been officially recognized by Constantine.

Monasticism, to which Bonaiuti dedicated much research, is seen as "the correction and the antidote" to the alliance between Christianity and Imperial politics.

> When the enthusiasm of the first Christian generations [. . .] began to wane, and the incandescent material of their experiences needed to coagulate into stable forms of belief and practice, the ideals of renunciation, previously kept alive by the great Messianic dream, also had to be committed to pedagogical manuals to be used in the everyday life of the community of believers, which had grown in number but not in fervor and purity. (Bonaiuti, 1928:158)

According to Bonaiuti, the monastic organization of the fourth century thus helps complete the translation of the philosophical asceticism of late Antiquity into Christian terms, a transformation that had already begun in the second century. The "laborious internal training" of the philosophical *áskesis* that makes it "possible to [. . .] succeed in becoming victorious athletes in the spiritual agon" (Bonaiuti, 1928:157), here takes on the shape of the "integral renouncing" of the first believers in Christ, keeping the evangelical ideals alive. However, the Church's recognition of Monasticism also enables ascetic practice to be made official as an effective disciplinary technique. For Bonaiuti, though, the monastic organization, seen as a continuous renewal of evangelical ideals, also fuels tensions within ecclesiastical institutions, tensions that remain alive and act as resistance against the official power of the Church. Fifty years prior to the publication of Bonaiuti's book, Overbeck had made more or less the same case.

In 1873 Overbeck published a one-hundred-page volume by the name of *Über die Christlichkeit unserer heutigen Theologie* (On the Christianity of Theology), which according to him remained almost unknown apart from a few minor reviews. However, interestingly, several implicit references to this work stand out in Harnack's *Essence of Christianity*. It is by no chance that the appendix added by Overbeck in 1903, only a year after the publication of Harnack's book, in the second edition of the "little work of 1873," should end with an attack on the *Essence of Christianity*, that is defined "the work 'of the century' (*Säcularschrift*)," "which—writes Overbeck—has shown

me 'the inessentiality' of Christianity in a much more convincing way than
it shows the 'essence,' the exposition of which the frontispiece announces"
(Overbeck, 2002:168).

The operation Harnack undertakes is, for Overbeck, the prototype of
the task that has been carried forward since the beginning of Christian theology: "it claims to have discovered a Christianity whose reconciliation with
mundane culture is no longer a problem" (Overbeck, 2002:69). Overbeck,
being the "allegorical" and undisputed heir of the critical-historical school
of Tübingen (Overbeck, 2002:11), opposes the noninnocuous character of
a scientific form that starts from concrete historical research to the pacifying
reconciliation of Christianity with culture carried out by theology on the
basis of a purely historical study of the phenomenon of religion. In particular, he states that as soon as the scientific form is applied to a religious
phenomenon like the origins of Christianity, its prehistory (*Urgeschichte*),
that is, the history of its origins (*Entstehungsgeschichte*), becomes obscured
by the tradition that, in the case of Christianity, coincides with its "canonization." Thus begins what Overbeck defines as the history of decadence.
The latter, however, as well as being intimately connected to the "progress"
of its duration, is also dependent on it in order to access the sources of its
*Entstehungsgeschichte*. The origins of Christianity do not and cannot have a
meta-historical nature, from which one may identify their essence. On the
other hand, he does not simply stop at what would seem an "antihistorical"
genesis, as could be inferred from Löwith's interpretation of his thought
(Löwith, 1965). This is precisely the point that leads us to the idea of Christian asceticism that Overbeck proposed.

Overbeck claims, "The negation of the world is the intimate soul
of Christianity and the world is no longer a possible and worthy dwell-
ing place for religion" (Overbeck, 2002:78). As the renunciation of the
worldly dimension, asceticism becomes the most characteristic feature of
the Christian conception of the world, one that has not only shaped all
the most authentic manifestations of this religion, but also significantly
determined its historical destiny. According to Overbeck, the point of
emergence of Christianity is to be found in the belief in the *parousía* or the
second coming of Christ: the peculiarity of this phenomenon consists in it
not being "a simple awaiting what shall arise within the world" but instead
expressing "a longing, through the abandonment of this world, to make
the ever eternal advent of the Kingdom of God become present" (Overbeck, 2002:75). "The early Christian waiting of the imminent coming of

Christ" was not "*simply* put aside after its lack of factual accomplishment",
otherwise "[. . .] the primitive Christian inclination to flee the world would
have waned" (Overbeck, 2002:74). "In this perspective," Overbeck states,
"there shall always be an insoluble enigma as to why a faith, whose conception of the world depended on its tangible accomplishment, did not dissolve
when this accomplishment did not occur" (Overbeck, 2002:74). What, in
his view, permitted Christianity to keep itself alive notwithstanding the
absence of the coming of Christ was precisely "the ascetic way of life," as
a "metamorphosis of the early Christian faith in the return of Christ" that
"continues to consider the world ripe for its decline and incites its followers
to withdraw from it" (Overbeck, 2002:74). This means that Christianity
"in actual fact [. . .] has desecrated the world, that is, it has allowed both
the use and the enjoyment of the world to continue, because it could not
deny them, but at the same time it has also deprived them of the consecration they enjoyed in antiquity" (Overbeck, 2002:78). "The most striking
example of this attitude towards ancient culture (*Cultur*) is Monasticism,"
thanks to which "the Church saved none other than its own life" (Overbeck, 2002:71; see also Overbeck, 1994).

For Overbeck, Monasticism "in actual fact is no less than the institution thanks to which the Church, just as it seemed to be handing itself
over to the pagan state entirely, managed to escape from its iron grip once
again" (Overbeck, 2002:72). On this point the positions of Overbeck and
Bonaiuti coincide; in fact, the latter dedicated part of his research to trying
to demonstrate how Monasticism was an expression of internal tensions in
the Church. Overbeck, too, goes as far as to state that "a theology which
views the ascetic conception of life solely as an inessential feature of Christianity exclusively relevant to a certain period, and a theology convinced
that it is possible to reconcile Christianity with worldly culture without
losing its power, will inevitably have to treat Monasticism as something
without which the Church is perfectly conceivable; but in so doing it will
make it impossible to understand not only this institution, but also the
deepest and noblest phenomena in the history of the Church up to the
Reformation" (Overbeck, 2002:72).

Overbeck returns to the "ascetic side of Christianity as the fatal flaw
in its character" also in one of the posthumous fragments collected by Carl
Albrecht Bernoulli in the volume *Christentum und Kultur*. This text is particularly significant: here, not only is asceticism called into question in relation to Christian life, but also more generally, as a key feature of human life

itself. In this text, Overbeck's position emerges as clearly radical and distant from the more complex and problematic theological position of Bonaiuti. As he writes,

> Christianity is undoubtedly ascetic in its fundamental traits and it is too much so. Rather than in asceticism itself, the incompatibility of Christianity with the evolution of humankind lies precisely in this excess of asceticism. In asceticism one finds the roots of the ascendancy it has acquired among men, for the ascetic impulse is as deep in humans as its opposite. Unless this fact is taken into account, no human culture can be built. The ascetic impulse and the desire for pleasure must express themselves with equal freedom. Only because it has succumbed to the danger of becoming too ascetic in humanity and thus of subjecting humanity to hyper-ascetic demands that clash with human life at its roots, only for this reason has Christianity entered into an irreconcilable conflict with humanity, or with that which it calls the world, and due to this it will disappear amongst men. (Overbeck, 1963:33–34)

Although when it comes to their critique of culture the affinity between Overbeck and Nietzsche is commonly acknowledged (after all, *On the Christianity of Theology*, in the words that Nietzsche dedicates to its author, is the "twin" of *The Untimely Meditations*), their positions tend to be viewed as different and even opposite on the subject of asceticism: one criticizes ascetic ideals due to their being the source of modern "philistinism"; the other sees in asceticism the original core of Christianity, which modern culture has repudiated. As is clear from the above fragment, the analysis is too superficial and does not account for the complexity inherent in both positions.

With a formulation and lexis that not only matches the complexity and the ambiguity of the ascetic ideal highlighted by Nietzsche, but also, in some respects, even seems to anticipate the Freudian dialectics between *Eros* and *Thanatos*, Overbeck here continues to face the problem of asceticism as the distinguishing feature of Christianity; but ascesis, especially in this passage, emerges as a life practice. At stake here is something that is intimately connected to the very nature of humankind, we could almost say something that concerns his biological evolution. Even though Overbeck finds excessive asceticism in Christianity to be responsible for its imminent demise, he also considers the ascetic impulse to be as deeply rooted as the opposing impulse, the "desire for pleasure," of which the history of Christianity is simultaneously traitor and custodian. The affinity with Nietzsche's analysis of the ascetic ideal, here, is evident. So much so that one can confront the ambiguity with which Nietzsche speaks of asceticism with greater conviction in light of Overbeck's position. However, the anthropological entrenchment of ascetic practice highlighted here, leads us to reconsider the link between Christian ascesis and the economy clearly underlined by Weber historically.

## Chapter 4

# Voluntary Poverty on the Market

If—following Weber's claim, that is, our starting point—there is a close link between asceticism and modern economics, then before establishing the continuing credibility of the Weberian notion directly, it would perhaps be worth carrying out a preliminary evaluation of the extent to which the Christian development of the concept of *oikonomía*, through the efforts of the ascetics we have focused on thus far, paved the way for the foundation of economic discourse. According to a recent body of research on medieval history that is particularly relevant for our purposes, the endeavors that built on the patristic idea of the "economy of salvation," or the divine ordering of the world, contributed significantly to the formation of the Western economic vocabulary. What is notable, in relation to our subject, is that this research has predominantly been based on interpreting texts from the ascetic monastic tradition precisely because of their economic and political nature.

The paradigm of a salvation transaction between God and human beings is the fundamental framework of these studies, but the origin of the economic lexicon is largely identified based on an analysis of ascetic practice, uncoupling it from its original objective of eternal salvation. Asceticism, therefore, emerges as a kind of investment, not in what can be permanently acquired in exchange for the sacrifice made to obtain it, but rather in what can be enjoyed, gained, and used from its practice, starting with the ability to make sacrifices.

In this sense, Western economic discourse did not begin with reflections on property and ownership, but rather the development of the possibility to invest in that which, while impossible to fully own, is associated with the inherent ultimate calling of human activity, and in the form of "common goods," becomes the fundamental operator of a political mechanism of inclusion and exclusion; a preferential methodology for governing communities, striking examples of which can still be identified to this day.

## Economics and Christianity: A Historical View

In the best-known historical research available on this issue, economics, and Christianity, proto-capitalism and Christian society have generally been seen as fundamentally antithetical to one another, in constant conflict, or at the very least compared, relatively belatedly and always as being in conflict with Scholasticism, recognized as the first conceptualization of economics. Swimming against the tide of scholarship that tended to agree on the total absence of genuine scientific economic thinking in the medieval Christian world, Jacques Le Goff sought to reframe the medieval economic debate on usury (Le Goff, 1990, 2012): ultimately, however, the ecclesiastical ban is still considered to have been conceived of as a "theological obstacle," a deliberate brake on economic development, with mainstream discourse proceeding to focus on the incompatibility of Christianity and economic systems. The majority of medieval historiography on this subject therefore continues to take its cue from the observation of a scientific limit: the resistance of Christian morality against the majority of economic practices that have to do with the production of money.

Furthermore, in all the research that proposes to recognize a relationship between Christianity and economics, scholars have analyzed sources to seek the origins of modern capitalism, but always based on the idea of a market economy. Even in the discussions that developed in the twentieth century around the contributions of Werner Sombart, Ernst Troeltsch, and Max Weber, the prevailing tendency has been to try and ascertain to what extent the message of the gospels participated in the theoretical definition of a supposed profit-based society, founded on the individual's search for profit. In other words, even these investigations sought to understand how medieval Christianity may have given rise to a modern world with which it was fundamentally irreconcilable. Ultimately, this perceived incompatibility derives from an abstract portrayal of the medieval world as being heavily Christianized and scarcely "capitalistic."

Troeltsch's analysis of Christian social teachings, which aims to synthesize Christian value systems with those of the market, paved the way for the idea of "Christian economics," nevertheless still a concept considered to be in conflict with the capitalistic model (Troeltsch, 1931). Weber was certainly the first to identify the Christian ethic, in its Calvinist formulation, as a stimulus rather than a hindrance to capitalist activity. Although his reasoning—as he tried to demonstrate and as we explore in more detail—is more complex than it might appear at first glance, many consider his work to indicate that the progress of economic rationality was based on the underlying opposition between a charity principle and rational calculation. In his interpretation, this incompatibility forms the foundation of the very process of economic rationalization, which is the indelible hallmark of the Western world.

More recently, however, another area of medieval historical research has opened up, with particularly interesting implications for the analysis reported thus far (see above all Todeschini, 2002 and 2004, but also Capitani, 1987, and Prodi, 2009). The question driving this research largely focuses on the formulation of medieval lexicons of economic thought. Acknowledging the fact that in medieval times economic discourse did not only concentrate on the problems posed by the accumulation of wealth, that which was framed as "chrematistics" by Aristotle, and therefore could not be reduced to the formulation of "Christian chrematistics" in opposition to usury, the sources studied here are not limited to texts concerned directly with economics. Instead they take into consideration reflections on nonmonetary issues from medieval times, from which emerge some specific discussions of trade and exchangeable goods that demand the attention of my work here.

## Commerce and Good Use of Worldly Wealth

Of particular importance, within the scope of the research carried out thus far, are recent studies of historical medieval materials relating to the regulations of institutional Christian life; namely, texts that examine monastic rules, which had hitherto been studied by historians specializing in the development of legal rather than economic thought. The interpretation proposed by these studies is particularly important for my argument, as it attempts to highlight a common feature of the sources analyzed: their ability to formulate a discourse around the way of conceiving and verbally expressing various aspects of wealth and deprivation in light of the practice of Christian life, which can be understood as a fundamentally economic experience. These historians suggest that when reading patristic sources, our focus should neither be on an adhesion to the "transcendental" and, in this sense, noneconomic message, nor on the possibility of detecting a primitive or advanced model of scientific economic analysis; the main focus of the research is language itself, the discourse of economics and of the economic behavior that was effectively being instituted in them, starting with the economic mode of Christian life.

The process of Christianization is reformulated here in terms of a translation or semantic adaptation of Greek and Roman vocabulary, used for the definition and juridical and moral evaluation of economic practices in a linguistic system based on the opposition between the terrestrial and the celestial. This method is used to interpret economic behavior in the context of a process based on the interaction between earthly actions and transcendent outcomes. The result of this process, however, is that not only do the sources studied not contain a simplistic condemnation of the worldly and the economic, defined as activities linked to survival and the accumulation of worldly wealth; there is actually room for a varied range of interpretations of how worldly goods should be used in light of what was considered to be the privileged trade of the Christian experience at a particular point in the history of Christianity: this is the *commercium* of the Incarnation. The "economy of salvation," the historical divine plan implemented through the Incarnation, is literally posed as an economic problem, and ascetic practice is also interpreted in economic terms. In these studies, the life in Christ described in the texts analyzed is viewed as a fundamentally economic activity, one where administrative organization and charitable practice, *dispositio* and *caritas*, are combined.

In previous medieval historiography, monastic literature, on which a significant part of the works in question are focused, had traditionally been catalogued as an ascetic discourse oriented toward the "idle" life of contemplation. Despite the renowned reference to work in the Rule of Benedict, seldom had monastic discipline been studied from an economic point of view. Thanks to this new body of research, headed by the works of Giacomo Todeschini, the fundamentally active nature of contemplation evidenced in the sources studied here—already implicit in Greek philosophy but brought to its fulfillment by the Christian translation of the main categories of ancient thought by the first Fathers of the Church—becomes substantial in the context of an economic interpretation of the monastic phenomenon. Even more relevant to my analysis is the fact that this research reconstructs the formulation of a conceptual framework linked to the act of embracing poverty that reproposes the patristic model of frugality and the imitation of Christ in

an economic, political and institutional form—the very form of the monastery—that involves a different perspective on ownership. The articulation of
ascetic practices—especially those relating to the use of wealth and money—
and the development of monastic asceticism as a way of life are traced back to
the collection of patristic teachings on the *good use* of worldly wealth.

Cassian's reflection on the mechanisms of desire is therefore transferred
into a discourse on ownership, not in terms of the definitive ownership
of possessions that are retained in perpetuity, but as the retention of command over the faculty of desire, the ability to exercise mastery over what the
world contains, and to control and enjoy worldly goods through rigorous
denial and constant suppression of desire (Toneatto, 2004). In this respect,
Todeschini writes that "the desire to own possessions led, according to
ascetic severity, to the origins of western economic thought, to understand
the value of possessions and the motive for desiring them; in conclusion, to
assume the economic and social sense of possession" (Todeschini, 2002:16).

Monastic economic principles as laid out by Cassian, who became the
point of reference for all subsequent monastic rules, hinge on organizing
monks' desires and the disciplined arrangement of consumption. In addition to aiding the inhabitants of the monastery in their attempt to achieve
perfection, this was even more useful to the community of believers living outside cloistered walls, in other words, wider Christian society. Salvian, author among other texts of a treatise entitled *De guvernatione Dei*
(On the Government of God) entirely dedicated to divine economy, spent
several years in the Saint Honoratus monastery on the Lerins Islands,
where he was ordained priest, then transferred to Marseille in around
439, whence he wrote a text entitled *Ad Ecclesiam*. The objective of this
text, studied in great depth in the research we have already mentioned,
was to discipline Christian economic life along the lines of monastic rules
(Salvian, 1971). According to Todeschini, Salvian's work reveals how economic discourse, focused on the monastic environment, was subsequently
applied to Christian society in its broadest definition. He contends that
monastic reality, in this case, should follow along the lines of De Vogüé's
interpretation: "as an economic organization outside of Christian society, but
linked with it by the emblematic importance it assumes as institutional salvation of that society, considered imperfect in virtue of the fact that it is not fully
ordered" (Todeschini, 2002:17; De Vogüé, 1961:213).

Thus, in both the *Rule of the Master* and the *Rule of Benedict*, the
ascetic discipline of self-denial does not correspond to renouncing worldly

riches, but rather to the management of a possession considered sacred, in that it does not belong individually to anyone, but is held in common and its good use serves the divine plan of salvation, when the Last Judgement becomes a form of divine calculation (*divina ratiocinia*, according to the Rule of the Master xvi, 29). Therefore, in the medieval Christian world, material wealth is not reduced to a false idol to be worshipped by misers, but rather the administration of property held in common in an orderly and scientific manner.

In this context, even the concept of evangelical perfection from which Francis of Assisi drew his inspiration to found a community based on the renunciation of worldly possessions is interpreted as an economic theory. Since the death of the order's founder, Franciscan identity has revolved around the formulation of a conceptual vocabulary focused on the semantic difference between "use" and "utilization," "property," and "possession," enabling the construction of a voluntary poverty in which self-denial took on an economic as well as an existential meaning. Indeed, with the Franciscans, renunciation becomes a concrete reality, which through a concise deciphering of the very condition of "poverty" leads to the explicit definition of an economic behavior. Poverty, as a strategy and way of ordering the use and consumption of goods and money without appropriation, does not mean withdrawing from the world. Rather, it enables to investigate the difference between needs and desires, enhances the possibility of benefiting from the world's resources and therefore allows for the formulation of the economic criteria functional to the notion of "common goods."

In the second half of the thirteenth century, the Franciscan Peter John Olivi carried out a detailed economic investigation on the "poor" or restricted use of goods (*de uso paupere*) that consisted of an analysis of the way of defining the useful value of the goods that make human life possible. "The notion of 'privation' [. . .] emerges conspicuously from Olivi's writing on 'evangelical perfection' as an emotional interpretation" (Todeschini, 2004:92). He linked the economic value of things to the manner in which they are used. The Franciscan definition of poverty drove Olivi to indicate privation as the founding principle for the valuation of goods, and therefore the assignment of a price to them. The poverty of the friars and the imitators of Christ emerged as a valuation paradigm. On the one hand, self-denial became an experience that teaches how to decipher and measure privation as a condition of life; on the other, worldly goods take on an economic character expressed in the utility identified in them, starting from that which can be done without or which is enjoyed only through its absence. From this stems Olivi's radical analysis of *de facto* "use" as opposed to property "rights."

Using and consuming goods does not signify owning them, but paves the way to the discovery of some benefit deriving from them that, while not having any relation to the possibility of appropriating them for oneself, makes a fair and accurate economic valuation of them possible. This, however, also means that the economic value of things (their market value) largely depends on human choice to use them (use value). Not only does this imply that the use of things is directly conditioned by the political meaning attributed to them by those who consume them, but above all use and value do not depend on ownership, but rather on the possibility of investing in that which, while not able to be owned definitively, is not useful in terms of the realization of a specific end, but relates instead to the ultimate calling of human life. The use of money, uncoupled from ownership, therefore acquires a socially positive political significance that is directly proportional to its circulation.

In this way, an awareness of the objective and absolute indefinability of the value of things drove Olivi to define the concept of *ius*, the "right" to money, distinct from "possession," which forms the basis for the publicly useful and institutionally accepted use of wealth. From the pauperistic awareness of denial and privation as the fundamental source of the valuation of the good use of common worldly goods, according to Todeschini's interpretation, Olivi then added "the recognition of market society as a collective capable of defining its own measurement of the useful" (Todeschini, 2004:120).

In this perspective, "the ascetic desire not to seek wealth," is seen to have "a lay equivalent in the desire to exchange money for goods, goods for other goods, currency with other currencies: in both cases underlying the path traced by the desire (the intention) of being poor or wealthy can and must be glimpsed a collective, members of which are dedicated not to accumulation but to distribution" (Todeschini, 2004:128).

## Having Everything while Owning Nothing:
## Voluntary Poverty and the Market Economy

According to Todeschini, the theological roots of the economic view at the basis of market society can be found in the charitable economic notion of gift that the Christian experience is built on. As made clear by Thomas Aquinas, who in his turn acknowledges and elaborates on the questions posed by Olivi and the Mendicant Orders, "commerce" between God and human beings personified in Christ is a trade that implies the obligation of repayment, and harks back to "an economy capable of producing the equivalent of the gift: a 'counter-gift' that incorporates the capacity of benefiting from the gift itself. What is given forms the basis, the starting point for a subsequent investment, potentially for the completion of virtuous acts" (Todeschini, 2002:195). The Mendicant Orders, Olivi, and finally Thomas propose that the urban society emerging in the second half of the thirteenth century adopt a gift economy, rooted in the experience of the economic ordering of grace in Christ, passing through the patristic reflections of the first five centuries of the Christian era and rapidly translating into a discourse on "the methods through which 'giving' proves to be the framework on which to build a social organization that arrives at economic trade starting from a social system founded on an association of the faithful" (Todeschini, 2002:196).

This doctrinal determination to represent "giving" as an integral factor of the economy of salvation, with the attached expectation of a "counter-gift," allows us to understand how, in the intellectual universe of Western Christianity—of which Augustine and Thomas are without doubt the leading representatives—it was important to "establish a model of economic organization that founded the contractual nature of trade and credit on the basis of the obligations expressed in the gift system" (Todeschini, 2002:196). In this system, it is of fundamental importance that the counter-gift given in exchange of the original gift is not simply "bought," but derives from the highly delicate and characteristic acquisition of "faith." As Todeschini rightly highlights, in this sense, the economic community is a community of the faithful, "The extremely close bond between religious faith and economic credibility" (Todeschini, 2004:171), or rather confidence in markets and merchants that operate therein, is based on the notion that it is their very belief that makes them credible, thus creating a divide between the "faithful" and the "faithless." The equivalence between voluntary poverty and the social use of wealth, that is, the renunciation of property and the continuing circulation of goods and money, is only possible, from this point of view, if the market is made up of persons linked by shared faith and reciprocal confidence.

Faith is therefore the fundamental operator of the political mechanism of social inclusion and exclusion that this embodies.

It is therefore no coincidence that it was the Franciscans who, in the late 1400s, succeeded in forming an institution that was of fundamental importance to the subsequent development of the Western economy: the Mount of Piety. A direct precursor to modern banks, the Mount of Piety was able to present itself to the world as the summary articulation of the Christian economic perspective based on the concept, both ethical and economic, of the implicit productivity of the circulation rather than the possession of wealth; it was therefore opposed to the "faithless" activity of usury, which in this context was particularly diffuse among the Jews, who as a result were excluded from the economic community of the faithful.

While Todeschini claims to have "never thought that the Franciscans discovered the 'laws of the market,' inaugurating modern economics like predecessors to Adam Smith," but rather to have maintained "that their concept of poverty [. . .] was intrinsically if inadvertently an economic language," which "formed some basic categories of western economic reasoning, starting from those of the western Protestants" (Todeschini, 2004:7) studied by Weber, his discourse nevertheless seems to lean toward an unequivocal confluence of the troubled Franciscan journey into the medieval mercantile system that was the point of origin of the modern market economy.[1] Even though he affirms that "the Franciscans weren't the 'first economists,' but rather the ones that made the arrival of economists in western Christianity in subsequent centuries possible" (Todeschini, 2004:8), it remains unclear within his formulation, to what extent the foundations for the development of modern economic scientific language can be identified within Franciscan economic discourse, albeit as an involuntary derivative of their works.

While it is impossible to disregard this contribution in my study of the relationship between economics and the Christian religion, and more in general an investigation of the connection between economic forms of power and the ascetic practice of self-denial, the purpose of any research is largely written in the margins, and often only expressed as a kind of foreword, thus leaving a degree of uncertainty over its ultimate destination. Todeschini clearly states that, in his case, the purpose is neither an attempt to "identify the 'spirit' of capitalism from a Catholic point of view" nor to "ascertain an earlier date of birth for the science of economics" (Todeschini, 2004:8). In his view, "the Franciscan approach to the market" actually reveals that "it was the most rigorously influential Christian religion in the formation of a large part of the western economic vocabulary" and therefore "that there was never the great divide between the Christian world and the market that was imagined in the nineteenth and twentieth centuries, nor was there a clear separation between morality and worldly affairs" (Todeschini, 2004:8). With the Franciscans, the fundamentally economic structure of the Christian religion proved to be a key element of the work carried out internally to provide reassurances that mercantile activity and worldly wealth were harmless from a social point of view. This was therefore how the conditions that made a market economy compatible with "common goods" are identified.[2] In this way, wealth for its own ends, based on self-denial rather than possession, was not an evil to be exorcised, but rather could rationally be justified within the economic system of Christian life experience as developed by the Franciscans.

Regardless of the more or less explicit possibility of identifying in these studies the development of a "spirit" of capitalism from a Catholic point of view, and regardless of the limitations of such a formulation—similar to those that are revealed in Weber—it seems that the two paths, while different, are in accordance on one point, which is not explicitly defined in either case, but of fundamental importance for the point of view developed here and therefore worth laying out clearly at this stage.

In Todeschini's research, ascetic Franciscan reflections tend to be studied purely in economic terms rather than as a function of the economy of salvation, even though the fact that they are inscribed in the finalistically focused system of salvation appears to be one of the keys to comprehending the phenomenon. The economic nature of asceticism, on the other hand, can be identified by the fact that its very practice fundamentally involves the ability to appraise and evaluate, and an intimate opportunity to invest in something that has no other end than itself. In the same way, in Weber, inner-worldly ascetic action in the Protestant tradition is the precondition of economic rationality, not only because it allows ascetic practice to be untangled from the extrinsic end of transcendent compensation suggested in the Catholic tradition, thus entrusting economic action to a formal rationality that is unequivocally focused on the calculation of the means required to deliver the desired end result as the only inherent criterion. Rather, the exclusion of a transcendent goal from the practice of inner-worldly asceticism and the inherent behavior that derives from it definitively reveals, in his discourse, the fact that human action is only possible if it is a performance that serves the defined end that character-izes it, which within capitalism assumes the "irrational" form of endeavor for no other reason than its own fulfillment. At this point it should also be investigated the extent to which, in either case, profit and investment capacity, rather than the relation to an extrinsic purpose, are connected to that which has its own ends, and in what sense this link reveals a close relationship between the capitalist economy and the religious experience.

## Chapter 5

# Capitalism as Religion

If, as Durkheim claimed, asceticism "is not [. . .] a rare, exceptional or even abnormal result of religious life," but, "on the contrary, an essential element of it" (Durkheim, 1976:372), our work now needs to turn to a discussion of *The Elementary Forms of Religious Life (EFRL)* and what characterizes the fact of religion, considering that it is consubstantial with ascetic practice.

Between the nineteenth and the twentieth century, the most important studies of the science of religions arose out of a similar perspective: on the one hand, they were stimulated by the need to see a real comparative history of different religious forms, while on the other hand they were encouraged by the attempt—internal to Protestant theology and historical studies on the "origins" of Christianity—to find an answer to the question of the "essence of religion" (this, not surprisingly, is the title of a famous book by the theologian Wilhelm Bousset, one of the most important representatives of the *Religionsgeschichtliche Schule*).

Other studies in this area were different and varied but, whether one sought to emphasize its social dimension (like Mauss, Durkheim, or the members of the Collège de Sociologie) or grant more importance to its ontological-existential aspects (like Rudolf Otto, Gerardus van der Leeuw, or Mircea Eliade), religious experience ultimately appeared, more radically than other types of experience, to not demand the accomplishment of extrinsic goals. In religion and its various expressions, humankind experiences its actions as ends in themselves. This proves an essential part of the practice of renunciation in asceticism and is manifested as a form of power with an end in itself that is capable of constraining human action.

Within this framework it makes sense for our discussion to read an early text by Walter Benjamin who, albeit in a fragmentary form, raises some important questions for the course here indicated, making it possible to envisage not only—as stated explicitly in the text—that capitalism is a true religion but, above all, that the religion of self-referentiality inherent to human life was definitively realized in capitalist forms of production.

## A Permanent Cult

Among the many unpublished notes of Walter Benjamin is an early fragment, written around the middle of 1921 and titled, precisely, "Capitalism as Religion." This we quote in full because, despite the incompleteness that characterizes it, it can help connect what has been discussed so far with the contemporary situation.

The divinatory character of the fragment has perhaps hindered its reception, privileging, in the study of Benjamin, other better known texts. But, just recently, the reflections that emerge from this text have been recovered by several authors whose contributions are gathered in a single volume (Baecker, 2003); with this it became possible to rethink our reading of Benjamin and, more generally, his almost prophetic intuition that saw capitalism as a real form of religion. Here is the text:

> A religion may be discerned in capitalism—that is to say, capitalism serves essentially to allay the same anxieties, torments, and disturbances to which the so-called religions offered answers. The proof of the religious structure of capitalism—not merely, as Weber believes, as a formation conditioned by religion, but as an essentially religious phenomenon—would still lead even today to the folly of an endless universal polemic. We cannot draw closed the net in which we are caught. Later on, however, we shall be able to gain an overview of it.
>
> Nevertheless, even at the present moment it is possible to distinguish three aspects of this religious structure of capitalism. In the first place, capitalism is a purely cultic religion, perhaps the most extreme that ever existed. In capitalism, things have meaning only in their relationship to the cult; capitalism has no specific body of dogma, no theology. It is from this point of view that utilitarianism acquires its religious overtones. This concretization of the cult is connected with a second feature of capitalism: the permanence of the cult. Capitalism

is the celebration of the cult *sans rêve et sans merci* [without dream or mercy]. There are no "weekdays." Here there is no "weekday"; no day that would not be a holiday in the awful sense of exhibiting all sacred pomp—the extreme exertion of worship. And third, the cult makes guilt pervasive (*verschuldend*). Capitalism is probably the first instance of a cult that creates guilt (*verschuldend*), not atonement (*entsühnenden*). Herein stands this religious system in the fall of a tremendous movement. An enormous feeling of guilt not itself knowing how to repent (*das sich nicht zu entsühnen weiß*) seizes on the cult, not to atone (*sühnen*) for this guilt but to make it universal, to hammer it into the conscious mind, so as once and for all to include God in the system of guilt and thereby awaken in Him an interest in the process of repentance (*Entsühnung*). This atonement cannot then be expected from the cult itself, or from the reformation of this religion (which would need to be able to have recourse to some stable element in it), or even from the complete renouncement of this religion. The nature of the religious movement which is capitalism entails endurance right to the end, to the point where God, too, finally takes on the entire burden of guilt, to the point where the universe has been taken over by that despair which is actually its secret *hope*. Capitalism is entirely without precedent, in that it is a religion which offers not the reform of existence but its complete destruction. It is the expansion of despair, until despair becomes a religious state of the world in the hope that this will lead to salvation. God's transcendence is at an end. But he is not dead; he has been incorporated into human existence. This passage of the planet "Human" through the house of despair in the absolute loneliness of his trajectory is the *êthos* that Nietzsche defined. This man is the superman, the first to recognize the religion of capitalism and begin to bring it to fulfilment. Its fourth feature is that its God must be hidden from it and may be addressed only when his guilt is at its zenith. The cult is celebrated before an un-matured deity; every idea, every conception of it offends against the secret of this immaturity.

Freud's theory, too, belongs to the hegemony of the priests of this cult. Its conception is capitalist religious thought through and through. By virtue of a profound analogy, which has still to be illuminated, what has been repressed, the idea of sin, is capital itself, which pays interest on the hell of the unconscious.

The paradigm of capitalist religious thought is magnificently formulated in Nietzsche's philosophy. The idea of the superman transposes the apocalyptic "leap" not into conversion, atonement, purification, and penance, but into an apparently steady, though in the final analysis explosive and discontinuous intensification. For this reason, intensification and development in the sense of *non facit saltum* are incompatible. The superman is the man who has arrived where he is without changing his ways; he is historical man who has grown up right through the sky. This breaking open of the heavens by an intensified humanity that was and is characterized (even for Nietzsche himself) by guilt (*Verschuldung*) in a religious sense was anticipated by Nietzsche. Marx is a similar case: the capitalism that refuses to change course becomes socialism by means of the simple and compound interest that are functions of guilt/debt *Schuld* (consider the demonic ambiguity of this word).

Capitalism is a religion of pure cult, without dogma.

Capitalism has developed as a parasite of Christianity in the West (this must be shown not just in the case of Calvinism, but in the other orthodox Christian churches), until it reached the point where Christianity's history is essentially that of its parasite—that is to say, of capitalism. (Benjamin, 2005)[1]

It is hardly obvious to see in capitalism, as does Benjamin, a real religious form that can satisfy the "same concerns," the same "pains and anxieties," that were once answered by "the so-called religions." First, we would have to understand what function, in general, can be attributed to religion and in what sense, then, capitalism would play the same role today that was previously performed by various religious forms.

Benjamin says that capitalism is "a purely cultic religion"; a religion that performs purely practical tasks. It is a practice that does not need a theoretical apparatus, a "specific body of dogma" or "a theology." In this perspective, even its object of worship does not possess supernatural characters, because "God's transcendence is at an end. But he is not dead; he has been incorporated into human existence." In this form of worship it is man who is due absolute devotion. In this sense then, according to Benjamin, "utilitarianism" assumes "its religious overtones." One would think that the useful is worshipped as the only thing worth pursuing. But Benjamin's text, albeit in a piecemeal fashion, offers an understanding that is entirely in line with what has emerged from our discussion so far.

However, one thing is clear in the words we just read: the veneration at stake in this cult is a constant worship that has no end, no interruptions. It is a cult of "permanent duration." There is no alternation between public holidays and weekdays, there are no festivals of passage or exceptional days that interrupt the regularity of daily life; there is but a single continuous party that takes the form of "the awful sense of exhibiting all sacred pomp—the extreme exertion of worship."

In the "permanent worship" of capitalism, the pursuit of utility is not, as it were, separate from that which has no other purpose than itself. Instead, it manifests itself in all of its "uselessness." If it can be said that the search for useful and uniquely identifiable purposes is naturally inscribed in man, in an autotelic move that constitutes its essential premise, the same activity emerges in capitalism as a single continuous motion that no longer has purpose or ends. In the capitalist forms of production, like a party that knows no rest, what is achieved is an uninterrupted veneration of what is useful to human life. But the satisfaction of needs ends up becoming a form of indebtedness for its own sake. As Benjamin says, it is "the celebration of the cult *sans rêve et sans merci*," which inscribes capitalist modes of production, not so much into a utilitarian rationality, but rather into a logic of pure waste. What needs to be understood is the sense in which this cult can correspond to a true religious form, able to satisfy the "pains" and concerns that were once answered by so-called religions.


## Religion Is Not a Worthwhile Experience

In a statement in the book devoted to the "elementary forms" of religious life, in 1912, Durkheim writes:

> Only one form of social activity has not yet been expressly attached to religion: that is economic activity. [. . .] Also, economic value is a sort of power or efficacy, and we know the religious origins of the idea of power. Also, richness can confer *mana*: therefore it has it. Hence it is seen that the ideas of economic value and of religious value are not without connection. But the question of the nature of these connections has not yet been studied. (Durkheim, 1976:419)

When Durkheim wrote these words, Weber's essay on "The Protestant Ethic and the Spirit of Capitalism," the first draft of his larger work, had already been published in the 1904–1905 issue of the journal *Archiv für Sozialwissenschaft und Sozialpolitik*. But the void indicated by Durkheim in the relationship between religion and economy will be mainly filled by Mauss's text on the gift, written 1923–1924, which must be added to the enormous amount of research that Weber himself subsequently dedicated to the "economic ethics of religions." These studies, on the one hand, are driven by the desire to find conclusive material for the thesis on the origin of the spirit of capitalism; on the other, they are born by the need to perform an analysis of the rationality of religious actions. This unveils an economics inherent to religious practice whose aims are predominantly economic and do not contradict, but indeed confirm, the full autonomy of religion (Weber, 1978).

The autonomy intrinsic to religion, repeatedly emphasized by Weber, is also one of the key points in Durkheim's work on the elementary forms of religious life. Contrary to a psychological-pragmatic framework that sees religion as configuring itself functionally to the practical effectiveness it purports to possess, as a "system of ideas whose object is to explain the world" (Durkheim, 1976:428), in short, a system with an aim that is extrinsic to itself, Durkheim identifies one of the decisive aspects of the religious experience in the fact that it is "foreign to all utilitarian ends" (Durkheim, 1976:380).

It is then possible to understand the close affiliation of the religious with the recreational or the aesthetic element, with play or the work of art, and that which, in human life, is "without purpose" and that takes place "only for the mere pleasure of affirming itself;" ultimately, all that is involved in "supplementary and superfluous works of luxury" (Durkheim, 1976:425, 381).

"This luxury is indispensable to the religious life; it is at its very heart" (Durkheim, 1976:15). Its uselessness consists in the fact of having no other purpose than itself. To this is connected, in the perspective of Durkheim, "the irreducibility of a moral ideal to a utilitarian motive, and in the order of thought, the irreducibility of reason to individual experience" (Durkheim, 1976:16).

"In so far as he belongs to society, the individual transcends himself, both when he thinks and when he acts" (Durkheim, 1976:16). This possibility of transcendence, which is inherent in the very nature of religious experience, is what, in its way of being, makes religion a social phenomenon of "active cooperation" (Durkheim, 1976:482), one that has nothing to do with all that is attributable to a purely individual gain.

The social dimension of religious experience (its being a "social fact") cannot be reduced to the simple sum of each individual event, but transcends it. This transcendence has to do with the same dichotomy as that of the sacred and the profane, the definition of which, in Durkheim, is the outcome of a complex process. Decisive was, in this sense, the theoretical contribution of students Hubert and Mauss. The sacred, in their studies, emerges as a universal force (mana), which goes beyond any natural or utilitarian element and that, according to the famous definition of Hubert, turns religion into an "administration du sacré," which is about what is different from all that only concerns the individual.

The experience of "collective effervescence" that, in Durkheim, characterizes this type of "administration," also emerges in studies of the Collège de Sociologie, which connect the idea of the sacred to an experience of "social paroxysm," through which it is possible to transcend the individual in social reality. The sacred is revealed here as the bearer of a "prerational" force that is the foundation of the social bond. "The gift of self" that, according to this perspective, belongs to it is sacred because it comes with that peculiar instance of overcoming the individual, which uniquely allows the formation of society. The "unproductive expenditure" that characterizes this dimension, beyond the orgiastic and paroxysmal logic that emerges in some positions of the members of the Collège, effectively reveals, however, the self-finality constitutive of the religious experience, from which social reality originates.

The autonomy of religious experience—the fact, namely, to be on the one hand an essentially useless experience, aimed at nothing but itself and, second, to originate exclusively from what is part of the scope of religion— is also apparent in studies that follow the phenomenological approach inaugurated by Rudolf Otto. Religion, according to Otto, "begins with itself"; it originates from the same "lived experience" (*Erlebnis*) of the sacred, which has in itself the contents of its experiencing. Otto's research (as the subtitle of his most famous book suggests) aims to analyze "the irrational in the idea of the divine and its relation to the rational." The Kantian framework of his discussion, first, tries to formalize an experience of the "noumenal" that helps to highlight the conditions of possibility of the religious a priori. The original "religious disposition" is then identified as a self-generating germ, which contains its own purpose in itself. The telos of the particular power of the sacred, for Otto, is implicit in its very experience.

The self-finality intrinsic to religious experience, which emerges from Otto's phenomenological investigation—often close to a psychological analysis of the irrational—is also highlighted in the work of van der Leeuw. The phenomenon of religion is revealed, for him, in the intimate relationship between a subject and the object to which it is directed. "The object of religion—for van der Leeuw—is subject for the faith. Reciprocally, the subject of religion is object to the faith. The science of religion [then] confronts a practicing man [. . .]. Faith sees a man to whom something happened. Phenomenology describes the conduct of man in regard to power, but it must not forget that this man himself determines his own conduct or changed it after being touched by power," which he lets himself experience (van der Leeuw, 1933:151).

Completely in line with this approach is the research of Mircea Eliade, which enjoys a degree of autonomy from other studies in this field. The sacred for Eliade is a matter of conscience, historically manifest in "hierophanies" (Eliade, 2004). Through these events, the unique "reality" of the sacred is expressed in many different ways, and yet they never exhaust its power, the purpose of which, according to Eliade, can only be itself.

## As a Separate Power

The auto-finality of religious practice manifests itself in the form of a power with a separate end in itself. The religious experience is one of a power, where a force, before affecting other forces or suffering from their effects, not only is exerted on itself, but above all separates from what is not like it, finding its own end in itself.

Hence, the impossibility to derive the dichotomy of the sacred and the profane, and the ambivalence of the sacred underlined in studies in this field; the fact, namely, of being something intimate, familiar, and, at the same time, strange and disorienting; being at once august, numinous and terrible, despicable; prohibited, forbidden and permitted, allowed. Of particular relevance to the discussion of this work is that this ambiguity emerges, for example, in Latin, in a comment on the saying "auri sacra fames," reported by Virgil (*Aeneid* 3, 57) and taken up in Weber's investigation into the origins of capitalism (Weber, 2002:41–44).

The passage in question is one where Servius notes that *sacer* can mean, in fact, both "saint" and "damned" (see Virgil's *Aeneid* 3, 57). A power seemingly familiar, like that of procuring money for the satisfaction of needs, becomes something completely alien and disturbing, precisely because it is a separate power that has no other purpose than itself.

According to the most famous studies on the sacred, in religious experience this separation basically takes place in two ways: in the form of social obligation, which is the binding force that, for example, according to Durkheim, is typical of the religious element, capable of making the individual transcend its individuality to establish collective bonds; or in the form of the complete otherness ontologically experienced, according to Otto, in the phenomenon of religion as *sensus numinis*.

Within studies on the sacred we are particularly interested in a text by Bataille titled *Theory of Religion*, first published in 1948. Although Bataille's research in this field is affected by problems that also emerge in the works of the other members of the Collège de Sociologie, this essay is of particular interest to us. Bataille explicitly identifies the religious form in a peculiar act of separation that is consubstantial with the experience of what is truly human. Decisive is, in this sense, the relationship with animal life, which is more complex than it might seem at first glance. The animal is not simply assumed by Bataille to be part of the same evolutionary chain that leads to humans. The traits of animality that belong to human life are not definitively superseded. Rather, they give rise to quite different modes of being from which the experience of the sacred derives.

Bataille writes "every animal is in the world like water in water" (Bataille, 1989:19). Nothing in the world is "useful" strictly speaking. This absolute continuity of animal life is not foreign to man. Indeed, says Bataille, "the animal opens before me a depth that attracts me and is familiar to me. In a sense, I know this depth: it is my own. It is also that which is farthest removed from me, that which deserves the name depth, which means precisely that which is unfathomable to me" (Bataille, 1989:22). This condition occurs due to the "limits of the human," to the need to build "utensils" with which to protect oneself.

The utensil introduces an exteriority into the human world, a separation; the ability to process purposes extrinsic to mere natural life and to identify the means to achieve them. Thus, the realm of the useful takes shape. Here, a constant reference to the means and ends to which the tools have to be directed is essential. This reference reveals, however, the meaninglessness intrinsic to human life: it is impossible for man to exhaust the meaning of his actions in the goals he sets himself. So we find a world where human beings are equally lost; "superfluous," of "no use" where building artificial protections is insufficient for the limitless opening to which man is naturally exposed.

At this point, human life experiences an intimate familiarity with the "continuity" of the animal environment. A certain opacity, a "nonknowledge" unites the two realms and makes them more familiar than extraneous. This familiarity proves disorienting; disturbing precisely because of what is most familiar. From a similar conjunction man comes to experience the sacred; an experience of what "serves no purpose," what "only has a value in itself, not with a view to something else" (Bataille, 1989:29).

The experience of the sacred, for Bataille, is one of power, never fully accomplished, a discontinuous finality that has no extrinsic goal; in this sense, it is "omnipotent." It could almost be said that the opacity of the animal world may prove familiar to humans precisely in the experience of the sacred. More than an expression of the final separation of man from the realm of animal life, the experience of the sacred is one of a detachment that is, so to speak, internal: the separation from the separation that was produced, in man, from the processing of the profane world of tools. "This continuity, which for the animal could not be distinguished from anything else, [. . .] offered man all the fascination of the sacred world, as against the poverty of the profane tool (of the discontinuous object)" (Bataille, 1989:35).

Technical-industrial progress and the capitalist economy result from the domination of the instrumental and utilitarian rationality that originated with the production of tools. Here, a process of autonomy from any form of sacredness seems accomplished. According to what Bataille wrote in a text we referred to in chapter 11, this separation was made possible thanks to the Protestant perspective highlighted by Weber, once the world of works had become definitively separated and made autonomous from the world of grace. The link between religion and economics would thus be confirmed, but only within a secularizing approach like the one proposed by Weber: instrumental reason would be imposed only when, in the age of capitalism, it could become autonomous from any munificent form of transcendence.

However, at the end of the text on the theory of religion—when Bataille speaks of the latest stage of development of capitalist forms of production—we find a perspective that somehow belies the path he had previously traced. The link between religion and capitalist economy seems more problematic than indicated by the process of secularization.

> Only the gigantic development of the means of production is capable of fully revealing the meaning of production, which is the nonproductive consumption of wealth [. . .]. But the moment when consciousness [. . .] sees production destined to be consumed is precisely when the world of production no longer knows what to do with its products. (Bataille, 1989:94)

Bataille recognizes that in the most recent contemporary modes of capitalist production, consumption is not the ultimate purpose of the production chain, extrinsic to the process as an ultimate goal to be achieved; rather, it is the end in itself, inherent to the production chain. At the foundation of the mechanisms of the capitalist economy and the development that fueled it, lies not utilitarian and instrumental rationality (as seems to be the case elsewhere in his writings). The basis on which the force of economic power rests is a self-finalized process like that of consumption for the purpose of consumption: the futility of consumption for consumption's sake.

For Bataille, a similar self-finality characterizes religious experience and resurfaces here as an essential component of the production chain. The link between the religious and the economic element appears, then, more stringent than that resulting from a logic exclusively marked by the idea of secularization. The hypothesis proposed by Benjamin in the early fragment—namely that of understanding capitalism as a real form of religion, and not only as "religiously conditioned conformation"—is thus reinforced.

The fact that "unproductive consumption" represents the "meaning" of capitalist production is still current to this day. Underpinning today's capitalist economy is not so much a utilitarianism made definitively autonomous from all references to transcendence that, in some interpretations, would appear to be the case for Weber or, in other respects, Bataille. What today fuels economic power seems to be, rather, an investment in the uselessness inherent to the experience of the sacred itself.

From this point of view, Benjamin's claim that "utilitarianism acquires its religious overtones" can be seen, perhaps, in a new light. It is not that utility is worshipped as the only thing worth pursuing. The obsessive search for useful purposes has become, rather, a single continuous motion that no longer has purpose. Satisfying needs or trying to delay their satisfaction in view of greater yields is no longer what counts; what matters is, instead, an extreme form of enjoyment and consumption that is not content with anything but itself. As the ultimate meaning of production, unproductive consumption introduces to the market objects that, rather than fulfilling desires, have the power to foment compulsive demand.

It seems difficult to see at the basis of this mechanism an ascetic practice in Weber's terms. But asceticism, which would be the origin of capitalist enterprise—as we have seen—is characterized by the ability to invest in that which cannot be definitively possessed and therefore is not useful to achieve a particular purpose or postpone it, but rather refers to the self-finality inherent to human action. Thus a paradoxical form of asceticism can be called back into question even in the offer of enjoyment for its own sake that is at stake in unproductive consumption, and which current capitalist production is geared toward. This technique refers to the process of decoding desire that characterizes Christian asceticism. Not only does the desiring subject take form thus as a subject of enjoyment, but through it, it even becomes possible to organize control mechanisms that coincide with its own ability to govern desires. Possible methods of consumption are thus channeled or stimulated or addressed, rather than being simply repressed through the removal of the impulses that generate them so as to obtain higher gains.

But above all, in the era of the "global market," a continuous "exercise on the self" is demanded as a freely chosen training for the "flexibility" that characterizes the current modes of production: the activity of work is fed into a process that invests life, and man as a "being in debt" is a form of capital.

Benjamin's claim that capitalism is the religion of our time somehow rings true. Thinking of capitalism as the ultimate form of religion may perhaps also help us understand the explosive return of the religious that we have witnessed in recent years. New religious demands have emerged, both inside and outside the so-called modern world, directly involving the international political order and powerfully demanding public attention. But a convincing response to the question of this renewed domination of the religious over the public realm is yet to be found. That such a return is linked to the perpetuation of a war that, instead of being created by a conflict between civilizations, is actually fueled by a real global economic clash seems only to confirm Benjamin's prophetic intuition. A perspective that wishes to deal radically with this question, cannot but reveal the extent to which the paradigm of secularization, in fact, has proven to be increasingly inadequate for a reading of the present, and how it has appeared totally reductive with respect to a phenomenon emerging as forcefully as the religious one.

The emergence of new religious demands globally may be then merely a response to the prevailing religion of our time that is still called "capitalism."

## Life as Fetish: Theological Arcane or Real Abstraction?

The inherently religious structure of capitalism identified by Benjamin in the fragment above, in many ways, finds confirmation in the latest mode of production. But, for Benjamin, thinking about capitalism as a religion also means implicitly assuming Marx's discussion on commodity fetishism. What should be understood in this framework, then, is how the cult religion that the capitalist economy is meant to have developed can be identified with the worship of the "fetishism of commodities" that Marx speaks of. In addition, it is necessary to look deeper into the extent to which Marx's thoughts on this issue may still be useful for an understanding of the present, to what extent it seems possible to confront, albeit partially, the problems he raised with what emerged in our discussion so far.

From a superficial reading of the first chapter of volume 11 of *Capital*, where Marx deals with the problem of fetishism in relation to the commodification of life carried out by the capitalist mode of production, one might see the fetishistic character of the commodity as simply consisting of its being separate from that which is not exposed to the market; hence, the incarnation of its value in money. According to Marx, "the first step made by an object of utility towards acquiring exchange value is when it forms a *non-use value*" (Marx, 1996:98). In this reading, commodities would be custodians of "value exchange," that crystallizes in the "*form of money.*" At the basis of this perspective lies the idea that both are nothing but "mere *symbols*" (Marx, 1996:102).

According to Montesquieu—whom Marx cites in a footnote on this issue—money is a symbol of a thing and represents it. Similarly, for Hegel—also referenced on this in *Capital*—the commodity, because of its value, is "a mere symbol" and "count not for what it is, but for what it's worth" (Hegel, *Philosophy of Right*, quoted in Marx, 1996:101). This perspective, seemingly innocuous, in fact tends to show an ambiguity.

If, as Marx claims, "every commodity is a symbol, since, in so far as it is value, it is only the material envelope of the human labor spent upon it" (Marx, 1996:101), the question becomes more complicated. If we regard as symbols the "social characters assumed by objects, or the material forms assumed by the social qualities of labor under the régime of a definite mode of production" (Marx, 1996:102), this constitutes a simplification, according to which they are no more than "arbitrary fictions sanctioned by the so-called universal consent of mankind" (Marx, 1996:102). Marx claims that this is a "bourgeois" interpretation of the phenomenon, an ambiguous way to simplify what in itself cannot be simplified; an interpretation that "suited the mode of explanation in favor during the eighteenth century. Unable to account for the origin of the puzzling forms assumed by social relations between man and man" (Marx, 1996:102). The point, however, for Marx, is to go to the heart of this enigma, without simplifying any of the ambiguities that may arise.

In the very title of the fourth part of the first chapter of the first volume of *Capital*, "the fetishism of commodities" is, as is known, presented as a "secret"; because "a commodity appears, at first sight, a very trivial thing, and easily understood. Its analysis shows that it is, in reality, a very queer thing, abounding in metaphysical subtleties and theological niceties" (Marx, 1996:81).

Its nature of "mysterious thing," which determines the "fetish character" is what, according to Marx, deeply connects it to "the mist-enveloped regions of the religious world" (Marx, 1996:82).

The religious structure of capitalism, identified by Benjamin in the fragment previously discussed, implicitly refers to this aspect of Marx's discussion of commodity fetishism. In this way, we must not forget that both Marx and Benjamin identify a special relationship between capitalism and the Christian religion. While for Benjamin, "capitalism has developed as a parasite of Christianity in the West, until it reached the point where Christianity's history is essentially that of its parasite—that is to say, of capitalism" similarly, for Marx, "for a society based upon the production of commodities, [. . .] Christianity [. . .] is the most fitting form of religion" (Marx, 1996:90).

This "suitability," Benjamin described as essential, and for Marx, too, it is not extrinsic. "Christianity is likewise the special religion of capital" because, "In both it is only men who count." In this sense, then, in both, "one man in the abstract is worth just as much or as little as the next man. In the one case, all depends on whether or not he has faith, in the other, on whether or not he has credit" (Marx, 33:369).

The Christian matrix of the capitalist economy, for Marx, is traceable to one of the most fundamental aspects of its framework; the essential characteristic mode of producing, socially and historically determined, what is known as capitalism. This intimately concerns the device that allows for the regulation of the movement of commodities: the unit of measure at the basis of this regulation coincides with the labor time that is socially necessary to the production of certain commodities, independently of the qualitative difference between laboring activities.

Marx claims that "*the equalization of the most different kinds of labor can be the result only of an abstraction from their inequalities,* or of reducing them to their common denominator, viz., *expenditure of human labor power* or human labor *in the abstract*" (Marx, 1996:84). Marx believes that this mechanism, normally presented as a law of nature, is, in fact, deeply connected with "the mist-enveloped regions of the religious world" (Marx, 1996:82). In particular, in his view, it has a privileged relation with the peculiar religious form expressed in Christianity: "for a society based upon the production of commodities in which the producers in general enter into social relations with one another by treating their products as *commodities* and *values*, whereby they reduce their individual private labor to the standard of homogeneous human labor—for such a society, Christianity with its cultus of abstract man [. . .] is the most fitting form of religion" (Marx, 1996:90).

For Marx, the capitalist modes of production are based on the distinction between the use and the exchange value of labor power. Exchange value originates precisely from this "cultus of abstract man" that Christianity has first organized. From this process, for the capitalist, a surplus value is generated that is the source of a profit deriving from the mechanism of "commodification" of labor. The labor that, in itself, is aimed not only at the production of an object, but also at the realization of the subject, becomes, under capitalism, a mere means of exchange, separate from the more proper and singularly different qualities of labor power. The shift is carried through in the process of abstraction that, according to Marx, not only intimately derives from the Christian religion, but is also "real" because it intimately concerns the activity of labor as a historically determined mode of production.

Marx's critique of the capitalist abstraction of life is based on a critique of the fetishist abstraction of the commodity. As the commodity that becomes fetish is a good that cannot be fully enjoyed without accumulation and exchange, so labor reduced to commodity is alienated and not oriented towards the realization of man in society. For Marx, labor cannot be separated, in man, from his social power, its use value, and the most intimate faculties that characterize him as a human being equipped with action and language that determine the "wealth of *human* needs" (Marx, 1996: 306). This is because man, in his view, "needs a totality of manifestations of human life" to satisfy himself, and "his realization is an inner necessity, a *need*" (Marx, 1996:306).

However, the enjoyment of life is not resolved in a natural and original relation of human beings with the world aimed at the satisfaction of primary needs through labor. If the full realization of life solely consisted of the satisfaction of needs, human beings would establish a utilitarian relationship with the world, and Marx's critique of the utilitarian ideology would become ambiguous. The critique would seem to be exclusively geared to defend the concreteness of the use value of worldly goods against the abstraction of exchange value. But, in fact, the "reality" of abstraction that the capitalist forms of production carry out is also due to the fact that the activity of abstraction, for Marx, is a primarily human one: it is rooted in praxis. In this sense, labor is no more than one partial aspect of it, insufficient, or in any case inherent to the primarily potential and self-finalized constitution of human beings who are central to the labor market in the form of labor power, rather than on the basis of the works effectively carried out (Virno, 2004). This shift also throws a different light on the connection Marx detects between Christian religion and capitalism.

The abstraction of the capitalist mode of production is not a mere instrumentalization of labor that turns it into something aimed at the production of commodities and the self-realization of the subject. Instead, the abstraction is accomplished in the separation, in human beings, between what is preventively aimless in character so as to become aimed at a purpose and thus open to the possible, and that which only thus becomes an end in itself and unlimited source of profit. Marx's critique of the separation of life from its needs, operated by abstraction in the historically determined capitalist mode of production is not satisfied with the return to a "concrete" use of things as opposed to the "abstract" one actualized by exchange value, as it has often seemed the case in some interpretations of his thought. After all, the "secret" of the commodity form is not simply that it is a mere object of use on which only subsequently a market value is ascribed. As a product of human labor, the commodity is *at the same time* both a use and an exchange value, thus presenting itself as "something useful to exchange." Freud makes a similar point: the fetish is not only a fictitious object; it is simultaneously the presence of something and the mark of its absence, which is why it irresistibly attracts desire without ever fully satisfying it while relating to it paradoxically as enjoyment. This highly complex process is fully called into question in Benjamin's work on commodity fetishism, as we will later see, in the draft materials for *Passagen-Werk*.

Next, we investigate what Benjamin calls the cult of man as a being-in-debt that results from the fetishism of life and the separation that arises from it, in order to explore the connection between capitalism and the Christian religion on the path also traced by Marx. As I have tried to demonstrate, the experience of Christian life becomes one of "debt" and the onerous condition is not, in itself, a mere void to fill, but the epicenter of its existence. Given the "parasitical" relation of capitalism and Christianity Benjamin outlines and Marx prospects, one might say that the debt becomes, here, the presupposition of a constant enslavement: an unfillable lack is constantly reproduced and turned into a powerful means of subjugation.

In order to understand this mechanism, we need to investigate, in anthropological term, the stakes of the "indebtedness" that pervades human life. In light of what emerged from Marx's discussion, it is worth carrying out a preliminary comparison with Benjamin's reflection on commodity fetishism.

## Phantasmagorias

Marx raised questions on fetishism that certainly have great influence on Benjamin's *opus postumum* (Desideri, 2001); the few fragments cited earlier can be better understood in the context and throw new light on the considerable amount of annotations that would later be incorporated in the preparatory materials of the book on Paris Arcades he worked on during the final years of his life.

In this unfinished work, the *arcade* is not only a special object of study, but also the form that modernity takes. In *arcades*, where commodities are exhibited in the market surrounded by an aura of *nouveauté* and where the *flâneur* passes by as if traversing "a time that disappeared" (Benjamin, 1999:895), Benjamin sees the typical place of modernity as an epoch of fetishistic self-representation. In his picture, the arcade is not a border (*Grenze*), but a threshold (*Schwelle*), a zone of transition (*Übergangsbereich*) between street and shops, home and street. "Threshold magic"; it is the announcement of a *rite of passage*: everyone who crosses it is transformed, what precedes it is not simply overcome but rather condensed in what appears. In the arcades Benjamin discerns the realization of the phantasmagoria of the fetishism of commodities. "Phantasmagoria" is a term he borrows from Marx and whose meaning he radicalizes. It best expresses, in his view, the fetishist nature of commodities that emerges from Marx's analysis, too. The commodity is constitutively ambiguous (*Zweideutigkeit*); an ambiguity that characterizes, in Marx, the reality of abstraction and that, in Benjamin, is embodied in the architecture of the arcade. The ambiguity is given in the fact that the elements that make it up are not successive in an evolutionary process nor do they subsist as components of parallel classes; instead, they exist in a constellation "charged with tension," a "dialectic at a standstill" (*Dialektik im Stillstand*) (Benjamin, 1999:943). As a union between street and home, the arcade provides a privileged image of that dialectic; either as a fetish of the commodity, whose use value and exchange value coexist, or as "real abstraction" where reality is one and the same with what is abstracted from it. In fact, one might say that the dialectical nature of the arcade, in Benjamin, derives from the evident connection between this physical place of the metropolitan topography and the metaphysical place of the commodity, which refers back to Marx's framework: abstraction, as a primary human mode, is nothing but the effectivity it arises from. Hence its exemplary role in Benjamin's work.

The architectonic structure of the arcades, as places where novelties take on the spectral semblance of the commodity, displays its ambiguity and that of the modern era, where the unpredictable coexists with the ever-the-same. The infinite progress that seems to characterize modernity, in fact, shows nothing but a continuous repetition of sameness. To Benjamin, modernity appears as the "Time of Hell," where the desire for the new, progress and eternally self-same are but variations of a single hellish time. Benjamin claims:

> What matters here is that the face of the world, the colossal head, precisely in what is newest never itself changes—that this "newest" remains in all respects the same. This constitutes the eternity of hell and the sadistic delight in innovation. To determine the totality of traits which define this "modernity" is to represent hell. (Benjamin, 1999:843)

Breaking this semblance of peace so that the hell animating the soul of the commodity can find a voice entails tracing one's way back to the fetish, its appearance now petrified by the thing in itself. But questioning the changing nature of the thing cannot correspond with a definitive return to its real nature; rather, it is the creation of an opening, of a *passage* in its comprising of a use value and exchange value at the same time. On this issue, the correspondence between Benjamin and Adorno is crucial.

In a letter dated August 2, 1935, Adorno harshly criticizes the *exposé* of the Arcades Project, known as *Paris, Capital of the Nineteenth Century.* He invites Benjamin to avoid falling into Brechtian attempts at tracing the seemingly Marxian shortcut that sees in use value a stronghold for the critique of the fetishism of the commodity. Adorno writes that from a standpoint internal to society the mere concept of use value is totally insufficient to critique the character of the commodity: it simply leads to the previous stage of the division of labor. This was always, he claims, his reservation toward Berta (pseudonym of Brecht). On this issue it is worth noting that Adorno sees a fundamental element of the critique of the fetishism of the commodity in its theological character: "A restoration of theology, or better still a radicalization dialectic introduced into the glowing heart of theology, would simultaneously require the utmost intensification of the social-dialectical, and indeed, economic motifs" (Adorno and Benjamin, 1999:108). The *restitution theological*, for Adorno, entails an accentuation of the economic motif, in the sense that it becomes inseparable from the society of exchange where all ambiguities are eliminated. Adorno writes:

> To understand the commodity as a dialectical image is also to recognize the latter as a motif of the decline and "sublation" of the

commodity, rather than its mere regression to an older stage. On the one hand, the commodity is an alien object in which use-value perishes, and on the other, it is an alien survivor that outlives its own immediacy. It is through commodities, and not directly in relation to human beings, that we receive the promise of immortality. (Adorno and Benjamin, 1999:107–108)

Following Adorno, Benjamin does not subscribe to the naive perspective that promotes a simple return to a previous stage of the division of labor. However, his and Adorno's frameworks are different. It is not possible to reconstruct their respective positions here, but what we are interested in is Benjamin's attempt to open a new and alternative path precisely where all exit routes seemed blocked. This is absent from Adorno, and allows his theory to maintain its currency over time, to our present. Like Adorno, Benjamin believes that the promise of immortality embodied in the commodities is linked to a time that does not want to know about death, the time of hell. This is the time of an endless transition, a constant passing that nails us in the torment of an eternal self-sameness and coincides, for Benjamin, with the ever-growing pace of fashion. For Benjamin, the time of hell is not something awaiting us, but this life here, which takes on the form of a modern ritual, not a rite of passage. The passage, the arcade that houses fashion, is denied its effective character of threshold. The cult of this form does not interrupt the regularity of daily life by introducing an alternation between festive and working days, recognizing seasonal festival, or exceptional dates. Instead, it is a "permanent cult," and its rituality is precisely adequate to the religion that is called capitalism.

All of Benjamin's work is aimed at showing how the *passage*, as a dialectical image of modernity, can include also another kind of opening, another possibility. The "phantasmagoria" typical of these places shows the commodity as a dream about something: "the exposition transfigures exchange value" and also "creates a realm where use value becomes secondary" (Adorno and Benjamin, 1999:204). Despite this, there is a perversely liberating force in the objects that are here not subjected to the utility limited to the satisfaction of immediate needs. The perverse form of the commodity seems to open up a gap, a condition that cannot resolve itself in the realization of useful goals that are clearly individuated, but rather the reference to a lack of determined purpose that essentially characterizes human life. The poverty of experience that for Benjamin characterizes those who only inhabit the phantasmagoria of commodities is linked to an experience of the poverty of spirit that refers back to that to which men and women are constantly exposed. In order to fight it, to overcome the advancing barbary, new spiritual means are not necessary, what is needed is a new positive concept of barbarism, "to start from scratch, to make a new start, to make a little go a long way, to begin with a little and build up further" (Benjamin, 1999a:732). Thus, it is possible to see the ability to do without that does not merely amount to a naive opposition of the exchange value of the fetish as an impediment to an authentic use of things. In the "real" separation actualized in them, the auto-finality inherent to the human ability to abstract, Benjamin seems to see the chance to exhibit the extreme effects of the poverty of experience that now characterizes human life. What remains unclear is the way man could finally use it fully.

The conditions under which Benjamin developed his analysis have changed. The Internet has become the virtual and privileged home of the universal exposition of commodities. Benjamin's analysis, while keeping some ambiguities, is still effective for our analysis of the present. The *passages*, the arcades as a physical place of fetishist self-representations, survive in the form of new shopping centers. The action aimed at purchasing and selling in order to satisfy a targeted demand has now lost priority. The power of commodities to compulsively feed demand has grown, and certainly there is a form of desire that is an end in itself that is artificially produced by the anonymous repetition of a self-same enjoyment. Like the Parisian arcades of the nineteenth century, these new universal shopping centers are hellish places. We should ask, then, if the time of hell, the eternal return of the same, and the possibility of blocking what simply appeared as an infinite progress can point to unexplored directions, as Benjamin suggested at the beginning of the last century.

In his fragment on capitalism, in a concise but incisive manner, Benjamin significantly links three figures of modernity that, aside from Marx, have largely contributed to the celebration of the capitalist cult and belong to its priesthood. These are Nietzsche, Freud, and Weber.

Nietzsche's "superman," for Benjamin, is the first to recognize the religion of capitalism and begin to bring it to fulfilment. [. . .] Freud's theory, too, belongs to the hegemony of the priests of this cult. Its conception is capitalist religious thought through and through. By virtue of a profound analogy, which has still to be illuminated, what has been repressed, the idea of sin, is capital itself, which pays interest on the hell of the unconscious. (Benjamin, 2005)

Finally, in Benjamin's view, Weber failed to identify an important link between the Christian religion and capitalism and misunderstood its properly religious form. Seeing only a formation that is conditioned by religion, Weber obfuscated the meaning of the network we find ourselves in, and the religious core that is present and keeps operating as a privileged driver of capitalist modes of production. In our view, the crucial point is that Benjamin mentions the three authors who develop, to different degrees, an original critique of the "ascetic ideal," and we are going to examine them seriously. The nexus between asceticism and economy investigated so far can benefit from an investigation of the unexplored possibilities Benjamin refers to and questions that can be renewed.

## Chapter 6

# A Philosophical Critique of Asceticism

As we have seen, in the 1921 fragment, Benjamin names Nietzsche, Freud, and Weber the "priests" of the capitalist religion (together with Marx). Regardless of the criticisms that can be made of the paths indicated by each of these, there is an aspect of their thought that is particularly relevant to the viewpoint we would like to expand upon in this context. All of them uncover a problematic link between asceticism and the constitutive economy of human beings. In their reflections asceticism is, explicitly or otherwise, identified as an anthropological device whose functional mechanism operates in broadly the same way in each case, albeit with a different argumentative focus: in none of their writings does the practice of restraint and self-denial, the central feature of asceticism, boil down to a simple negation of being. On the contrary, in the three analyses asceticism is the way in which human life, which has no predetermined biological purpose, finds ways of sustaining itself.

Nietzsche's "ressentiment," Freud's "repression" and the process of "rationalization" identified by Weber pave the way for an analysis of this mechanism, but their investigations reveal a surplus, something beyond these initial concepts. The "will to nothingness," connected to the will to power (in Nietzsche), the "economic problem of masochism" (in Freud) and the "meaninglessness" of the rational and self-referencing logic of profit (in Weber)—the starting point for our reflections—are the three ways in which this something beyond, surplus or excess becomes manifest.

First and foremost, we should therefore try and understand the extent to which, within the Christian framework, this excess is connected to the theme of "lack" that is at the origin of human life, and its reading as both "guilt" and "debt." Then we can see how another anthropological mechanism emerges, one that is more sophisticated than what we previously identified and described as the mechanism of mere self-preservation.

An analysis of these three paths calls for a reassessment of the most widely recognized interpretations in this field. Above all, the view of man as an "indebted being" that emerges in different ways in the reflections of each of the three authors leads this investigation to call into question the underlying forces currently in effect within capitalist modes of production, which have turn the indebtedness of individuals into instrument of their subjugation, as Benjamin insightfully envisaged.

## Guilt and/or Debt?

In many ways, the sense of guilt is one of the cornerstones of Western morality. It is normally associated with the concept of responsibility, innocence, judgment, or absolution, and thus traced back to a tacit superimposition of ethical and judicial concepts, or judicial concepts and theological ones. The blurring of these lines has certainly yet to be fully exposed. Carl Schmitt's endeavors in this area are important. Around ten years before the publication of his notorious essay on political theology, where he focused on sovereignty as a "limit concept" of the law and on the "evil" nature of man—as an anthropological precondition (Schmitt, 1985)—Schmitt published a dissertation entitled "Uber Schuld und Schuldarten" where he outlined the difficulties of defining guilt in legal terms. These difficulties do not only derive from the religious and moral implications associated with the concept. In his view, the main problem is that "the question of guilt is from all points of view a meta-legal (*meta gesetzlich*) one," as it does not relate to "positive criminal law" (positives Strafrechte) or to "the theory of premeditated (Vorsatz) and guilty action (Fahrlässigkeit)" (Schmitt, 1910:155). Rather than in its "material sense" (materielle Inhalt), he believed the legal determination of the concept of guilt should be examined starting from its "formal sense" (formale Inhalt) (Schmitt, 1910:1), as defining the limit of the law.

Benjamin tackles this problem further, tracing guilt back to the theological and legal domains, in two texts that were contemporary to the previously analyzed fragment "Capitalism as Religion" and also connected to one another. These writings implicitly appear to be in dialogue with contemporary themes espoused by Schmitt, given the links and differences that—as has been noted elsewhere (Taubes, 1969; Stimilli, 2004a:117–119 and 249–265) both unite and divide the two authors. In his 1921 essay "A Critique of Violence," and also in "Fate and Character," composed in the same year, Benjamin considers the "guilt of mere natural life," as that on which "the rule of law over the living" is exercised, leading to a separation, within man himself, of "the marked bearer of guilt" (Benjamin, 1995:200–202). The basis of such a formulation, which to a certain extent appears, as has been noted (Agamben, 1998:72–76; Esposito, 2011:29–36), to be a radicalization of similar concepts expressed by Schmitt, may have been nothing other than a "myth": the premise of a sovereign subject, fundamentally autonomous and its own master, formally legitimized to judge and exercise its power through violence, separating in the living human being from the "bearer" of the guilt. Indeed, it is no coincidence that Benjamin traces back the origin of this power to that violence that he defines precisely as "mythical," where, as in the German word Gemalt used for this purpose, there is a crossover between violence and legal power.

The problem of guilt also forms a central theme of the fragment we examined previously. The power described here, however, does not simply isolate guilt, separating the "bare life" of man and identifying in it a "bearer" on which to exercise violence; rather it becomes a generative force. Indeed, according to Benjamin capitalism is nothing other than a religion, to which "an enormous sense of guilt, not itself knowing how to repent, grasps [. . .] not in order to report for this guilt, but to make it universal," to such an extent that, based on his words, it should be seen as the first religion that "engenders blame" (Benjamin, 1995, 100). Following Benjamin's reasoning we could almost say that capitalism, through the definition in economic terms of the theological and legal concept of guilt and its definitive translation into debt has somehow made possible the exercise of power in a way that is similar to the perpetration of legal violence while demystifying its effects: a situation envisaged by Schmitt. Above all, it is clear that starting from this premise, a genealogical investigation into Western moral concepts that does not first and foremost deal with economics, even before considerations of law and theology, is destined to fail.

Nietzsche's *On the Genealogy of Morality* is without doubt the most radical attempt to reconstruct the economic origin of the formation of Western ethics. It is indicative, from our point of view, that one of the key processes it outlines is tracing back the "sense of guilt" to the experience of debt. When seeking to investigate the "gloomy business" of "bad conscience," employing the derisory tone determined to sweep away all that preceded him; Nietzsche poses the question "Have these genealogists of morality up to this point allowed themselves to dream, even remotely, that [. . .] that major moral principle 'guilt' derives its origin from the very materialistic idea 'debt'?" (Nietzsche, 2006:161).

According to Nietzsche the conflation of guilt and debt (it is always worth remembering that the German word "Schuld" encompasses both meanings), derives from the "contractual relationship between creditor and debtor," which refers back to "basic forms of buying, selling, bartering, trading, and exchanging goods" (Nietzsche, 2006:162), and which from his point of view is the "oldest and most primitive personal relationship there is and was." Indeed, it is in such commercial transactions, that Nietzsche claims "for the first time one person encountered another person and measured himself against him" (Nietzsche, 2006:268). The "value" is what is used to measure the debtor against the creditor, thus revealing the original economic nature.

From this link is developed a feeling of "obligation," a duty to settle debts to which, according to Nietzsche, the sense of guilt, the common condition of those that feel that they are in debt, can be traced back. In Nietzsche's reflections, justice also takes on a fundamentally economic character that takes precedence over ascertaining the truth or proclaiming the law. In this respect, it is none other than an "extremely late achievement, indeed, a sophisticated form of human judgment and decision making," which feeds on the retributive force of the punishment; the notion that inflicting pain can provide "compensation" for the injury suffered.

Among post-Heidegger interpretations of Nietzsche, it is in the works of Gilles Deleuze that this aspect is most clearly emphasized. He writes:

> The creditor-debtor relationship expresses the activity of culture during the process of training or formation. Corresponding to prehistoric activity this relationship itself is the relationship of man to man, "the most primitive of individuals" preceding even "the origins of any social organization." It also serves as a model "for the crudest and most primitive social constitutions." Nietzsche sees the archetype of social organization in credit rather than exchange. The man who pays for the injury he causes by his pain, the man held responsible for a debt, the man treated as responsible for his reactive forces: these are the means used by culture to reach its goal. (Deleuze, 2002:135)

In the passage earlier, Deleuze's approach of contrasting credit and exchange within Nietzsche's theory on the origin of culture implicitly seems to want to maintain a distance between Mauss's research in social anthropology and Nietzsche's broader view. According to Mauss, as has been shown, the "total social facts" originated from a liberal exchange, a gift, and not from a creditor/debtor relationship (Mauss, 1966).[1] Effectively, the two adopt contrasting positions on many points; on closer inspection, however, Nietzsche's theory actually seems to confirm Mauss's research. Although the latter aims to distinguish economic exchange from the "total" exchange of the gift (at the origin of the social relationship), evidently the "total social fact" he speaks of is triggered by a chain of exchanges that are born out of the obligation to return a gift, to provide a counter-gift. This obligation precedes any clear distinction between the economic and religious spheres, or the legal and the moral; for this very reason (despite the version Mauss prefers to put forward), there is actually very little difference between his position and Nietzsche's. Clearly Nietzsche's is more definitive: the obligation to settle debts, which originates from the oldest social relations between men—and where "for the first time [. . .] one person measured himself against another"—is clearly born out of an economic exchange and not a gift; but the starting point in both cases, that is, the credit relationship (in Nietzsche) and the liberal one (in Mauss), is obligation. This notion needs to be investigated for our purposes, as we examine the link between guilt and debt in more depth, in an attempt to expose the intrinsic anthropological problem.

## Man between Biological Deficit and Public Debt

Phylogenetically, Nietzsche perceives obligation as being formed in the relationship between debtor and creditor. Indeed, according to his theory the first development of the phenomenon can be traced back to the origins of man. From an evolutionary view, Nietzsche contends that man emerged from a compensation for an original lack of animal instinct. Human life is effectively an economy in the true sense of the word, a way of administering a natural deficit, a biological debt that man is "obligated" to repay. This obligation distances man from the key link of predetermination that characterizes the instinctive animal reaction to its environment, and comes into its natural domain in the sphere of possibility, or to put it better in

Nietzsche's own terms, of "power," which is nevertheless always connected to the "weakness" from which it arises. For him, human life derives from "the most radical of all metamorphoses" that nature has ever witnessed. He writes:

> Just like the things water animals must have gone through, when they were forced either to become land animals or die off, such was the fate of this half-beast so happily adapted to his wild state, to adventure—suddenly all their instincts were devalued and "disengaged." From this point on, these animals were to go on foot and "carry themselves"; whereas previously they had been supported by the water. A terrible heaviness weighed them down. In performing the simplest things they felt ungainly. In dealing with this new unknown world they no longer had their old leader, the ruling unconscious drives which guided them safely. These unfortunate creatures were reduced to thinking, inferring, calculating, bringing together cause and effect, to their "consciousness," their most impoverished and error-prone organ! I believe that on earth there has never been such a feeling of misery, such a leaden discomfort—while at the same time those old instincts had not all at once stopped imposing their demands! Only it was difficult and seldom possible to do their bidding. For the most part they had to find new and, as it were, underground satisfactions for them. (Nietzsche, 2006:283–284)

If, from Nietzsche's perspective, human life fundamentally appears to be an economy, the way of managing an initial discomfort, or a debt that must be repaid, then to an extent we ought to understand how to discern a certain flourishing ambiguity in his reasoning. The uncertainty arising from this problem is connected to the idea that there is nothing stable and well defined at the origin of life, but rather different "forces" that exert themselves in various ways.

On the one hand, deprived of the conditions in which it can be exercised and separated from what it can influence, the natural, intrinsic power of man appears to turn inwards against itself; it transforms from action to reaction, directed internally: "All instincts which are not discharged to the outside—Nietzsche affirms, are turned back inside—this is what I call the internalization of man [. . .] that is the origin of 'bad conscience'" (Nietzsche, 2006:285). On the other hand, however, he still maintains that the "fact that there was on earth an animal soul turned against itself, taking sides against itself, meant there was something [so] new, profound, unheard of, enigmatic, contradictory, and full of the future, that with it the picture of the earth was fundamentally changed. [. . .]" Since then, he contends, "man [. . .] arouses for himself a certain interest, a tension, a hope, almost a certainty, as if something is announcing itself in him, something is preparing itself, as if the human being were not the goal but only a way, an episode, a bridge, a great promise" (Nietzsche, 2006:289).

On Nietzsche's path, to identify a link between anthropology and economy, we need to understand the substance of his regular references to "evolution"; to what extent his works discuss a final destination for man that at the same time marks a genuine step beyond existing limitations; and therefore, to what extent he attempts to redefine the human species, positing that the boundaries of what is not human (the animal and the inorganic) are not definitively fixed, but can be continuously shifted.

For Nietzsche, evolution is not "*progressus* towards a single goal, even less so the short-lived, logical *progressus*, achieved with minimal expenditure of power and resources, but rather the sequence of processes of overpowering [. . .] together with the resistance which arises against this process, the changes of form attempted for the purpose of defense and reaction, as well as the results of successful counter-measures" (Nietzsche, 2006:277). In this scenario, "bad conscience," which originated from the internalization of natural force, separated from what it can influence, should not be understood as the "goal" of the evolutionary process that unequivocally led from animal to man. Rather, Nietzsche contends that the sense of guilt formed from it is not a "matter of fact, but much rather only the interpretation of a factual condition, that is, of a bad psychological mood" (Nietzsche, 2006:333). In this sense, the faculty of interpretation is considered wholly innate to the force from which human life originates (Butler, 1997:63–82).

In Nietzsche, interpreting entails evaluating, determining what it is that endows an object with value. Genealogically, human life is prospective by nature, originating from the economic evaluation of a biological deficit. Values are not principles that are appreciated for themselves, nor do they simply relate to a point of view; rather their worth is a function of the process of evaluation from which they themselves derive. They cannot, therefore, be considered separately from the process from which they draw their value. In some ways, this is a similar argument to the one made by Marx in relation to the "reality" of abstraction. Valuation, restored to its original genealogical setting, is not simply the assignment of objective values; it is an inherent trait of man. This brings into play the very method by which values are produced, and not their inherent validity. Herein lays their economic origin, so much so that Nietzsche affirms:

> To set prices, to measure values, to think up equivalencies, to exchange things—that preoccupied man's very first thinking to such a degree that in a certain sense it's what thinking itself is. Here the oldest form of astuteness was bred; here, too, we can assume are the first beginnings of man's pride, his feeling of pre-eminence in relation to other animals. Perhaps our word "man" (manas) continues to express directly something of this feeling of the self: the human being describes himself as a being which assesses values, which values and measures, as the "inherently calculating animal." Selling and buying, together with their psychological attributes, are even older than the beginnings of any form of social organizations and groupings; out of the most rudimentary form of personal legal rights the budding feeling of exchange, contract, guilt, law, duty, and compensation was instead first transferred to the crudest and earliest social structures [. . .]. The eye was now adjusted to this perspective, [. . .] but then inexorably proceeding in the same direction, people soon reached the great generalization: "Each thing has its price, everything can be bought"—the oldest and most naive moral principle of justice, the beginning of all "good nature," all "fairness," all "good will," all "objectivity" on earth. (Nietzsche, 2006:269)

Nietzsche, therefore, interprets the economic origin of human life in a "historical manner," within the relationship "between those people presently alive and their ancestors" (Nietzsche, 2006:288). "Here the reigning conviction was that the tribe exists only because of the sacrifices and achievements of their ancestors, and that people must pay them back with sacrifices and achievements. In this people recognize a debt which keeps steadily growing" (Nietzsche, 2006:288), which gives rise to a "fear of ancestors." "So the ancestor is necessarily transfigured into a god;" to the extent that, according to Nietzsche, "here perhaps lies even the origin of the gods, an origin out of fear!" (Nietzsche, 1968:288).

Of all the deities, it is no coincidence that Nietzsche favors the Jewish god, toward which man has an unfathomable sense of guilt. "He sees in 'God' the ultimate contrast he is capable of discovering to his real and indissoluble animal instincts. He interprets these very animal instincts as a crime against God" (Nietzsche, 2006:293). This is until the emergence of "the paradoxical and horrifying expedient" devised by Christianity: "God's sacrifice of himself for the guilt of human beings, God paying himself back with himself, God as the only one who can redeem man from what for human beings has become impossible to redeem—the creditor sacrifices himself for the debtor" (Nietzsche, 2006:292). The Christian idea of "remission," for Nietzsche, does not imply liberation from debt, but its radicalization; pain only pays the interest on the debt, leaving man chained to eternal indebtedness. With Christianity "in a fit of pessimism, the prospect of a final instalment must once and for all be denied. Now, our gaze is to bounce off and ricochet back despairingly off an iron impossibility, now those ideas of 'debt' and 'duty' are supposed to turn back. But against whom? There can be no doubt: first of all against the 'debtor,' [. . .] and finally [. . .] even against the 'creditor': the creditor (*who*) sacrifices himself for the debtor" (Nietzsche, 2006:291).

Christianity, therefore, appears as the most radical interpretation, the most extreme variant of the original evaluation through which, according to Nietzsche, human life was formed as the management of a natural deficit, of a biologically unpayable debt. It is a reactive interpretation, however, a result of "ressentiment" that acts exclusively by separating and diverting from the original force; depriving the active force of its power in order to deflect it away from its primary direction. Reaction, in these terms, is not "counteraction," but rather simply "nonaction." Having destroyed any form of action, it ends up destroying itself, as it finds no other way of staying alive than by continuing to feed the originally contracted debt.

The viewpoint outlined in Benjamin's 1921 fragment—which identified capitalism as a religious movement that reproduces itself in the form of a worldwide debt, and that developed from Christianity in a parasitical relationship—was first elaborated theoretically in Nietzsche's analysis of the Christian religion. It is nevertheless worth investigating for what reason, in the same text, Benjamin maintains that "capitalist, religious thinking magnificently reconciles itself in Nietzsche's philosophy," to the extent that he names Nietzsche as one of the "priests" of the religion. This kind of reflection may help contribute to an understanding of the mechanism of indebtedness that to this day, in the form of both public and private debt, serves to feed the working of the global economy.

What is particularly important in this respect is the fact that the problem of debt is also taken seriously into consideration in the capitalist economic analysis carried out by Marx. The twenty-sixth chapter in the eighth section of the first volume of *Capital*, which is entirely dedicated to the delicate issue of "so-called primitive accumulation," is in actual fact a chapter on debt or guilt (in which Marx also uses the word Schuld). What is called into question here, however, is "the system of public credit (des öffentlichen Kredit), that is, of national debt (die öffentliche Schuld)" that "marked with its stamp the capitalistic era" (Marx, 1996:874).

According to Marx, the issue is the way in which money is transformed into capital.

> The public debt becomes one of the most powerful levers of primitive accumulation. As with the stroke of an enchanter's wand, it endows barren money with the power of breeding and thus turns it into capital [. . .]. The state's creditors actually give nothing away, for the sum lent is transformed into public bonds, easily negotiable, which go on functioning in their hands just as so much hard cash would. [. . .] The national debt has given rise to joint-stock companies, to dealings in negotiable effects of all kinds, and to speculation: in a word to stock-exchange gambling and the modern bankocracy. (Marx, 1996:919)

In Marx's formulation, public debt is the tool with the power to transform cash into capital. The increase, the growth that is produced in this way, originates from a lack, or more precisely from a debt. The link between debt and accumulation is so persuasive, that Marx even goes so far as to state that "the only part of the so-called national wealth that actually enters into the collective possessions of modern peoples is their national debt." Hence, as a necessary consequence, he claims, derives "the modern doctrine that a nation becomes the richer the more deeply it is in debt. Public credit becomes the credo of capital. And with the rise of national debt-making, want of faith in the national debt takes the place of the blasphemy against the Holy Ghost, which may not be forgiven" (Marx, 1996:920).

The fact that the economic form of credit, at the very stage of primitive accumulation, obtains in Marxist discourse the sacramental nature of a "credo"—a belief that "plays in Political Economy about the same part as original sin in theology" (Marx, 1996:925), lends further weight to Benjamin's diagnosis of capitalism as a structurally religious phenomenon. Marx also confirms this viewpoint elsewhere.

In the section dedicated precisely to the transformation of money into capital, Marx represents the sacramental process of debt, from which the very productivity of capital originates, as an intra-divine genesis endowed with a "motion of its own, passing through a life-process of its own." In describing this development, Marx maintains: "instead of simply representing the relations of commodities, it enters now, so to say, into private relations with itself. It differentiates itself as original value from itself as surplus-value; as the father differentiates himself from himself qua the son, yet both are one and of one age" (Marx, 1996:188).

And whereas according to Marx, the circulation of goods, in its abstract form, remains a "means of carrying out a purpose unconnected with circulation, namely, the appropriation of use-values," "the circulation of money as capital is, on the contrary, an end in itself, for the expansion of value takes place only within this constantly renewed movement" (Marx, 1996:185).

Marx identifies the capitalist form of production, founded on the exploitation of labor and on enhancing the value of capital as an end in itself, with the process through which the Christian theory of the "economy of salvation" claims that God reveals himself from nothingness in his incarnation through the Son. In both cases, from an original absence a "movement" of growth and development is created, although this movement proves to be an end in itself. In many ways, this process is similar to the evolution described by Nietzsche, which sees man drawing his origins from the compensation that he makes for his formational lack of animal instinct.

If human life—like the life of divinity or of capital—evolves from an initial deficit (out of nothingness, or from an originally contracted debt), to preserve its existence, and therefore according to Nietzsche's thinking to survive, it is simply incapable of doing other than to negate its own vital essence, which in itself is negative. In this way, however, it separates from itself into an abstract form that is an end in itself. In Nietzsche, this signifies using life against life and limiting death with death; this path leads to weakness and degeneration, with life heading in the opposite direction of its own creation and triggering the process that characterizes the

entirety of Western civilization, to which both Christianity and capitalism—apparently occupying opposite ends of the scale but actually following the same logic—intrinsically belong. However, in his desire to oppose
this degeneration by simply negating it, Nietzsche in his turn risks being
completely enmeshed in the self-same process. Benjamin therefore states
that Nietzsche's *Ubermensch*, is the "first who knowingly begins to realize the capitalist religion," so much so that "capitalist, religious thinking,"
in Benjamin's view, "magnificently reconciles itself in Nietzsche's philosophy." The key point to understand is therefore in what way Nietzsche's
Ubermensch can be seen as the representation of the final form of capitalist domination, and above all, what new horizons his reflections could
open up for present day consideration.

## The Ambiguity of the Ascetic Ideal

The person who with more conviction interpreted Nietzsche, seeing the
"realization" of the technical-metaphysical perspective of the West in
his thinking, was Martin Heidegger. Heidegger interpreted Nietzsche's
"Thinking is meant purely 'economically' here, in the sense of 'machine
economy.' What we think is, as something thought, 'true' only insofar
as it serves the preservation of will to power" (Heidegger, 1991:130). In
Heidegger's reading of the concept of will to power, the final outcome of
the direction of metaphysics is implied from the outset. The economic
slant of his interpretation of Nietzsche is not at all secondary to his better
known theory of technique.

For Heidegger, the form of domination in question here consists precisely in the fact that, for Nietzsche, it is the will to power that establishes
its own conditions, which are called, in fact, values. According to Heidegger, "Being, the beingness of beings, is interpreted as will to power. In a
covert yet utterly comprehensible way, the history of metaphysics appears
in the light of valuative thought. [. . .] But the fact that Nietzsche explains
the history of metaphysics from the horizon of will to power arises from
his metaphysical thought and is not simply a subsequent historiological
insertion of his own 'views' into the teachings of earlier thinkers. Rather,
the metaphysics of will to power, as a revaluating stance toward previous
metaphysics, first determines the latter in the sense of valuation and valuative thought" (Heidegger, 1991:69–70). According to Heidegger, for

Nietzsche what appeared to be of value unconditionally and objectively is found to have its origin and its scope of validity in the will to power. Values are, in this sense, "results of particular perspectives of utility, for the preservation and enhancement of human constructs of domination" (Heidegger, 1991:47). Values are essentially related to "domination." Dominance is the being in power of power (Heidegger, 1991:50). In this sense, according to Nietzsche, "power itself" "requires no aims." It is aimless, just as the whole of beings is valueless. Such aimlessness pertains to the metaphysical essence of power. If one can speak of aim here at all, then the "aim" is the aimlessness of man's absolute dominance over the earth (Heidegger, 1991:82). This aimlessness is, according to Heidegger, precisely what the "will" transforms into power as an end in itself.

This is a very delicate point for our interpretation of both Heidegger and Nietzsche, and for the development of the argument followed so far. At stake is precisely that lack of definitive aims essential to human life; the potential character of human nature that since Aristotle has been presented as a question for Western thought and, at the same time, counterbalanced by the autotelic movement of an abstract power as an end to itself. Pivotal for this step is the fact that, in Nietzsche's view, the potential character of human action, its lack of defined objectives has assumed the characteristics of a deficit, of a "biological debt." According to Heidegger, this lack of pre-established objectives is the condition of possibility because man's behavior can be found inscribed in a movement that has no other end than itself and which is definitively resolved, in Nietzsche, in the full unfolding of a power as an end in itself: a "power of power," that does not aspire to the creation of an "act," but on the contrary considers every implementation as just a step toward the acquisition of a higher power.

This need to continually go beyond itself, according to Heidegger, is not a simple consequence of the will to power; but is the constituent part of its very essence. It is what which, in it, makes power a simple exercise of power (De Carolis, 1989). In this sense, power is such only if it pursues more and more power. Since, according to Heidegger, it is referred to the conditions of the will, power as an end in itself becomes separated power in the form of a power that does not escape the metaphysical statute of the subject, because at the same time it is the objective of the will. It becomes a will that, being "will of will," wants the power of domination.

Heidegger's argument on this issue ends up agreeing with what Benjamin affirms in his passage on capitalism where he states that the religious thinking of capitalism can be found, in this sense, beautifully expressed in the philosophy of Nietzsche. Thus, in Nietzsche, the accomplished theoretical formulation of the mechanism at the basis of economic power that has been investigated until now, emerge in this way: an investment in auto finality inherent in human life is at work in the capitalist forms of production and is perpetrated in the form of an endeavor whose universal control has no other end other than itself.

All the same, the Nietzsche an "will to power" presents an unsolved problem and it might be worth asking whether it really is true that the "power of power" is, effectively, none other than the ultimate objective of the will, its essential motivation, what this will desires (as gathered from Heidegger's and, in a sense, Benjamin's interpretation).

The debate on Nietzsche that took place in Germany, Italy, but especially France, following Heidegger's contribution, over and above certain differences that are also important, seems to stimulate the questioning of a fundamental issue, not just relevant to Nietzsche's critique. Once again I think that Deleuze poses the problem in the clearest terms: "Will to power must be interpreted in a completely different way: power is the one that wills in the will. Power is the genetic and differential element in the will. This is why the will is essentially creative. [. . .] The will to power is essentially creative and giving: it does not aspire, it does not seek, it does not desire, above all it does not desire power. It gives" (Deleuze, 2002:85).

Deleuze attributes "the genetic and differential element in the will" to power, leading back to the problem of the "difference" he identifies at the foundation of human life. French theory, and the whole of post-Heideggerian philosophy, has continued to question this, moving from Nietzsche and Heidegger himself. It is impossible to reconstruct this theoretical development now. But we must not forget that Heidegger's last work appeared closer to Nietzsche, in many ways, than Heidegger himself would have ever admitted. Reiner Schürmann's reading is enlightening in this sense; according to him "Heidegger's recent texts could be interpreted as an attempt to develop the essential traits of an economy of the future which is the irreducible presence of an Arche, the features of a plural economy" (Schürmann, 1982:40). The economic interpretation of Heidegger's thinking proposed here—that ultimately coincides with the description of a passage "from a main economy," still linked to the definition of metaphysical premises, "to an anarchist economy of presence" (Schürmann,

1982:99)—leads his discourse back to the Nietzsche an prospective of an economic origin of man.

Heidegger's economy of being, the "ontological difference," albeit irreducible to an Arche, does not appear, however, to fully get to the root of the problem of "nothingness" as the basis to which it subtended. The "not," as guilt or as debt (Schuld), identified in *Being and Time* as a dark underbelly, like an unbridgeable "lack," from which it gives rise, for the being of being there, to the call of "conscience" and the possibility of its "authentic" healing (see Heidegger, 1978: § 58, 59, and 60).[2] Although it is problematic and, as such, later reviewed by Heidegger himself, it never completely loses its traces of ambiguity, manifesting an intrinsic connivance with what he would have wished to criticize.

Nietzsche instead calls hierarchy the genetic element that Deleuze attributes to the question of "difference," thereby indicating the ratio of forces from which human life would seem to originate and from which it would continue to be sustained: an original power relation expressed in the same form as the will to power. This means that, for Nietzsche, there is not just a lack to be filled at the origin of human life, a nothing to dominate. Rather, in each submission there is a corresponding resistance, a tension where one is never entirely depleted in the other. There is no total domination, just as there is no complete freedom. And yet one cannot be carried out without the other. What is human practice in his view?

The action of man is, at first glance, according to Nietzsche, like a generic activity on which reactive forces that distort and divert from its meaning are triggered, precisely because they originate from the resentment against a life constantly in debt, thus transforming man, the gregarious animal, into a docile and domesticated creature. On the other hand, however, in his argument, it seems that the reactive being of man—what appears like a "natural deficit"—must be recovered on another plane. The experience of the possible, which essentially relates to human life, resurfaces in Nietzsche's argument, though in an inherently ambiguous manner.

This is the framework wherein Nietzsche suggests something quite different from the man who, in order to restrict and dominate his own vital content, becomes subjected to his own naturally inadequate life. On the one hand there is, then, his attempt to reconnect everything that has been separated from the fundamentally destructive tendency of life that he also aimed at safeguarding, to the reasons of the body; on the other hand, however, there is a need to subtract the body from a mere natural degradation.

This is the point at which Nietzsche's critique of the ascetic ideal manifests all its effectiveness, even in its ambiguity.

The ascetic ideal, ultimately, is the interpretative lens through which Nietzsche sees the entire Western civilization and, more generally, human action as such. Devaluation and negation of life, which constitute the cardinal principle of "ascetic practice," guarantee, in reality, its preservation and survival, even in the form of a reactive life, to the point that Nietzsche considers the ascetic ideal as a real "strategy for the preservation of life" (Nietzsche, 2006:250). Emblem of the ascetic ideal is the priest, the pastor. What moves him "is the desire, made flesh, of a being-in-another-world, of being in-another-place"; however, "the supreme level of this desire [. . .] the power of his desire is the strain which pins him here;" so much so that the priest "becomes the tool forced to work to create favorable conditions for being-here and being-man—and it is precisely with this power that he keeps the entire flock anchored to existence." The inhibitory mechanism typical of the ascetic ideal, through which the vital energies become sublimated and transposed onto a different plane ("in-another-world," "in-another-place") reveals itself, in reality, as being functional to the preservation of life and, therefore, the preservation of the power of whoever—the priest in this case—is able to maintain control over it. More than an experience of the possible inscribed in human life, the ascetic practice becomes then an exercise of power in this sense; not only, however, a power over mere biological preservation, but rather over man's capacity to shape his life. Nietzsche even goes as far as stating that "this ascetic priest, this apparent enemy of life, this person who denies belongs precisely" not only "to the greatest conservative forces," but also to those which are "affirmative creators of life" (Nietzsche, 2006:224). Thus, not only preservation but also innovation. But how can preservation, here, be in agreement with a creative activity?

The ascetic ideal manifests, then, in Nietzsche, a fundamental ambiguity and in the critique Nietzsche allows his fundamentally profitable being to emerge (see Fink, 1960:169; Di Marco, 1984:35), which does not end with the capacity of preservation of an abstract form of power; an advantage that is perhaps possible to revive at the origin of the human species. Not only does this, for Nietzsche, not resolve the fundamentally perspective nature of the human animal, his originating from the economic evaluation of a biological deficit in a form which is evolutionarily, in line with self-preservation and for self-control commencing from an initial lack of it. The constitutively being-alive of man is, for him, not only a "being-indebt," a gap to be filled, but as like a lack by excess (Esposito, 2008:78–109): biologically a nonlife, whose essentially potential nature requires continuous strengthening—in Nietzsche's terms a will to power. This power does not end in the mere establishment of a form of domination as an end in itself, but opens rather to the experience itself of opportunity. In this framework, the peculiarity of the ascetic practice, for Nietzsche, lies not so much in its definitively repressive action with respect to the impulses; in it, that is, there is not only the reaction process at stake through which the active force becomes reactive and turns against itself. The ascetic practice, rather, in Nietzsche a discourse, properly becomes a technique of life not only because of its constantly self-preserving strength; and not even because of the abstract self-reference aspect of his domination, but above all because of its implied capacity for expansion of power. This possibility lies exactly in the contact that it continually establishes with excess, which relates to human life. The strategy of containment, which also is typical, coexists with that of the unleashing of the possibility from which it originates as well. The reactive force also, therefore, that turns against itself if carried to excess, becomes a denial that is destined to negate itself and present itself in the form of affirmation. Deleuze's argumentation in this regard is completely convincing: not an overturned Hegelianism, a negative, in turn, denied in a dialectical process of the overcoming of alienation, but a negativity that is affirmed as such; which itself becomes a vital affirmation. In this sense Nietzsche might say with Overbeck that "the ascetic impulse is as deep in man as the opposite impulse."

This excess of the vital element has an effect, for Nietzsche, on the very biological life of man. As such, as unstable and precarious balance, human life can continually redefine itself, strengthening itself, to the point that preservation coincides, in it, with the same opportunities for innovation, with a new act of creation. If the statement is not the synthetic result of a double negation, but the free expression of the forces that are produced in the self-suppression of the negation itself, the Nietzsche an overman, does not seem to be that or as Heidegger would want, just the fulfillment of the technical-metaphysical essence of man, but is rather his "active destructive" (Nietzsche, 1969 "Because I am a destiny," § 2). In the ambiguity that emerges from Nietzsche's critique of ascetic ideals it is therefore possible to discern the formulation of an ascetic economy of existence and a biological nature of asceticism from which an overman as "active destruction" of the human being may have its origin (Sloterdijk, 2009). This is a point of view that, while not losing some traces of opacity, may help to identify different possibilities even for the present day. At stake is an innovative liberation of that "purposiveness without purpose" from which the life of men and women is constitutively marked and which, today, is exactly what tends instead to be univocally neutralized in a universal enterprise as end in itself.

## Economic Mechanisms and Flows of Desire

An "avatar of the *ascetic ideal*" described by Nietzsche was expressly recognized in the context of psychoanalysis in the 1970s (Deleuze and Guattari, 1983:269). During that period, in which the analytic method had not yet been displaced by other less burdensome techniques, it held a near monopoly over the "care of the self." Therefore, reference to the "ascetic ideal" in the context of psychoanalysis meant not only attacking its position, but more than that, it meant stripping away its limit with the prevailing device of capitalist power. This attack arrived in the form of a ground-breaking book. In fact, after *Anti-Oedipus*, reference to collusion between psychoanalysis and capitalism (as per Benjamin back in 1921) became, to some extent, taken for granted. The connection identified here "is not merely ideological." Instead, psychoanalysis seems to depend "directly on an economic mechanism (hence its relations with money) through which the decoded flows of desire, as they are understood in the axiomatic of capitalism, must necessarily be reduced to a familial field, where this same axiomatic is applied: Oedipus as the last word of capitalist consumption" (Deleuze and Guattari, 1983:312). The implicit defense of capitalism in psychoanalysis, the fact that, as stated by Benjamin, it is essentially part of the "sacerdotal power of this cult," is condensed here in the Freudian theory of the Oedipus complex, to which psychoanalysis did no less than concede "a last territoriality, the couch, and a last Law, the analyst as despot and money collector" (Deleuze and Guattari, 1983:269). But the link to capitalism also comes from another equally significant connection: the one between psychoanalysis and political economy, as perceived by Foucault also (Deleuze and Guattari, 1983:302–304; Foucault, 2010a). The abstract subjective work, which is the discovery of political economy, coincides entirely with the abstract and subjective production of the libido on which psychoanalysis is based: "in short, the discovery of an activity of production in general and without distinction, as it appears in capitalism, is the identical discovery of both political economy and psychoanalysis, beyond the determinate systems of representation" (Deleuze and Guattari, 1983:302).

The important point to note here is that both are supposed to be organized "on the basis of a pre-existing need" (Deleuze and Guattari, 1983:28), a void to be developed and set in motion, in which "desire then becomes this abject fear of lacking something" (Deleuze and Guattari, 1983:27).

> The deliberate creation of lack as a function of market economy is the art of a dominant class. This involves deliberately organizing wants and needs (manqué) amid an abundance of production; making all of desire teeter and fall victim to the great fear of not having one's needs satisfied; and making the object dependent upon a real production that is supposedly exterior to desire (the demands of rationality), while at the same time the production of desire is categorized as fantasy and nothing but fantasy. (Deleuze and Guattari, 1983:28)

The abstraction of desire as a "familial" psychoanalytic tactic, "the reduction of sexuality to the *dirty little secret*," all its "priest's psychology" on guilt, are the basic elements that make psychoanalysis a "new avatar of the *ascetic ideal*" (Deleuze and Guattari, 1983:269). The psychoanalytical mechanism would not encounter obstacles, if the economic problem of desire were only "quantitative": it would mean strengthening the ego against the drives. But even Freud, perhaps too late, realized that the desiring-economy includes "qualitative" factors that obstruct treatment and whose importance he himself ultimately recognized, almost reproaching himself for not having valued them sufficiently (neither do they escape the attention of Deleuze and Guattari). It is a matter, therefore, of understanding what happened to the qualitative flows of the libido in light of the perpetually latent defeat of its quantitative economy; and most importantly, what happens once the pleasure principle no longer tends to be limited, but, in the abstract form of enjoyment, is elevated to a principle of social obligation.

## Sublimations

In 1928, the Norwegian theologian Kristian Schjelderup wrote *Die Askese*, published in Germany by Walter de Gruyter. The book is a psychoanalytical reading of the religious phenomenon of asceticism and, more generally, as the subtitle indicates, "a study of the psychology of religion," which not only positions itself in the debate between Catholic thought, the Pietist movement and Lutheran Protestant theology on the subject of asceticism, but also represents an attempt to compare, in Freudian terms, ascetic practice with neurosis. Contrary to the "praiseworthy" image of the Catholic Church and its attempt to legalize ascetic practice, and in contrast to the harsh criticism of asceticism instigated by Lutheran Protestantism, Schjelderup's book, starting with the problem of the unconscious raised by Freud, is centered on the need to question the genesis of ascetic practice. Ultimately, the psychological study conducted here seeks an answer to the question regarding the origin of the "need for asceticism present in man." In this context, Schjelderup not only reads Freud's discourse in the light of Nietzsche's criticism of the ascetic ideal, but more importantly distinguishes the pathological aspects identifiable in certain radical forms of asceticism, which can be traced back to neurotic behaviors and the problem of the way of life that underlies the phenomenon of asceticism.

The attempt to interpret asceticism as a reaction against the temptations of the flesh cannot, according to Schjelderup, disregard repression and sublimation, around which Freud built his theory of the unconscious. If, in Freudian terms, the repressed sexual drive is not eliminated, but continues to exist unconsciously, ascetic practice is still motivated by vital unconscious drives, which, through a process of sublimation, are directed and dynamically channeled once again. The "exoneration of the primary functions of impulse" and the "activation of new forces" (Schjelderup, 1928:159) are the two poles at work in the sublimation created by an ascetic life. In this manner, Schjelderup reaches the conclusion that "asceticism is not a denial of impulse, but an affirmation of the same"; in the sense that, it is at the same time a means to "satisfaction (Triebbefriedigung)" and an "achievement of desire (Wunscherfüllung)" (Schjelderup, 1928:98). This "positive" aspect of asceticism, which supposedly comes from an intimate cobelonging of religion and sexuality (Schjelderup, 1928:168), leads Schjelderup to identify in it a constitutive practice of human praxis.

In the second of the *Contributions to the Psychology of Love*, originally published in 1912, regarding the obstacles to the libido, which, apart from his natural resistances to fulfillment, man is supposed to have constructed over centuries of human history "to enjoy the joys of love," Freud himself admits, entirely in line with Schjelderup's reading, that,

The ascetic tendency of Christianity had the effect of raising the psychical value of love in a way that heathen antiquity could never achieve; it developed greatest significance in the lives of the ascetic monks, which were almost entirely occupied with the struggles against libidinous temptation. (Freud, 1997:57)

Even in Freudian discourse, monastic-ascetic life resembles a privileged situation for exercising and encoding desire, which, by nature, exists thanks to the obstacles it creates for itself, diverting and investing libidinous impulses in a sublimated manner. The process of sublimation that lies at the heart of ascetic praxis is, therefore, the issue a stake.

Considering the "long and difficult evolution the instinct goes through," as claimed by Freud, "the ultimate object selected is never the original one but only a surrogate for it;" some components of the original sexual impulse "cannot be carried on into its final form; some have to be suppressed or turned to other uses" (Freud, 1997:58). This other use for desire is the preferred fuel of sublimation, which, for Freud, is at the source of the process of civilization and which in many ways, appears in the same Freudian perspective, as a genuine alternative to repression. Indeed, one of the main aims of analytical therapy seems to consist in substituting sublimation for repression. On the other hand, the difficulty in finding complete satisfaction through sublimation, the fact that very few of us seem capable in this respect and the impossibility of completely sublimating the libido, create more than a few problems for Freudian theory.

According to Freud, "Sublimation is a process that concerns object-libido and consists in the instinct's directing itself towards an aim other than, and remote from, that of sexual satisfaction; in this process the accent falls upon deflection from sexuality" (Freud, 1961:94). Every sublimation includes a process of desexualization that cannot be generated by the sexual drive itself; a lethal component exists in the very life of the body, a principle of self-denial and denial of the body element, which, even though, according to Freud, originally part of the process of identifying and civilizing man, does not free itself from the guilt from which it originates, and makes drawing a clear distinction between neurosis and civilization so difficult.

Phylogenetically, an "archaic heritage" that can be traced back to the murder of "the father of primitive times," at the source of the Oedipus complex (Freud, 2010:33), led Freud to identify the history of humanity with the origins of "man's sense of guilt." From this point of view, it seems that the same already psychoanalyzed society must restore and cultivate an ever increasing sensitivity towards guilt and the original debt to which it is connected. "The repressed, the sinful imagination," as claimed by Benjamin in his fragment on capitalism, "is, at bottom, still an illuminating analogy to capital—to which the hell of the unconscious pays interest" (Benjamin, 2005:260). In *Civilization and Its Discontents* Freud writes,

> That which began in relation to the father ends in relation to the community. If civilization is an inevitable course of development from the group of the family to the group of humanity as a whole, then an intensification of the sense of guilt—resulting from the innate conflict of ambivalence, from the eternal struggle between the love and the death trends—will be inextricably bound up with it, until perhaps the sense of guilt may swell to a magnitude that individuals can hardly support. (Freud, 2010:34)

The disillusioned form of guilt without expiation proposed by Freud, finds its only outlet, according to his theory, in a "sane" conscious acknowledgement. However, in *Moses and Monotheism*, he recognizes the power of expiation present in the "delirious" version of the "good book" proposed by St Paul the Apostle. According to him, the obstacles that hinder complete recovery, a definitive release from guilt, led Freud to reflect (almost at the end of his life) on the difficulties involved in contemplating a "finished" analysis, leaving, among other things, more than a few doubts about psychoanalysis. His notable admissions on this subject seem, however, to open the discussion to different possibilities.

## The Economic Problem of Masochism

Of the three perspectives through which Freud studied psychical phenomena, the economic view was the most problematic. The premise underscoring psychoanalytical theory is that psychological life is the result of diverging and converging tensions that act dynamically in analogy with a physical field of forces. Alongside the "dynamic" perspective, Freud places the "topographical" aspect, which has a sort of completeness even though it has evolved from the spatial model of the psyche to the relational definition of the second topographical view of the 1920s. Even the energetic model, which is at the foundation of the economic perspective, was revised over the years, without, however, reaching a definitive theory. In one of his last works, *Analysis Terminable and Interminable*, Freud admits to having failed "to give the same importance to the economic as to the dynamic and topographical aspects of the case;" and he adds, "So my excuse must be that I am drawing attention to this omission" (Freud, 1937:382).

*Beyond the Pleasure Principle*, published in 1920, is the essay that ignited new thought in this area by presenting the problem in clearly philosophical terms. If the issue of the "principles" at stake, then we must consider, according to Freud, the meaning of a "beyond" that exceeds the pleasure principle itself. Functional disorders or transference phenomena, through which a wholly unpleasant event is obstinately reproduced, in fact, seem to contradict the economic principle of pleasure underlying all psychological phenomena, which are essentially concerned with defending and expanding the life of the psyche. The logic of self-preservation, with which the pleasure principle is concerned, ends up not being able to provide an account of all the components of the psyche. Therefore, for the first time in the essay, it became necessary to admit the existence of another principle, seemingly contrary to the first, of a destructive nature, which has its origins in the death drive and, as such, is essentially anti-economic for the psyche's self-sufficiency.

However, in this essay from 1920, the issue already appeared more complex in comparison to the way in which it had previously been understood and commonly represented in Freudian texts. Here we encounter the idea of a psychological economy that is not connected exclusively to self-sufficiency and, therefore, the fact that the death drives are not exclusively contrary in a dualistic manner to the life drives, which are motivated by the pleasure principle. In other words, for Freud, it seems that there is no exception to the pleasure principle; if anything there are singular complications that lead toward its different articulations. What complicates the dominion of the pleasure principle are the ways in which it is administered.

In this context, what is notable is the particular interest with which Freud, with increasing conviction, observes psychological phenomena from the economic point of view. The legal approach, mostly connected to the topographical configuration (according to which the psyche is spatially divided into overlapping regions, which culminate in the dominion of the Super-ego) is progressively supplemented by the economic view, which, in turn, undergoes changes that are significant for Freudian thought. According to Freud, the dynamic management of psychological phenomena is essentially based on the logic of costs and benefits, which is ultimately consistent with the legal structure of the topographical perspective.

In this respect, we can hypothesize a relationship between the Austrian school of thought on economics and the economic approach to psychological phenomena led by Freud, since, in a way, there are obvious analogies between the two. The idea of optimizing the practice underlying the economic theories of the main exponents of the Austrian school, who were working in Vienna during the period in which Freud was preparing his thoughts on psychoanalysis, was clearly supported by the economic aspect of Freud's theory, which sought to calculate the necessary dynamic expenditure that the psychical economy must endure to reach a sane balance of drives. However, optimization of psychical phenomena does not end with a linear calculation of costs and benefits.

If, as Freud suggested in his essay of 1920, there is a force that pushes toward a compulsion to repeat, throwing the self-preservation logic of the psychical apparatus into crisis, without, however, effectively opposing it in a complete manner, it seems necessary to turn to a more complex form of economic management. Apart from the pleasure principle, there is no other contrasting principle. Instead, a paralysis of this principle limits its total dominion over psychical life. Therefore, not only for Freud is the ego no longer master in its own home; but more importantly (contrary to an economic perspective concerned with a linear optimization of results, entirely consistent, in this sense, with Darwinian evolutionary theory, which was also important to Freudian discourse) self-preservation no longer appears, in this context, as the sole objective pursued by man. It must therefore be understood in terms of the overwhelming compulsion to repeat, seemingly contrary to self-sufficiency, as an enactment of the death drive, pain itself becomes the objective of a drive to be pursued and, as such, retains its predominantly economic function, which connects it fundamentally to pleasure. These are the foundations from which "the economic problem of masochism" arises and to which Freud turned his attention in his essay of the same name written in 1924, which is particularly relevant in this respect.

Here masochism seems not to be a mere anti-economic phenomenon, as would be the case if it only followed the logic of self-preservation; but neither is it presented, in terms of a developing economic view, as an internalized form of sadism, an evolutionarily selected method of internalizing the violence instinctively directed toward the outside, which is concerned with the struggle to survive. On the contrary, Freud himself later refuted his previous analysis of sadomasochism.

In this work, "the existence of a masochistic trend in the instinctual life of human beings may justly be described as mysterious from the economic point of view" (Freud 1961:159). It is not, therefore, a phenomenon that is completely incomprehensible in economic terms, as it would be in relation to absolute dominion over the pleasure principle; but an economic enigma, since it benefits from the same disadvantaged position, with the profit being self-generated and not simply derived from paying a price to obtain it.

The premise on which this is built is that "pleasure and displeasure, [. . .] cannot be referred to an increase or decrease of a quantity"; that is, they do not depend on a "quantitative factor" but on some characteristic of it which we can only describe as a "qualitative one" (Freud, 1961:160). Here Freud touches on a crucial point, but quickly brings the matter to an end with what is almost an admission of failure: "If we were able to say what this qualitative characteristic is, we should be much further advanced in psychology" (Freud, 1961:160). However, one thing remains clear: his previous economic view of psychical phenomena undergoes a radical mutation at this point; a quantitative approach aimed at demonstrating the investments and divestments of the libido is now taken over by a new economic perspective, which, although obviously unclear, nevertheless seems to open up a perspective filled with consequences.

The death drive does not oppose the pleasure principle and the changes that this undergoes through the reality principle. "None of these three principles is actually put out of action by another" (Freud, 1961:161). The pleasure principle remains the "watchman" over psychical life, but without being able to completely dominate all its phenomena, because it is repeatedly paralyzed, "narcotized" within itself. Beyond the pleasure principle there is no topographical afterlife, situated in another place or attributable to a different principle. Instead, the death drive is within the pleasure principle itself, that is, there is no this side and that side, the death drive leads us not beyond the pleasure principle, but digs into it (Derrida, 2005), thereby making it possible to halt the automatic functioning of that guarantor of psychical life.

The idea of a "primary masochism" that we encounter in this book, but which had already been discussed elsewhere, and which refutes the previous Freudian analysis of sadomasochism, supports this view. The "moral masochism" that it derives calls into question the issues raised by the phenomenon of sublimation, which is, as we have seen, also at the heart of ascetic practice. At stake is the process of desexualization connected to the subject's constitution and to the very development of human culture (Brown, 1959). But here Freud claims that, "Conscience and morality have arisen through the overcoming, the de-sexualization, of the Oedipus complex," "through moral masochism morality becomes sexualized once more" (Freud, 1961:169). Hence, we see the possibility of a libidinous investment in the very sacrifice of drives; the sacrifice becomes a new and paradoxical drive objective in which, as Jacques Lacan would say, an increase in "enjoyment" originates (Recalcati, 2010:68–69, 291–303; Moroncini and Petrillo, 2007). The repression of drives, on which civilization is founded, therefore leads to "an intensification of masochism." On the one hand, "its danger lies in the fact that it originates from the death instinct" (Freud, 1961:170). Since, however, "we never have to deal with pure life instincts or pure death instincts but only with mixtures of them in different amounts" (Freud, 1961:164), moral masochism, as a "classical piece of evidence for the existence of fusion of instinct"( Freud, 1961:170), it holds an "erotic component" originally present, in man, in his capacity for self-destruction not only as an opposite choice to the positively constructive choice of pleasure, but to this originally concomitant one.

This component, beyond its mortiferous implications that are evident in civilization's current forms of discontent (no longer tied to renunciation of drives, but to the elevation of enjoyment to a position of social obligation) seems as though it could even merge into that form of "destructive activity" discussed by Nietzsche: not only the ability to stay alive continuously depriving ourselves in an evolutionary process; and not only the drive toward death in life, as per the current economic forms of power; but above all the possibility inherent in humanity of constantly re-creating ourselves starting with the destructive capacity that seems to be within us. In this context of negativity, not only is an absence of life at stake, but rather what exceeds it as a simple capacity for self-preservation. Perhaps it is from this point, in Freud's theory, that the possibility originates of suspending the unilateral form of dominion that is the foundation for constructing a merely self-preserving process (for which even he continued to argue throughout his work). However, the possible implications of such a view remain unclear, if they are confined within Freudian discourse.

## Primary Masochism

In 1967 Deleuze wrote *Coldness and Cruelty*, in praise of Leopold von Sacher-Masoch, motivated by the belief that the latter's work had been treated unfairly. "Not because his name was unfairly given to the perversion of masochism, but quite the reverse, because his work fell into neglect whereas his name passed into current usage" (Deleuze, 1971:13). While "Sade is becoming more thoroughly known; clinical studies of sadism are considerably enriched by literary studies of the work of Sade, and vice versa. Even the best writings on Masoch, however, show a surprising ignorance of his work." Also unjust, according to Deleuze, is above all "that in clinical terms he is considered complementary to Sade. [. . .] The theme of the unity of sadism and masochism and the concept of a sadomasochistic entity have done great harm to Masoch. He has suffered not only from unjust neglect but also from an unfair assumption of complementarity and dialectical unity with Sade" (Deleuze, 1971:13).

For Deleuze, the world of Masoch is entirely different from that of Sade. "Their techniques differ, and their problems, their concerns and their intentions are entirely dissimilar" (Deleuze, 1971:13). Despite the complexity of Freud's position on this subject (on which the Deleuzian reading of Masoch is based), the fact that psychoanalysis "has long shown the possibility and the reality of transformations between sadism and masochism" (ibid.), speaks volumes about his project: it is the very unity of what has been named sadomasochism that is at issue here and not the characteristics of the two different behaviors. Deleuze claimed that, "Sado-masochism is one of these misbegotten names, a semiological howler" (Deleuze, 1971:134). Restoring the distinction is therefore essential, in his view, in order to better define the peculiarities of the two projects.

On the basis of the clinical experience available to date, it is difficult to
analyze masochism in its "literary" uniqueness, as Deleuze often tends to
do in his presentation of Masoch. Nevertheless, the striking aspect of his
argument is the need to identify what characterizes the project underlying
masochistic practice. According to Deleuze, masochism has "a particular
way of 'desexualizing' love and at the same time sexualizing the entire history of humanity" (Deleuze, 1971:12). Essentially, this is what he was trying to demonstrate.

What is particularly important for our argument is that, in his
"Freudian" reading of Masoch, Deleuze aims to identify the uniqueness
of masochism by setting out the paradox that arises from Freud's theory.
According to Freud's analysis, it is not the renunciation of drives that
results from moral conscience, but moral conscience that, in contrast, is a
product of renunciation, on the basis of that particular relationship with
the "law," which makes it fundamentally impossible to carry out its principles, to the extent that one is initially guilty in terms of the law, and
then more guilty the more rigidly one adheres to it. According to Deleuze,
"while the sadian hero subverts the law, the masochist should not by contrast be regarded as gladly submitting to it. [. . .] He simply attacks the law
on another flank" (Deleuze, 1971:87–88). In masochistic practice it is,
"By scrupulously applying the law we are able to demonstrate its absurdity
and provoke the very disorder that it is intended to prevent or to conjure.
By observing the very letter of the law, we refrain from questioning its
ultimate or primary character; we then behave as if the supreme sovereignty of the law conferred upon it the enjoyment of all those pleasures
that it denies us; The masochist regards the law as a punitive process and
therefore begins by having the punishment inflicted upon himself; once
he has undergone the punishment, he feels that he is allowed or indeed
commanded to experience the pleasure that the law was supposed to for-
bid" (Deleuze, 1971:88). If "the law increases the guilt of the person who
submits to it, the masochist [. . .] he stands guilt on its head by making
punishment into a condition that makes possible the forbidden pleasure"
(Deleuze, 1971:89).

In this context, what Freud defined as the "economic problem" coincides with the same masochistic way of engaging with the law: at stake
is the capacity to find benefit in an inherently unfavorable situation. It
could be argued that this is no coincidence, since even what we would
have grounds for considering as the first masochistic experience in relation

to the law was defined, by St. Paul the Apostle, in economic terms. The currently prevailing "capitalist's discourse" is nothing but a radical expression of this experience; but in a completely lethal form, since it is capable of neutralizing every innovative aspect, even those intrinsic to masochism as a human way of life. Of great interest in this context is the work of the Canadian artist Rodney Graham inspired by Freud's essay on masochism, for which he suggests an entirely "economic" reading.[3]

*Chapter 7*

# The Spirit of Capitalism and Forms of Life

The best-known analysis of the masochistic practice of asceticism as the propelling engine of the capitalist economy is offered by Weber, who has been the red thread of our discussion. The most convincing category of Weber's production, in this regard, is undoubtedly the "spirit of capitalism." Despite the numerous criticisms that have been leveled against it, it continues to inspire fresh attempts to interpret the present that do not limit themselves to a purely descriptive investigation. For instance, Luc Boltanski and Eve Chiappello saw in Weber's thesis a key to interpret the so-called managerial ethics that has become common in the last decades of the last century and is still prevalent in contemporary capitalist modes of production (Boltanski and Chiappello, 2005; Donaggio, 2009).

However, despite various attempts at updating it, Weber's theory still causes suspicions even within the *Weberforschung*, which is mostly of interest to historians of religion, and its development is certainly absent from economic discourse. With the boom of the Asian tigers first, and China and India second, the link between Protestantism and the spirit of capitalism appears feebler; it suffers from a Eurocentrism that is hardly reconcilable with the logic of globalization (Goody, 2004). To conclude our discussion, I explain, more analytically than I have so far, both the limits and the present relevance of Weber's position.

The expression "spirit of capitalism" was coined by Werner Sombart in 1902 in his book *Modern Capitalism*. Weber recovers and changes the meaning of the expression, using it to indicate a constellation of motivations and expectations of meaning that social actors are driven to adopt when selecting a conduct that can "electively" be integrated within the capitalist modes of production. The mechanism behind the "spirit" of capitalism leads to a revolutionary overall reshaping of the satisfaction of human needs, favoring and definitively imposing the free establishment of conducts that, while seeming to enjoy full autonomy, are actually moved by self-referential instances of valorization of capital. In Foucault's terms, one might say that the "spirit" of capitalism emerges out of the intersection between governmental drives and biographical needs, between forms of power and techniques of life. It is the source of the motivation that feeds the anonymous and often dissimulated and masked coaction of power; constantly suspended between self-realization and submission, freedom and constraint. Ultimately, it innervates capitalism as a form of life.

## Religion and the Economy: More than a Mere "Reflection"

The problematic nexus between asceticism and capitalist forms of production that Weber first presented in his 1905 essay (Weber, 2001) immediately found a following, stimulating considerable debate. Weber identifies the origin of the "spirit" of capitalism with the ascetic ethics of Calvinism. This was a highly original thesis for the discussion on the nature, genesis, and specific characters of the capitalist economy that was unfolding in Germany at the beginning of the 1900s. His position is definitely different from that of, for instance, Sombart in *Modern Capitalism* (1902) and *The Jews and Modern Capitalism* (1912), and that of Lujo Brentano in *The Origin of Modern Capitalism* (1916). Weber was not concerned with identifying the origin of modern capitalism starting from its inner workings, thus, unlike Brentano who instead identifies capitalism with the monetary economy, Weber did not search for its premises in medieval Europe. In this respect, Weber is closer to Sombart, who rejects the thesis that sees in the medieval merchant a precursor of the modern capitalist entrepreneur. However, Weber differs from Sombart in his assessment of the role of the Jewish people in the formation of modern capitalism: the historical premise of the capitalist spirit is not to be sought in the Jews, but in Calvinism, which seeks in the "world" and in economic activity the "signs" of grace. Hence, Weber establishes a peculiar relationship between this religious form and the economic mentality of capitalism, which is "unique" precisely because of the particular rationality that is borne out of the capitalist economy whereby accumulation becomes an end in itself.

Immediately after its first publication, Weber's thesis gave rise to a heated polemic on the journal *Archiv fur Sozialwissenschaft und Sozialpolitik* between 1907 and 1910. First Hans Karl Fischer and subsequently Felix Rachfahl harshly critiqued Weber's interpretation, contesting the relation he instituted between these two planes. The historiographical debate on the relationship between Protestantism and capitalism, religion and the economy became rather lively during the 1930s thanks to the contributions of Richard Henry Tawney, Hugh M. Robertson, and Talcott Parson, and even more heated in 1957 when Kurt Samuelsson published his critical work. The debate continues in the present (Schluchter and Graf, 2005; Böhl, 2007).

Weber's position on the responses to his thesis is collected in the so-called *Antikritiken*: four replies to Fischer and Rachfahl published in the *Archiv fur Sozialwissenschaft und Sozialpolitik* (Weber, 2002:231–321). There he reviews the "idealist" or "spiritualist" interpretation of history attributed to him, whereby he was meant to have simply "derived" capitalism from Luther and Calvin. He also shows no hesitation in critiquing the materialist view of history and the distinction between "structure" and "superstructure," opposing the privileging of one aspect of the historical process—the economic structure—and the attribution of a phenomenon like religion to the superstructure. In fact, his inquiry on the origin of the spirit of capitalism moved in the opposite direction, trying, in some ways, to demonstrate the dependency of a particular economic development on religious motives. Hence, his insistence on the religious origin of economic ethics is affirmed without excluding the possibility of an economic conditioning of religious action itself. What Weber denies is, rather, the notion that there is a simple "reflection" of economic situations, and he is also critical of simplistically spiritualist views of history.

As Karl Löwith writes,

> the so-called spirit of capitalism is understood by Weber neither in the vulgar Marxist sense as a merely ideological spirit of capitalist relations of production, nor as an autonomous and primordial religious spirit which is quite independent of capitalism; instead, the spirit of capitalism exists for him only in so far as there is a general tendency towards a rational conduct of life, borne along by the bourgeois stratum of society, which establishes an elective affinity between the capitalist economy on one side and the Protestant ethic on the other. (Löwith, 1993:121)

The fact that subsequently Weber would bolster his critique of economic materialism and assume a more markedly anti-Marxist position should not lead us to jump to the wrong conclusions. This is the same Weber who warns us of such misunderstanding when claiming that he does not at all intend to defend a thesis whereby capitalism, as an "economic system," is the outcome or "result" of the Reformation. In fact, in *The Protestant Ethic and the Spirit of Capitalism*, he claims:

> It is, of course, not my aim to substitute for a one-sided materialistic an equally one-sided spiritualistic causal interpretation of culture and of history. *Each* is *equally possible*, but each, if it does not serve as the preparation, but as the conclusion of an investigation, accomplishes equally little in the interest of historical truth. (Weber, 2001:125)

The debate on Weber's thesis was primarily based on a presupposed and simplistic distinction between "economic structure" and "ideological superstructure," moved by the reductive opposition between a "materialist" and a "spiritualist" interpretation of history. Because of this, an aspect of Weber's argument that for us is of most interest has remained in the shadows. In our view, at stake for our understanding of Weber's position, is the nexus he establishes between this-worldly asceticism and the rationality of modern capitalism.

## Ascesis and Dilation

Previous investigations of the nexus Weber identifies between asceticism and capitalist forms of production have concluded that in his view the economic process of the accumulation of capital is founded on the ascetic ability to defer. Thus Weber seems to suggest that whoever is able to delay the satisfaction of their needs and accumulates wealth in order to invest it and produce greater wealth exercises power over those who do not carry out such displacement. The deferrer manages to articulate the vital connection between need, demand and consumption in a relation of domination based on his ability to defer in view of a goal: accumulation. Profit is, then, the goal of ascetic life.

According to Weber, this action results from the selection of a goal to which one attributes value in itself, so it is not a simple goal-instrumental action (*zweckrational*), but a particular value-oriented action (*wertrational*). Profit is thus assumed as a value in itself independently of the satisfaction it can procure. Understood in this way, as something that does not refer to an outside finality, according to Weber, profit "is thought of so purely as an end in itself, that from the point of view of the happiness of, or utility to, the single individual, it appears entirely transcendental and absolutely irrational" (Weber, 2001:18). The irrationality of the accumulation of profit as an end in itself, as the basic justification of rational action proper to professional work, is such that man, Weber writes, is "dominated by the making of money, by acquisition as the ultimate purpose of his life. Economic acquisition is no longer subordinated to man as the means for the satisfaction of his material needs" (Weber, 2001:18).

In reply to Lujo Brentano's criticism, who claims that the discipline of ascesis is nothing but a form of "rationalization" toward an "irrational mode of life," Weber claims: "If this essay makes any contribution at all, may it be to bring out the complexity of the only superficially simple concept of the rational" (Weber, 2001:140). The means becomes autonomous and turns into an end in itself, losing what seemed to be its initial meaning and original purpose, that is, a rationality aimed at the satisfaction of man's needs. In this, Weber sees an irrationality that characterizes the whole of modern civilization. Its institutions and organizations are so rationalized that they lock the man who inhabits them in an "iron cage." The form of life that gives rise to these institutions must now conform to them unreservedly.

This is the problem of civilization: rationalization that turns into irrationality (Rossi, 2007:115–232), a view Weber also shared with Marx, Freud, and Nietzsche. Weber's argument, however, is not a rejection; he does not regard the process of rationalization as something "inhumane," as Marx did in some ways, as a "neurosis" in Freudian terms or as a "deadly disease" as in Nietzsche. Neither does he endorse it as if it was a stage of human progress. Weber's position is much more complex, and perhaps more ambiguous: on the one hand, he looks for freedom inside the "iron cage," though a mere inner freedom; on the other hand, he is rather accepting of what he sees as "destiny" (Taubes, 1984).

Economic rationality understands profit as an end in itself and ends up turning into a fatal irrationality because of its contradiction. On the one hand, it separates away from the purposiveness without purpose that characterizes human action and identifies profit as an end in itself, something that must be pursued in the abstract, without goals extrinsic to the very process of accumulation. On the other hand, economic rationality does not withdraw from the theological logic that has characterized the rational action of the Western ethos since its origins. This is the neuralgic core of the ambiguity of Weber's argument, one that Marx, Freud, and Nietzsche also share.

## Rational Action and Its Goals

For Weber, on the one hand rational action is developed in the relationship between means and ends; on the other hand, it identifies an end in itself for action. This places his argument in the classical tradition on praxis that starts with Aristotle, who was the first to offer an imprint for this logic. We have already seen how, in the *Ethics*, Aristotle distinguished between technical-productive activity (*poíesis*), which has as its goal a product separate from the activity that produces it, and real action (*práxis*), whose end is inherent to itself. For Aristotle, the full circularity of action that contains both its end and its principle is a fundamental characteristic of human agency and differentiates praxis from the mere productive activity that finds its realization in ends extrinsic to it. Despite the clarity of Aristotle's differentiation between poíesis and praxis, which in some ways corresponds to Weber's distinction between goal-instrumental (*zweckrational*) and value-oriented action (*wertrational*), the difference between these two is much less linear than it appears at first sight. The meaning of an action and its product are not so easily separable in Aristotle, so much so that he uses the word *télos* (goal, end) for both. We find the same in Weber, when he ends up identifying the rational action that conceives of profit as an end in itself with practical rationality as a whole. Moreover, when it comes to profit, the auto-finality of praxis seems to fit into a teleological framework. This framework characterizes, from Aristotle, the thinking of action in the west, even in Christianity (when the "divine economy" becomes driven by a search for salvation in the afterlife). This is the path on which one can inscribe Weber's theory of economic rationality.

Jürgen Habermas is correct in describing Weber's concept of rational action as teleological (Habermas, 1985), but this is not simply due to Weber's privileging goal-instrumental over value-oriented action (Löwith,

1993). On the contrary, practical rationality, as a whole, is configured in teleological terms the moment economic rationality becomes its main form of expression. This is because it is capable of identifying profit as a separate end in itself toward which human action can be methodically directed. It is precisely at this point, at the apex of what since Aristotle had been regarded as Western practical rationality, that Weber sees a side to human action that is irremediably irrational.

Weber's analysis not only points to the false alternative between means and ends that paralyzed Western *ethos*; it also highlights the neutralization of aimless finalities inherent to human action that has been perpetrated until this fatal turn to the irrationality characteristic of capitalism and modernity in general. If an end without means seems as alienating as a means that only acquires meaning in relation to an end, it is now time to turn to Weber's view of asceticism as a methodical and rational conduct of life that lies at the foundation of the process of rationalization accomplished by capitalism.

## Asceticism and Methodical Existence

Important to our understanding of the teleological orientation underscoring the auto-finality of profit that characterizes economic rationality is the fact that, according to Weber, worldly asceticism is the condition of emergence of capitalist forms of production, but it cannot be exclusively reduced to a sacrificial practice of deferment of desire. Such practice has, in various interpretations of Weber's thesis, been associated with being functional to the achievement of profit as an end in itself. However, the deferral of immediate gratification teleologically oriented to the accumulation of capital as an extrinsic goal does neither comprehends nor exhausts the meaning of the methodical control over existence that, for Weber, lies at the very heart of Protestant ascetic practice as a presupposition of economic action in modern capitalism.

One of the most recent interpretations in this direction is that of Richard Sennett, who believes that Weber's theory is no longer relevant to our times. Sennett claims that in view of the current logic of work flexibility, it seems that Weber's paradigm of delayed gratification in the pursuit of long term goals is no longer relevant. Sennett believes that this is the hidden core of the "iron cage" in which men let themselves be locked up, reassured by the rigidity of the institutions and the recompense of a future promise. In his *The Culture of New Capitalism*, Sennett writes:

> The time-engine driving the Protestant Ethic is delayed gratifica-
> tion in the present for the sake of long-term goals. This time-engine
> Weber believed to be the secret of the iron cage, people immuring
> themselves within fixed institutions because they hoped finally to
> empower themselves in a future reward. Delayed gratification makes
> possible self-discipline; you steel yourself to work, unhappily or not,
> because you are focused on that future reward. (Sennett, 2006:77)

Despite Sennett's customary lucidity in dealing with the main aspects of the new forms of capitalist production, on this point, his argument does not seem to grasp the problem of Weber's framework, thus casting a shadow on the rest of his interpretation. In Weber, what makes "self-discipline" possible is not deferred gratification, quite the opposite. If anything, the condition of possibility for deferral is the methodical control over existence typical of ascetic practice. The current relevance of Weber's argument is rooted in this fact, that even though in a period so-called post-Fordism the iron cage has broken, a mode of self-discipline is still functional to the contemporary globalized form of economic power. Within this framework, I intend to investigate the meaning that Weber ascribes to worldly asceticism.

As some have underlined, Weber basically sees ascetic practice as a conduct of life (*Lebensführung*) (Schluchter, 1988). Then the question is to understand how asceticism, as a mode of life, triggers a mechanism that is both coercive and free, totalizing and individuating, and decisive for the genesis of power that turns the accumulation of capital into a goal to be pursued for its own sake.

## Power or Domination?

The centrality of the notion of power in Weber's political theory is not only an expression of the lucidity with which he prematurely identified the signs of the crisis of the modern state, which he only sees as a particular and historically conditioned form of Western power; it also more broadly allows for a definition of the political form of modernity. In Weber's theory, power is not reduced to the realm of domination (*Herrschaft*), but, as power (*Macht*), it is basically a relation of forces that is not simply reducible to the juridical state form of command and obedience. For power to function and be a relation of forces, it needs to be *legitimate*. Its legitimation is not secured principally by means of the law; nor does it derive from the domination and external control to which one subjects oneself; rather, it assumes the capillary form of self-domination and self-control. It is crucial to understand the meaning of this "interiorization" of command as its mode of individualization (Lemke, 2007:23–29). Undoubtedly, for Weber the assumption of legitimacy advanced by every form of power requires a recognition that constitutes its "inner" dimension, so to speak. However, for Weber, legitimacy is not resolved in this: the main operator of the legitimation of power is not "recognition," it is "faith": it is not a case of recognizing, once and for all, something previously existing, it is a case of continuously producing its validity. In this sense, radicalizing Weber's theory, one might say that the consensus of democratic power and the global market, however spectacular it has become in our day, is not only founded on the acclaim of an external public, but constantly produced within each individual's life conduct. The paradigm of this form of legitimation of power is the Protestant faith and this worldly asceticism connected to it (Weber, 2002), not only as a matrix of the self-discipline functional to the genesis of capitalism, but also and above all as a privileged form of life that shares an elective affinity with it.

Karl Löwith is right, then, when he writes:

> The form taken by the economy is not a direct consequence of a particular faith, nor is this faith an "emanatistic" consequence of a "substantive" economy. Rather, both are shaped "rationally" on the basis of a general rationality in the conduct of life. In its primarily economic significance, capitalism per se cannot be regarded as the independent origin of rationality. Rather, a rational way of life—originally motivated by religion—let capitalism in the economic sense grow into a dominant force of life. (Löwith, 1993:63–64)

In Weber's perspective, this implies that had a tendency to some forms of practical rational conduct in life been absent, the development of the rational economic conduct proper to capitalism would not have occurred.

Hence, the peculiarity, or "uniqueness," of modern capitalism: the form of rationalization of modernity (Schluchter, 1988; Schiera, 1999:81–94).

## Capitalism and Secularization

In the section *Economy and Society* on religious communities, Weber traces a "genesis of religions" and claims that any action motivated by religious factors is addressed to *this world*. Almost as if to explain what he means by "economic ethics of religion" (*Wirtschaftethik der Weltreligionen*), he adds that one should not separate "religious action or thought from the sphere of daily goal-oriented action, especially given that its goals are prevalently economic" (Weber, 1978:49). It seems that the origin of religion is to be sought in the economic search for the conditions of possibility that guarantee human existence. However, in order for survival to coincide with the form that life takes on, and in order for this to be such, it is necessary to have a meaning that orients its development, and this meaning is religion, which for Weber has an economic ethos that needs investigating.

These are the premises on which he understands the relationship between economy and religion as a decisive aspect of the relationship between religion and the world. This relationship is fundamental to all world religions and characterized, following his ideal type schema, by a radical antithesis between "adaptation" to and "rejection" of the world. Only in the case of a religion that does not aim to adapt itself to the status quo and its rules, but that rejects it instead, severing all links to the world, is it possible to speak of "religion of salvation," as is the case, for instance, with Judaism and Christianity. The point for Weber is that the tension implicit to the attitude of "rejection of the world" proper to religions of salvation is not limited to a devaluation of human action: it also creates the conditions for its possible potentiation. In fact, Weber claims that the rejection of the world is indissolubly linked, as its other side, to the desire to dominate the world (Weber, 2002).

According to Weber, the search for an ethical "remuneration" in the rationalizing form of theodicy is typical of religions of salvation (Accarino, 2005). But thanks to a decisive turn during the Reformation, it became possible to separate various spheres of life from the subordination to a redemptive compensation, without reducing, in fact reinforcing the fundamentally economic shape of religious existence. Crucial in this development and thus to the genesis of the capitalist economy was the concept of the "state of grace" proper of Protestant religions, especially in their Calvinist version.

In Weber's interpretation of Protestantism, the "state of grace" is a peculiar condition where man is free from the damnation of creation, from the "world"; its possession cannot be guaranteed by "magical sacraments," by "individual good works," but only with "*proof* in a specific type of conduct unmistakably different from the way of life of the natural man" (Weber, 2001:100). Here Weber introduces inner-worldly asceticism: "this ascetic conduct meant a *rational* planning of the whole of one's life in accordance with God's will" (Weber, 2001:100), not a concentration on the redemptive actions willed by God. The rationalization of the world is carried out despite, or because of an ascetic rejection of the world. The rational domination of the world becomes possible because for Calvinist asceticism the rejection of the world is not dependent on an escape from it, but on an action that is disconnected from ends extrinsic to it. In this perspective, if the meritorious aspects of human action that could lead to salvation becomes secondary, and human conduct becomes proof of an elective state, then its success coincides with man's ability to rationally dominate the world, which is a sign of divine grace in itself.

The rational domination of the world becomes directly proportional to the success of a methodical rationality of life. Self-control, characteristic of Calvinist ascetic ethics, allows for the production "in the individual of the most completely conscious, willful, and anti-instinctual control over one's own physical and psychological processes, and insuring the systematic regulation of life in subordination to the religious end" (Weber, 1993:203). The repression of the mean desire for profit and the related notion that economic success is proof of divine grace are aspects of inner-worldly asceticism. Weber believes that these do not obstacle economic development, in fact they unintentionally help it, thus constituting the indispensable precursor for "methodical bourgeois life." Above all, they demonstrate that the "acquisitive drive," the attribution of high and exclusive value to wealth, and utilitarian "rationalism" have in themselves very little to do with modern capitalism at this point (Weber, 1993).

Weber recognizes the connection between the life conduct of Protestant asceticism and the medieval monastic asceticism that we examined earlier. However, he claims that due to the rationalization carried out by Protestantism, the ascetic conduct no longer lived outside the world in monastic communities, but *within* the world and its institutions; now it strode into the market-place of life, slammed the door of the monastery behind it, and undertook to penetrate just that *daily* routine of life with its method-icalness, to fashion it into a life *in* the world, but *neither of nor for* this world. (Weber, 2001:100–101)

This is the reason the Protestant drive to the methodical control of the state of grace reveals its peculiarity when compared with previous forms of asceticism; what turns the ascetic conformation of existence into an actual matter of "calculation."

The watchful self-control of the Puritan referred to something positive, to an action informed in a determinate manner, and to something interior, the systematic domination of one's own inner nature, which is deemed cor-rupt by sin. The Pietist effectively made an inventory of the soul, as a matter of accounting, similarly, Weber claims, to Benjamin Franklin's daily practice.

The accounting of existence implicit in the methodical control of inner-worldly asceticism allows for the "sanctification of life" to assume the character of a commercial enterprise.

Aside from the formulation of a historically critical assessment of Weber's thesis, most of all I wish to point out that through his analysis of Protestant inner-worldly asceticism, Weber points to the emergence of the figure of the entrepreneur who must first be a self-entrepreneur in order to look after his enterprise methodically. Weber's thesis on the "spirit" of modern capitalism seems to be at the foundation of the notion of capitalist enterprise as a form of accumulation of that peculiar form of capital that is "human capital," which we mentioned at the beginning of this chapter (Boltanski and Chiappello, 2005; Bröckling, 2007).

But in Weber's argument, this shift also allows for a "rational-formal" orientation of the modern capitalist enterprise based on the calculation of capital and the relative profit that is continuously pursued systematically as an end in itself, with no other end. Although the Protestant religion, in its most extreme forms be it Calvinism or Puritanism, has made the process of "disenchantment" at the basis of modern rationality possible, starting from Weber's theory it is difficult to see a mere "religiously con-ditioned formation" in capitalism, rather than, as Benjamin claims in the fragment analyzed earlier, an "essentially religious phenomenon." The sec-ular translation of inner-worldly ascetic conduct, in some ways, allows for a separation of the rationality of praxis from the extrinsic finality of a transcendental ethical remuneration, which used to be connected to "religions of salvation" such as Christianity. The modern world thus becomes the privileged realm of realization for formal rationality, the ability to preventively calculate the means needed for the achievement of a determined goal, and to assess the consequences implicit in its realization; finally, the fact that "there are no mysterious incalculable forces that come into play, but rather that one can, in principle, *master all things by calculation*" (Weber, 1946:131). The planned exclusion of what is deemed "irrational" and the referral of conduct to its self-referentiality leaves modern man to himself, alone in dealing with the intrinsic auto-finality that characterizes capitalist accumulation, the apex of the process of rationalization but also the expression of renewed forms of irrationality. The process of "secularization" that characterizes modernity according to Weber in fact leaves the (religious) mechanism from which it sought to emancipate itself somewhat untouched.

The fact that economic action is separated from the extrinsic finality of transcendent remuneration on which the Christian worldview depends, and entrusted in the secularized perspective to a formal rationality univocally aimed at the calculation of the necessary means for the achievement of definitively determined ends that are immanent, does not free praxis from the self-referentiality that essentially characterizes it. The planned exclusion of transcendent finality and this resulting immanent orientation allow for the emergence of an auto-finality that characterizes human action and that in capitalism assumes the "irrational" form of the enterprise as an end in itself. In both cases, profit and the ability to invest are connected to something that is an end in itself rather than relating to an extrinsic goal. Like in religion, in the capitalist economy power as an end in itself, separated from human beings but intrinsic to their praxis, is the most effective tool for constraining their action.

Though seemingly distant from the inner-worldly asceticism Weber described, the extreme forms of enjoyment and consumption currently prevailing are still the expression of a "method of existence" that shows elective affinities with the development of capitalism. Unproductive consumption is now the ultimate goal of production: it is not satisfied with anything other than itself, it is not geared towards the satisfaction of needs, nor is it interested in deferring gratification in view of a greater profit. Instead, it presupposes a sort of constant exercise able to nurture a form of enjoyment for enjoyment's sake. This is a technique that allows desire to be ever more flexible, malleable, and, above all, functional to the power on which it is based.

The detachment from the world experienced by most "professional" managers ascetically dedicated to the vocation of financial gain is the contemporary version of inner-worldly asceticism. But the "spirit" of capitalism in our days is embodied in the living bodies of the human material required to work with increasing flexibility precisely starting from the flexibility that characterizes their lives. Through a slow and subtle training these lives change and take on the semblance of capital, transposing their whole existence in its "purchasing power," including their desires and modes of being (Sloterdijk, 2009).

## Self-Discipline and Power

Weber refers the methodical technique of life, as a reasoned calculation of existence, to an ideal type of power as a process of rationalization whose goal is profit, an abstract end in itself capable of neutralizing the potentialities inherent in human life and thus to orient it towards an irreversible movement. The methodical conduct of life seems such only if aimed at a rational conduct, whose end is a self-control that is functional to the form of domination that programmatically tends to exclude any irrationality. Weber writes:

> Inner-worldly ascetic is a rationalist, not only in the sense that he rationally systematizes his own conduct of life, but also in his rejection of everything that is ethically irrational, whether aesthetic, or personal emotional reactions within the world and its orders. The distinctive goal always remains the "conscious," methodical mastering of one's own conduct of life. (Weber, 1993:223)

But the methodical conduct of life aimed at the programmatic rejection of every element of irrationality, which Weber believes to lay the foundations of the capitalist process of accumulation, fails to explain the capsizing into irrationality that characterizes capitalism and modernity in general. Hence, following Weber's thesis, derive the perplexities in identifying modernity with a univocal process of rationalization; suffice it to mention, here, the debate of the Frankfurt School. Similarly, the current preferential use of the term "globalization" to identify what has happened following the expansion of the market on a world scale, which can hardly be interpreted as the development of an exclusively rational regime. The problem is the antinomy Weber sees in "rationality" and "irrationality," because whether rationalization is regarded as an evolutionary process or a degenerative one, it presupposes the absolute value of "reason," which seems inadequate for an analysis of the present.

All of Foucault's work on this issue has opened up the scope for further investigations that are still to be carried out. During a roundtable discussion in 1978, in one of his rare references to Weber, Foucault tries to confront his research with Weber's notion of rationality, and says:

> If one calls "Weberian" those who set out to take on board the Marxist analyses of the contradictions of capital, treating these contradictions as part and parcel of the irrational rationality of capitalist society, then I don't think I am a Weberian, since my basic preoccupation isn't rationality considered as an anthropological invariant. I don't believe one can speak of an intrinsic notion of "rationalization" without on the one hand positing an absolute value inherent in reason, and on the other taking the risk of applying the term empirically in a completely arbitrary way. I think one must restrict one's use of this word to an instrumental and relative meaning. The ceremony of public torture isn't in itself more irrational than imprisonment in a cell; but it's irrational in terms of a type of penal practice which involves new ways of calculating its utility, justifying it, graduating it, etc. One isn't assessing things in terms of an absolute against which they could be evaluated as constituting more or less perfect forms of rationality, but rather examining how forms of rationality inscribe themselves in practices or systems of practices, and what role they play within them, because it's true that "practices" don't exist without a certain regime of rationality. To put the matter clearly: my problem is to see how men govern (themselves and others) by the production of truth (I repeat once again that by production of truth I mean not the production of true utterances, but the establishment of domains in which the practice of true and false can be made at once ordered and pertinent). This is neither a history of knowledge-contents (connaissances) nor an analysis of the advancing rationalities which rule

our society, nor an anthropology of the codifications which, without our knowledge, rule our behavior. (Foucault, 1991:78–79)

To describe the relationship between his work and Weber's, Foucault later claims that "'Discipline' isn't the expression of an 'ideal type' (that of 'disciplined man'); it's the generalization and interconnection of different techniques themselves designed in response to localized requirements (schooling; training troops to handle rifles)" (Foucault, 1991:80). And he adds that there is no rigid difference between "the purity of the ideal and the disorderly impurity of the real"; rather, there are "different strategies which are mutually opposed, composed and superposed so as to produce permanent and solid effects which can perfectly well be understood in terms of their rationality, even though they don't conform to the initial programming: this is what gives the resulting apparatus (*dispositif*) its solidity and suppleness" (Foucault, 1991:80–81).

Despite their differences, the affinity between Foucault's and Weber's argument is deep (Gordon, 1987; Neuenhaus, 1993; Szakolczai, 1998). Toward the end of his life, while trying to bring to light the techniques of economic and governmental power that are expressed in liberalism, Foucault engages in an investigation of ascetic practices and self-government that in some ways recalls Weber's thesis (Foucault, 2005, 2009, 2010a, 2010b). There are many affinities between them although they differ in their approach to the question of power.

For Foucault, an analysis of power should not start with the juridical notion of the state, with its legal representation, or with what Weber would call "domination" (*Herrschaft*). Instead, it should start from its real functioning, its power relations, and what Weber would term power (*Macht*). However, while Weber starts from the fact of consensus and its legitimation, Foucault moves from what allows the acceptance of its validity. In his view, one cannot neglect the techniques of subjectivation that realize it. For Foucault, in asceticism life itself becomes proof, the result of a power relation between what can be governed and what cannot be governed, the rational and the irrational. Ascesis is a technique of life where at stake is a series of complex and accurately elaborated processes that can change when power relations change and do not respond to a single schema univocally directed toward man and his history, as is the case for Weber and in the history of Western thought to date in general. As a complex and multiple activity, ascetic practice interests

Foucault not in the Weberian terms of an ideal type process that follows one direction and is abstracted and functional to the management of the power in which it is inscribed. What interests Foucault instead is their ability to change everything they are applied to, including the power relations that regulate them.

In Foucault's view, power only exists as the act of execution of a technique, fundamentally one of the self onto the self and one's existence. It is never reduced to the simple manifestation of a passive consent; its nature does not consist merely of a renunciation of freedom or the transfer of a right; nor is it exhausted in the exercise of violence over a passively opposed object. Instead, power "is a total structure of actions brought to bear upon possible actions" (Foucault, 1983:223). This means that it can only be exercised on free subject and in so far as they are free. There is no exclusion between power and freedom; the game is more complex, and freedom appears to be the condition of possibility of power. On these grounds, during the same period of his study of technologies of the self, Foucault began to investigate liberal governmentality. His interpretation fundamentally joins together the different forms assumed by liberalism over the centuries of its history: the defense of freedom liberalism champions is not free of constraints, it is a minute and ever more precise modality of power. By ensuring each individual has the maximum level of self-control as an expression of freedom, the liberal technique of governmentality is a form of domination without constraints that guarantees power and absolute efficiency. In this framework, biopolitics is not reduced, in his view, to the reconstruction of the ways power is applied onto life depriving it of its singular qualities and turning it into mere biological life; rather, it coincides with the development of the same modalities whereby techniques of power and the free ability to give form to life intersect to almost completely merge, as in the case of neoliberalism.

For Foucault, "freedom may well appear as the condition for the exercise of power (at the same time its precondition, since freedom must exist for power to be exerted, and also its permanent support, since without the possibility of recalcitrance, power would be equivalent to a physical determination)" (Foucault, 1983:225). This is one of the most critical aspects of this last phase of his research. Some go as far as claiming that between power and resistance there is a vicious circle (Žižek, 2003). Clearly, the fact that Foucault's last work remains unfinished adds an opaque character to his reflections that find different interpretations; this does not help overcome, as was Foucault's intention, the *impasse*, to which Weber's argument on Western rationalization eventually leads.

In a 1984 interview, in reply to a question on practices of freedom and liberation, Foucault claims: "When an individual or a group of individuals come to block a field of power relations—by economic, political or military means, and to make them immobile, fixed, and prevent any reversibility of movement, one can speak of a state of domination. Surely, in such a state, practices of freedom either do not exist, or are circumscribed and limited; therefore, liberation sometimes coincides with the political and historical condition for a practice of freedom" (Foucault, 2001a:1530). And yet, freedom for Foucault is never identified with a final state, with a definitive form of liberation; it is a practice that inheres to the "technique of life" and its creativity. What characterizes it is the constant reversibility of its movement.

This is one of the most fertile points of Foucault's theory; it opens the possibility of an exercise one ought to tend to today, not only in order to activate "counter-conducts" against those one is directed, but also to find points of "resistance" to the power by which we are governed (as Foucault also suggests). Its power is not its ability to acquire a definitive form, on the contrary, it is the ability to never crystallize in one, its being able to no longer be what it has become. Instead of its realization, we should look to the constant possibility of its annihilation, the demolition of the limits that define it: "a labor of ourselves on ourselves as free subjects" (Foucault, 2001a:1394). This destruction is not a moment that follows on from a construction; it is its point of insurgence. Finally, it is the practice of freedom: the only thing that can prevent techniques of the self from turning into rigid tools of domination. At stake here is the possibility of reactivating, in ever different ways, the same finality without end that is inherent to human action and that, when not incorporated into an empty mechanism that is an end in itself, such as the one Weber describes, can coincide with its innovative ability to change. Then we need to assess the extent to which it is possible to find in the current separation of auto-finality inherent in human action, realized in the self-destructive form of the global enterprise that is an end in itself, ways of demolishing it critically.

# Notes

## Chapter 2. Oikonomía and Asceticism

1. The Christian question of "flesh" has emerged with all the urgency of a philosophical problem even in the contemporary debate. Particularly relevant to the perspective followed here is that the "immune dispositif" of modern power and its biopolitical implications, as recently highlighted by Roberto Esposito, an inherent irreducible otherness to it is detected precisely in the "carnal" element of Christian origin (Esposito, 2011; Esposito, 2008). On the subject we cannot fail to mention also the dialogue between Jean Luc Nancy and Jacques Derrida, of which there is evidence in particular in the book by Derrida, *On Touching—Jean-Luc Nancy*, 2005. With regard to problem of the "flesh," in its twentieth-century reception, primarily in reference to Merleau-Ponty whose reflections on the subject are absolutely worthy of note, see also Lisciani Petrini, 2002:95–139. For a discussion on the theme, in the writings of late antiquity, particularly interesting is the work of Theresia Heimerl that, in its textual research on Patristic, Gnosis, and Manichaeism, takes account of Foucault's and Brown's work as well as historical research; but the "flesh," which, according to the title, should have been the subject of his book, is, however mostly confused with the "body," which the author tends to focus her attention on (Heimerl, 2003).

2. In the second half of the last century, after the recovery in Nag Hammadi of a whole Gnostic library, the debate on this issue became intent on offering an interpretation of gnosis relevant to the present. Hence, the discussion became entangled with the debate on secularization and the relations between Christianity and modernity (Jonas, 1958; Vögelin, 1952; Blumenberg, 1966; Taubes, 1984, to mention a few).

## Chapter 4. Voluntary Poverty on the Market

1. For confirmation of this it perhaps should not be forgotten that, in most recent managerial publications, a significant number of texts aims to apply monastic rules to the organization of companies and the management of financial affairs. Just as an example, refer to the vast bibliography on this issue in Skrabec, 1998.

2. For an economic analysis that takes into account the medieval studies cited here see Berti, 2006.

## Chapter 5.  Capitalism as Religion

1. To this more homogeneous part followed a series of scattered notes that, for completeness and for interest, are reproduced here, even if only in an extract:

Comparison of images of saints of various religions on the one hand and banknotes of different states on the other.

The spirit, which talks about the art of adornment of banknotes.

Capitalism and right. Pagan character of right Sorel, *Réflexions sur la violence*, p. 262

Overcoming capitalism through migration Unger, *Politik und Metaphysik*, p. 44

Fuchs: structure of capitalist society or s.

Max Weber: *Ges. Aufsätze zur Religionssoziologie*, 2 Bd. 1919/20

Ernst Troeltsch: *Die Soziallehren der chr. Kirchen und Gruppen* (*Ges. W.* 1912)

First see the literature cited in Schönberg under ii

Landauer: *Aufruf zum Sozialismus*, p. 144

Concerns (*Sorgen*): a disease of the spirit that is proper of the capitalist epoch. Spiritual (non-material) lack of a way out of poverty, monasticism—vagrants—beggars. A state, which is so lacking a way out, is guilt inducing. The "concerns" are an index of this consciousness of guilt by the absence of an escape. "Worries" occur in the anguish of the absence of a common and non-individual-material exit route.

The Christianity of the Reformation did not favour the rise of capitalism, but has turned into capitalism.

Methodologically one should investigate in the first place which ties with myth money has established in history, up to the time when it was able to draw from Christianity so many mythical elements towards itself, to constitute its own myth.

Wergild/Thesaurus of good works/compensation that is due to the priest. Pluto as God of Wealth.

Adam Müller: *Reden über die Beredsamkeit*, 1816, pp. 56 ff. Connection with the capitalism of the dogma of the nature of knowledge, resolute and, for us, in this quality, at the same time redemptive and murderous: the budget as redemptive and dismissive as knowledge. It contributes to the knowledge of capitalism as religion to remember that original paganism certainly conceived religion in the first place, not as an interest "superior" "moral", but as the most immediate practical one, in other words, that like today's capitalism, it was not at all clear about its "ideal" or "transcendent" nature, indeed, in the irreligious or heterodox individual of the community it saw one of its members in the same way as today's bourgeoisie sees in its non-productive members one of their own.

## Chapter 6. A Philosophical Critique of Asceticism

1. The relationship between Mauss and Nietzsche is explicitly reexamined in Deleuze and Guattari's *Anti-Oedipus*, however, which states: "The great book of modern ethnology is not so much Mauss's *The Gift* as Nietzsche's *On the Genealogy of Morals* [. . .] Nietzsche has only a meagre set of tools [. . .]. But he does not hesitate, as does Mauss, between exchange and debt" (Deleuze and Guattari, 1983:180).

2. In § 58 of *Being and Time* Heidegger writes: "The meaning of the call becomes clear if our understanding of it keeps to the existential meaning of being-guilty, instead of making basic the derivative concept of guilt in the sense of an indebtedness 'arising' from some deed done or left undone. Such a demand is not arbitrary if the call of conscience, coming from Da-sein itself, is directed solely to this being. But then summoning to being-guilty means a calling forth to the potentiality-of-being that I always already am as Da-sein. Da-sein need not first burden itself with 'guilt' through failures or omissions; it must only be authentically the 'guilty' that it is" (Heidegger, 1978:265).

3. From January 30 to May 18, 2010, this work created in 1996 and entitled *Schema: Complications of Payment*, was shown at the MACBA in Barcelona (where I had the opportunity of seeing it) as part of the *Through the Forest* exhibition dedicated to the artist.

# Bibliography

Accarino, B. 2005. *Le frontiere del senso. Da Kant a Weber: male radicale e razionalità moderna*. Milan: Mimesis.

Adorno, T., and W. Benjamin. 1999. *The Complete Correspondence 1928–1940*. Translated by Nicholas Walker. Cambridge, MA: Harvard University Press.

Agamben, G. 1998. *Homo Sacer. Sovereign Power and Bare Life*. Translated by D. Heller-Roazen. Stanford: Stanford University Press.

———. 2005. *The Time that Remains*. Translated by P. Dailey. Stanford: Stanford University Press.

———. 2011. *The Kingdom and the Glory. For a Theological Genealogy of Economy and Government*. Translated by L. Chiesa (with M. Mandarini). Stanford: Stanford University Press.

Aristotle. 2014. *Ethics*. Edited by J. Barnes and A. Kenny. Translated by W. D. Ross. Princeton: Princeton University Press.

Assmann, J. 2000. *Herrschaft und Heil. Politische Theologie in Altägypten, Israel und Europa*. Munich: Hanser.

Badiou, A. 2008. *Saint Paul: The Foundation of Universalism*. Translated by R. Brassier. Stanford: Stanford University Press.

Baecker, D. 2003. *Kapitalismus als Religion*. Berlin: Kulturvergal Kadmos.

Bataille, G. 1989. *Theory of Religion*. Translated R. Hurley. New York: Zone Books.

———. 1998. *The Accursed Share*. Translated by R. Hurley. New York: Zone Books.

Bazzicalupo. L. 2006. *Il governo dell evite. Biopolitica e economia*. Bari: Laterza.

Becker, G. S. 1964. *Human Capital. A Theoretical and Empirical Analysis*. Chicago: University of Chicago Press.

———.1976. *The Economic Approach to Human Behavior*. Chicago: University of Chicago Press.

Benjamin, W. 1995. *Reflections: Essays, Aphorisms, Autobiographical Writings*. Edited by P. Demelz. Translated by E. Jephcott. New York: Schocken Books.

———. 1999. *The Arcades Project*. Translated by R. Tiedermann. Cambridge, MA: Harvard University Press.

———. 1999a. *Selected Writings. Vol. 2, 1927–1934*. Translated by R. Livingstone. Cambridge, MA: Harvard University Press.

———. 2005. "Fragment 74: Capitalism as Religion." In *Religion as Critique: The Frankfurt School's Critique of Religion*, 259–262. New York: Routledge.

Benveniste, E. 1969. *Le vocabulaire des institutions indo-européennes*. Paris: Minuit.

Berti, L. 2006. *Il mercato oltre le ideologie*. Milan: Università Bocconi Editore.

Blumenberg, H. 1966. *Die Legitimität der Neuzeit*. Frankfurt: Suhrkamp.

Böhl, M. 2007. *Das Christentum und der Geist des Kapitalismus. Die Auslegungsgeschichte des biblischen Talentegleichnisses*. Köln-Weimar-Wien: Böhlau.

Boltanski, L., and E. Chiappello. 2005. *The New Spirit of Capitalism*. Translated by G. Elliott. London: Verso.

Bonaiuti, E. 1928. *Le origini dell'ascetismo cristiano*. Pinerolo: Casa Sociale Editrice.

Bousset, W. 1913. *Kyrios Christos. Geschichte des Christusglaubens von den Anfängen des Christentums bis Irenaeus*. Göttingen: Vandenhoeck and Ruprecht.

Brentano, L. 1916. *Die Anfänge des moderne Kapitalismus*. Munich: Verlag der K. B. Akademie der Wissenschaften.

Bröckling, U. 2007. *Das unternehmerische Selbst. Soziologie einer Subjektivierung*. Frankfurt: Suhrkamp.

Brown, N. O. 1959. *Life against Death*. Middletown, CT: Wesleyan University Press.

Brown, P. 1988. *The Body and Society Men, Women and Sexual Renunciation in Early Christianity*. New York: Columbia University Press.

Buber, M. 1950. *Zwei Glaubensweisen*. Zurich: Manesse Verlag.

Butler, J. 1997. *The Psychic Life of Power*. Stanford: Stanford University Press.

Cacciari, M. 2004. *Della cosa ultima*. Milan: Adelphi.

Caillé, A. 1989. *Critique de la raison utilitaire*. Paris: La Découverte.

Campenhausen, H. 1949. *Die Askese im Urchristentum*. Tübingen: Mohr.

Capitani, O., ed. 1987. *Un'economia politica nel Medioevo*. Bologna: Pàtron.

Cassian, J. 2012. "The Conferences." In *The Works of John Cassian*. Translated by E. C. S. Gibson. Buffalo: Christian Literature.

Clement of Alexandria. 2015. *The Stromata, or Miscellanies*. Edited by J. Donaldson and A. Cleveland Coxe. Translated by A. Roberts. London: Perfect Library.

Coccia, E. 2008. "Inobedientia. La disobbedienza di Adamo e l'antropologia giudaico-cristiana." *Filosofia Politica* 22:21–36.

Cova, B. 1993. "Le don dans les theories du management." *Revue de Mauss* 2:158–174.

Cullmann, O. 1948. *Le prime confessioni di fede cristiane*. Rome: Centro Evangelico di Cultura.

De Carolis, M. 1989. "Dynamis e Macht. Il problema della potenza in Nietzsche e Aristotele." In *Sulla potenza. Da Aristotele a Nietzsche*, edited by M. De Carolis, F. Fusillo, G. Russo, M. Zanardi, 7–52. Naples: Guida.

———. 2004. *La vita nell'epoca della sua riproducibilità tecnica*. Turin: Bollati Boringhieri.

Deleuze, G. 1971. *Masochism: An Interpretation of Coldness and Cruelty.* Translated by J. McNeil. New York: Braziller.

———. 2002. *Nietzsche and Philosophy.* Translated by H. Tomlinson. London: Continuum.

———, and Guattari, F. 1983. *Anti-Oedipus. Capitalism and Schizophrenia.* Translated by R. Hurley, M. Seem, and H. R. Lane. Minneapolis: University of Minnesota Press.

Derrida, J. 1992. *Given Time: I. Counterfeit Money.* Translated by P. Kamuf, Chicago, and A. Bass. London: University of Chicago Press.

———. 2005. *Writing and Philosophy, Difference.* Translated by H. Tomlinson. London: Continuum.

———, and Gianni Vattimo, eds. 1998. *Religion.* Translated by D. Webb and Others. Stanford: Stanford University Press.

———, 2005. *On Touching—Jean Luc Nancy.* Translated by C. Irizarry. Stanford: Stanford University Press.

Desideri, F. 2001. "Teologia dell'inferno. Walter Benjamin e il feticismo moderno." In *Figure del feticismo,* edited by S. Mistura. Turin: Einaudi.

De Vogüé, A. 1961. *Monachisme et église dans la pensée de Cassien, in Théologie de la vie monastique. Études sur la tradition patristique.* Paris: Aubier.

Devoto, G. 1967. *Avviamento all'etimologia italiana.* Florence.

Di Marco, G. A. 1984. *Marx, Nietzsche, Weber. Gli ideali ascetici tra critica genealogia e comprensione.* Naples: Guida.

Donaggio, E. 2009. "Spiriti del capitalismo. Variazioni sul tema." *Quaderni di teoria sociale* 9:71–103.

Duchatelez, K. 1970. "La notion d'économie et ses richesses théologiques." *Nouvelle revue théologique* 92:267–292.

Durkheim, E. 1976. *The Elementary Forms of the Religious Life.* Translated by J. W. Swain. London: George Allen & Unwin.

Eliade, M. 2004. *Shamanism: Archaic Techniques of Ecstasy.* Translated by W. R. Trask. Princeton: Princeton University Press.

Esposito, R. 2008. Bios: *Biopolitics and Philosophy.* Translated by Timothy Campbell. Minneapolis: Minnesota University Press.

———. 2011. Immunitas. *The Protection and Negation of Life.* Translated by Z. Hanafi. Cambridge and Malden: Polity Press.

———. 2015. *Categories of the Impolitical.* Translated by C. Parsley. New York: Fordham University Press.

Evagrius, P. 1970. *The Praktikos.* Translated by J. Bamberger. Collegeville, MN: Cistercian.

Filoramo, G. 2007. *Ascèse et temps dans le christianisme antique.* Turnhout: Brepols.

Fimiani, M. 1984. *Marcel Mauss e il pensiero dell'origine.* Naples: Guida.

Fink, E. 1960. *Nietzsches Philosophie*. Stuttgart: Kohlhammer.

Foucault, M. 1983. "The Subject and Power." In *Michel Foucault: Beyond Structuralism and Hermeneutics*, edited by H. Dreyfus and P. Rabinow, 208–226. Chicago: University of Chicago Press.

———.1991. "Questions of Method." In *The Foucault Effect: Studies in Governmentality*, edited by G. Burchell, C. Gordon, and P. Miller, 73–86. Hemel Hempstead: Harvester Wheatsheaf.

———. 2001a. *The Order of Things: An Archaeology of the Human Sciences*. London: Routledge.

———. 2001b. *Dits et écrits II, 1976–1988*. Paris: Gallimard.

———. 2005. *Hermeneutics of the Subject*. Translated by G. Burchell. London: Palgrave.

———. 2009. *Security, Territory and Population*. Translated by G. Burchell. London: Palgrave.

———. 2010a. *The Birth of Biopolitics*. Translated by G. Burchell. London: Palgrave.

———. 2010b. *The Government of the Self and Others*. Translated by G. Burchell. London: Palgrave.

Freud, S. 1937. "Analysis Terminable and Interminable." *International Journal of Psycho-Analysis* 18:373–405.

———. 1961. "On Narcissism: An Introduction." In *The Standard Edition of the Complete Psychological Works of Sigmund Freud*, edited and translated by J. Strachey. London: Hogarth Press.

———. 1964. "*Moses and Monotheism: An Outline of Analysis, and Other Works*." In *The Standard Edition of the Complete Psychological Works of Sigmund Freud, Vol.23 (1937–1939)*, edited and translated by A. Freud and J. Strachey. London: Hogarth Press.

———. 1997. "Contributions to the Psychology of Love." In *Sexuality and the Psychology of Love*. New York: Touchstone.

———. 2010. *Civilization and its Discontents*. Mansfield: Martino.

Fumagalli, A., and S. Mezzadra, eds. 2009. *Crisi dell'economia globale. Mercati finanziari, lotte sociali e nuovi scenari politici*. Verona: Ombre Corte.

Gnilka, J. 1997. *Paulus von Tarsus. Apostel und Zeuge*. Freiburg: Herder.

Goody, J. 2004. *Capitalism and Modernity. The Great Debate*. Cambridge: Polity.

Gordon, C. 1987. "The Soul of the Citizen: Max Weber and Michel Foucault on Rationality and Government." In *Max Weber. Rationality and Modernity*, edited by S. Whimster and S. Lash, 293–316. London: Allen & Unwin.

Habermas, J. 1985. *Theory of Communicative Action*. Translated T. McCarthy. London: Beacon Press.

Hadot, P. 1995. *Qu'est-ce que la philosophie antique?* Paris: Gallimard.

Hafner, J. E. 2003. *Selbstdefinition des Christentums: Ein systemtheoretischer Zugang zur frühchristlichen Ausgrenzung der Gnosis.* Freiburg: Herder.

Harnack, A. 1901. *Das Wesen des Christentum.* Leipzig: Hinrich Verlag.

Hayek, von A. 1982. *Law, Legislation and Liberty.* Chicago: University of Chicago Press.

Heidegger, M. 1978. *Being and Time.* Translated by J. Macquarrie and E. Robinson. London: Blackwell.

———. 1991. *Nietzsche. Vol. 3 and 4.* Translated by D. F. Krell. San Francisco: Harper and Row.

———. 2010. *The Phenomenology of Religious Life.* Bloomington: Indiana University Press.

Heimerl, T. 2003. *Das Wort gewordene Fleisch.* Frankfurt: Peter Lang.

Hirschman, A. O. 1977. *The Passions and the Interests. Political Arguments for Capitalism before Its Triumph.* Princeton: Princeton University Press.

Hudson, M. 2003. *Super Imperialism. The Origins and Fundamentals of US World Dominance.* London: Pluto Press.

Hume, D. 1994. *Political Essays.* Cambridge: Cambridge University Press.

Hurtado, L. W. 2003. *Lord Jesus Christ. Devotion to Jesus in Early Christianity.* Grand Rapids: Eerdmans.

Insel, A. 1991. "L'enchássement problématique du don dans la théorie économique néo-classique." *Revue du Mauss* 12:110–119.

Irenaeus of Lyons. 2012. *Against Heresies.* Edited by A. Roberts and J. Donaldson. London: Perfect Library.

Jonas, H. 1958. *The Gnostic Religion.* Boston: Beacon Press.

Justin M. 2015. *Dialogue of Justin Philosopher and Martyr with Trypho a Jew.* London: Perfect Library.

Kretschmar, G. 1964. "Ein Beitrag zur Frage nach dem Ursprung frühchristlicher Askese." *Zeitschrift für Theologie und Kirche* 61(1): 27–67. Tübingen: Mohr.

Kuhn, K. G. 1957. "Askese IV. Im Urchristentum." In *Die Religion in Geschichte und Gegenwart. Handwörterbuch für Theologie und Religionswissenschaft,* Bd. I:642–644. Tübingen: Mohr.

Latouche, S. 2009. *Farewell to Growth.* Cambridge: Polity.

Laval, C. 2007. *L'homme économique. Essai sur les racines du néoliberalisme.* Paris: Gallimard.

Le Goff, J. 1990. *Your Money or Your Life: Economy and Religion in the Middle Ages.* Translated by P. Ranum. Cambridge, MA: MIT Press.

———. 2012. *Money and the Middle Ages.* London: Polity Press.

Lemke, T. 2007. *Gouvernementalität und Biopolitik.* Wiesbaden: Verlag für Sozialwissenschaften.

Lettieri, G. 2001. *L'altro Agostino. Ermeneutica e retorica della grazia dalla crisi alla metamorfosi del De doctrina christiana.* Brescia: Morcelliana.

Lisciani Petrini, E. 2002. *La passione del mondo. Saggio su Meleau-Ponty*. Naples: Edizioni Scientifiche Italiane.

Löwith, K. 1949. *Meaning in History. The Theological Implications of the Philosophy of History*. Chicago: University of Chicago Press.

———. 1965. *From Hegel to Nietzsche. The Revolution in Nineteenth Century Thought*. Translated by D. F. Green. London: Constable.

———. 1993. *Max Weber and Karl Marx*. Translated H. Fantel. London: Routledge.

Lübbe, H. 1965. *Säkularisierung*. Freiburg: Verlag Karl Albert.

Marquard, O. 1981. "Lob des Polytheismus." In *Abschied von Prinzipiellen. Philosophische Studien*. Stuttgart: Reclam.

Marramao, G. 1981. *Tecnologia e potere nelle società post-liberali*. Naples: Liguori.

———. 1985. *Potere e secolarizzazione. Le categorie del tempo*. Rome: Editori Riuniti.

———. 1994. *Cielo e terra*. Bari: Laterza.

Marx, K. 1996. *Capital, Vol. I*. In *Collected Works*, vol. 35, by K. Marx and F. Engels. Translated by B. Fowkes. New York: International.

Mauss, M. 1966. *The Gift*. London: Routledge.

Meineke, F. 1924. *Die Idee der Staatsräson in der neueren Geschichte*. Berlin: R. Oldenbourg.

Monod, J. C. 2002. *La querelle de la sécularisation. Théologie politique et philosophies de l'histoire de Hegel à Blumenberg*. Paris: Vrin.

Moroncini, B., and Petrillo, R. 2007. *L'etica del desiderio. Un commentario del seminario sull'etica di Jacques Lacan*. Naples: Cronopio.

Nancy, J. L. 2008. *Dis-Enclosure: The Deconstruction of Christianity*. Translated by B. Bergo, G. Malenfant, and M. B. Smith. New York: Fordham University Press.

Neuenhaus, P. 1993. *Max Weber und Michel Foucault. Über Macht und Herrschaft in der Moderne*. Pfaffenweiler: Centaurus.

Neumann, F. 1942. *Behemoth. The Structure and Practice of National Socialism*. New York: Oxford University Press.

Nietzsche, F. 1969. "Ecce homo." In *Werke. Bd. vi. 3*. Berlin: Walter de Gruyter.

———. 2006. *On the Genealogy of Morality*. Translated by C. Diethe. Cambridge: Cambridge University Press.

Origen. 1885. *De Principiis*. Translated by F. Crombie. In *Ante-Nicene Fathers*. Vol. 4, edited by A. Roberts, J. Donaldson and A. Cleveland Coxe. Buffalo, NY: Christian Literature.

Ornaghi, L., ed. 1984. *Il concetto di interesse*. Milan: Giuffré.

Overbeck, F. 1963. "Christentum und Kultur." In *Gedanken und Anmerkungen zur modernen Theologie*, edited by C. A. Bernoulli. Darmstadt: Wissenschaftliche Buchgesellschaft.

———. 1994. "Über die Anfängen des Mönchtums." In *Werke und Nachlass. Schriften bis 1873*, 13–37. Stuttgart and Weimar: Metzler.

———. 2002. *On the Christianity of Theology.* Translated by J. E. Wilson. London: Pickwick.

Padovese, L. 2002. *Cercatori di Dio. Sulle tracce dell'ascetismo pagano, ebraico e cristiano dei primi secoli.* Milan: Mondadori.

Peterson, E. 1948. "L'origine dell'ascesi cristiana." *Eunter Docete* 1(1–2): 195–204.

Plato. 2007. *The Republic.* Translated by H. D. P. Lee and D. Lee. London: Penguin Classics.

Polanyi, K. 2001. *The Great Transformation.* Boston: Beacon Press.

Ponticus, E. 1970. *The Praktikos.* Translated by J. Bamberger. Collegeville, MN: Cistercian.

Prodi, P. 2009. *Settimo non rubare. Furto e mercato nella storia dell'Occidente.* Bologna: Il Mulino.

Rabbow, P. 1954. *Seelenführung. Methodik der Exerzitien in der Antike.* Munich: Kosel Verlag.

Rajan, K. S. 2006. *Biocapital. The Constitution of Postgenomic Life.* Durham: Duke University Press.

Recalcati, M. 2010. *L'uomo senza inconscio. Figure della nuova clinica psicoanalitica.* Milan: Raffaello Cortina.

Reumann, J. 1966. "Oikonomía-terms in Paul in comparison with Lucan Heilsgeschichte." *New Testament Studies* 13(2): 147–167.

Richter, G. 2005. *Oikonomía. Der Gebrauch des Wortes Oikonomía im Neuen Testament, bei den Kirchenvätern und in der theologischen Literatur bis ins 20.* Berlin/ New York: Jahrhundert. Walter de Gruyter.

Rose, N. 2007. *The Politics of Life Itself. Biomedicine, Power and Subjectivity in the Twenty-First Century.* Princeton: Princeton University Press.

Rossi, P. 2007. *Max Weber. Un'idea di Occidente.* Rome: Donzelli.

Salvian of Marseilles 1971 and 1975. *Oeuvres, Sources Chrétiennes 176 and 220.* Paris: Les éditions du cerf.

Sand, A. 1967. *Der Begriff «Fleisch» in den paulinischen Hauptbriefen.* Regensburg: Verlag Friedrich Pustet.

Sandri, A. 2007. *Autorità e Katechon. La genesi teologico-politica della sovranità.* Naples: Jovene.

Schiera, P. 1999. *Specchi della politica. Disciplina, melancolia, socialità nell'Occidente moderno.* Bologna: Il Mulino.

Schjelderup, K.1928. *Die Askese. Eine religionspsychologische Untersuchung.* Berlin: Walter de Gruyter.

Schlatter, G. 1990. "Askese." In *Handbuch religionswissenschaftlicher Grundbegriffe,* edited by H. Cancik, B. Gladigow, M. Laubscher, 60–82. Stuttgart-Berlin-Köln: Kohlhammer.

Schluchter, W. 1988. *Religion und Lebensführung. Studien zu Max Webers Religions und Herrschaftssoziologie.* Frankfurt: Suhrkamp.

————, and F. W. Graf, eds. 2005. *Asketischer Protestantismus und der «Geist» des modernen Kapitalismus. Max Weber und Ernst Troeltsch.* Tübingen: Mohr.

Schmitt, C. 1910. *Über Schuld und Schuldarten.* Breslau: Schletter.

————. 1985. *Political Theology. Four Chapters on the Concept of Sovereignty.* Translated by G. Schwab. Cambridge, MA: MIT Press.

Schnackenburg, R. 1957. "Askese." In *Lexikon für Theologie und Kirche*, 930–932. Vol. I. Freiburg: Herder Verlag.

Schürmann, R. 1982. *Le principe d'anarchie. Heidegger et la question de l'agir.* Paris: Seuil.

Sennett, R. 2006. *The Culture of the New Capitalism.* New Haven: Yale University Press.

Skrabec, Q. R. 1998. *St. Benedict's Rule for Business Success.* Purdue: Purdue University Press.

Sloterdijk, P. 2005. *Im Weltinnenraum des Kapital.* Frankfurt: Suhrkamp.

————. 2009. *Du Mußt dein Leben ändern.* Frankfurt: Suhrkamp.

Spinoza, Baruch de. 1951. *A Theologico-Political Treatise.* Translated by R. H. Elwes. New York: Dover.

Stimilli, E. 2004a. *Jacob Taubes. Sovranità e tempo messianico.* Brescia: Morcelliana.

————. 2004b. "Per una «governamentalità» dell'esistenza. La vita come opera d'arte e ricreazione." *Forme di vita* 2(3): 209–222.

————. 2008. "Metodica dell'esistenza e capitale umano." In *Biopolitica, bioeconomia e processi di soggettivazione*, edited by A. Cedola, L. Bazzicalupo, F. Chicchi, and A. Tucci, 193–200. Macerata: Quodlibet.

Stolz, A. 1943. *L'ascesi cristiana.* Brescia: Morcelliana.

————. 1979. *La Scala del Paradiso. Teologia della mistica.* Brescia: Morcelliana.

Szakolczai, A. 1998. *Max Weber and Michel Foucault. Parallel life-works.* London: Routledge.

Taubes, J. 1969. "Kultur und Ideologie." In *Spätkapitalismus oder Industriegesellschaft? Industrie-gesellschaft? Verhandlungen des 16. Deutschen Soziologentages vom 8–11 April 1968 in Frankfurt/M*, edited by Th. T. W. Adorno, 117–138. Stuttgart: Enke.

————. 1984. "Das stählerne Gehäuse und der Exodus daraus oder ein Streit um Marcion, einst und heute." In *Religionstheorie und Politische Theologie: Gnosis und Politik*, edited by J. Taubes, 9–15. Munich: Schöningh.

Tarot, C. 2008. "Repères pour une histoire de la naissance de la grâce." In *La société vue don. Manuel de sociologie anti-utilitariste appliquée*, edited by P. Chanial, 479–497. Paris: édition la Découverte.

Todeschini, G. 2002. *I mercanti e il tempio. La società cristiana e il circolo virtuoso della ricchezza fra Medioevo e età moderna.* Bologna: Il Mulino.

————. 2004. *Ricchezza francescana. Dalla povertà volontaria alla società di mercato.* Bologna: Il Mulino (2009. *Franciscan Wealth. From Voluntary Poverty to Market Society*, New York: Franciscan Institute).

Toneatto, V. 2004. "I linguaggi della ricchezza nella testualità omiletica e monastica dal III al IV secolo." In *Economia monastica. Dalla disciplina del desiderio all'amministrazione razionale*, edited by V. Toneatto, P. Černic, S. Paulitti, and G. Todeschini, 1–88. Spoleto: Cisam.

Troeltsch, E. 1931. *The Social Teaching of the Christian Churches*. Translated by O. Wyon. London: George Allen & Unwin.

Uhrig, C. 2004. *"Und das Wort ist Fleisch geworden." Zur rezeption von Joh 1, 14a und zur Theologie der Fleischwerdung in der griechischen vornizänischen Patristik*. Munster: Aschendorff Verlag.

Van der Leeuw, G. 1933. *Phänomenologie der Religion*. Tübingen: Mohr.

Virno, P. 2004. *A Grammar of the Multitude*. Translated by G. Ambrosino, I. Bertoletti, and J. Cascaito. New York: Semiotext(e).

———. 2015. *When the Word becomes Flesh*. New York: Semiotext(e).

Vitiello, V. 1995. *Cristianesimo senza redenzione*. Bari: Laterza.

Vögelin, E. 1952. *The New Science of Politics*. Chicago: University of Chicago Press.

Weber, M. 1946. "Science as a Vocation." In *Max Weber: Essays in Sociology*, edited and translated by H. H. Gerth and C. Wright Mills, 129–156. New York: Oxford University Press.

———. 1978. *Economy and Society: An Outline of Interpretive Sociology*. Berkeley: University of California Press.

———. 1993. *Sociology of Religion*. Translated Talcott Parsons, London: Beacon Press.

———. 2001. *The Protestant Ethic and the Spirit of Capitalism*. Translated T. Parson, London: Routledge.

———. 2002. *The Protestant Ethic and the Spirit of Capitalism: and other writings*. London: Penguin.

Žižek, S. 2003. *The Puppet and the Dwarf: The Perverse Core of Christianity*. Cambridge, MA: MIT Press.

———. 2003. *Il soggetto scabroso. Trattato di ontologia politica*. Milan: Raffaello Cortina.

# Index